# Reading Faulkner's
# Best Short Stories

# Reading Faulkner's Best Short Stories

Hans H. Skei

University of South Carolina Press

© 1999 University of South Carolina

Published in Columbia, South Carolina, by the
University of South Carolina Press

Manufactured in the United States of America

03 02 01 00     5 4 3 2

### Library of Congress Cataloging-in-Publication Data

Skei, Hans H., 1945–
    Reading Faulkner's best short stories / Hans H. Skei.
      p.  cm.
    Includes bibliographical references (p. ) and index.

    ISBN 1-57003-286-6
    1. Faulkner, William, 1897–1962—Criticism and interpretation.
2. Short story.   I. Faulkner, William, 1897–1962. Short stories. Selections.
II. Title.
PS3511.A86 Z9689   1999
813'.52—dc21                              98-40293

Permission to quote from William Faulkner's *Collected Stories* as given by
Random House, Inc., and by permission of Curtis Brown, London.

Chapter 1 incorporates material taken from *Dictionary of Literary Biography*,
volume 102. Edited by Bobby Ellen Kimbell. © 1991 Gale Research. All rights
reserved. Reproduced with permission.

# Contents

# Preface

*Reading Faulkner's Best Short Stories* gives an introduction to William Faulkner as a short story writer and offers close readings of twelve of Faulkner's best short stories selected on the basis of literary quality. The selection of stories is not meant to be representative of Faulkner's overall short story achievement, nor to represent typical narrative strategies or thematic interests. Most of the stories should be expected to be among the best known of Faulkner's stories. They are often anthologized and frequently commented on, in addition to being taught in classrooms at all levels of the educational system. They have not been chosen on these bases, however, but rather because they represent Faulkner's most successful achievements with the short story as a literary form. They are highly literary stories, and they offer concentrated images of conflicts and confrontations of a kind that the short story genre seems particularly suitable for. The selection does not represent my private list of favorite stories, and I feel confident that it includes a number of stories about which most Faulkner scholars would agree. In chapter 4 I have discussed some of the reasons for choosing my twelve stories.

The stories differ very much in subject material, in setting, in narrative handling, in thematic impact. They are chosen from among all of Faulkner's stories, so that stories later reworked into novels stand alongside "pure" stories from magazines and story collections. As could be expected, all twelve stories stem from Faulkner's major years both as a novelist and as a short story writer. Since literary quality and not representativeness is my main criterion for selection, there is no "best" story published before 1930, and it is very difficult to find stories which are more than competent after 1942 and do not draw extensively on previous material or reiterate scenes and conflicts described in earlier stories and novels.

The book is divided into two main parts. Part 1 deals with Faulkner's short story career and questions of genre and explains the principles behind the selection of the "best" short stories. Part 2 gives fairly extensive readings of the twelve stories. A separate, brief introduction is given for each part. A selective but fairly extensive bibliography is included. Part 1 may be of special interest to Faulkner scholars and those particularly interested in the short story as a literary form who want to see how Faulkner contributed to this genre, since he was, after all, first and foremost a novelist. Part 2 is perhaps most useful to students of Faulkner at all levels, since it attempts to present and analyze central short story texts and, I hope, make them more easily accessible and add to their richness.

Preparing this study of a dozen of what I deem Faulkner's best stories, I have felt free to draw upon everything I have written on Faulkner's short story achievement over the years, and my two volumes published more than a decade ago form a necessary basis and point of departure for this book. *Reading Faulkner's Best Short Stories* is nevertheless not a recycling of previously published material; it offers new material, organized in new and more accessible ways, and since the study is limited to twelve stories only, this has given me ample space to treat each individual story at length and not just as an example of some particular storytelling technique or prevailing thematic interest.

The idea for this book came out of the 1995 International Faulkner Symposium on Faulkner's short fiction in Oslo, Norway. It was later followed up by a number of fellow Faulknerians and friends. I am thus indebted to a number of people, and grateful because they gave me the necessary push to return to what was once an all-consuming interest.

# Biographical Sketch

William Cuthbert Falkner was born in New Albany, Mississippi, on September 25, 1897, the first child of Maud Butler Falkner and Murry Cuthbert Falkner (he added the "u" to his name in 1918). Shortly after his first birthday the family moved to Ripley, Mississippi, and four years later to Oxford, where Faulkner spent most of his life. His great grand-father, Col. William Clark Falkner, had a literary reputation based main-ly on his novel *The White Rose of Memphis* (1881) and must be seen as a major influence on his descendant, not the least because of his active if not violent life, which Faulkner transformed and fictionalized as that of Col. John Sartoris. Growing up in an area of the United States that was just advancing from frontier status, Faulkner led an adventurous life as the oldest of four brothers, learning to handle guns and to hunt. His father had a livery stable for many years, and the boys lived among hors-es and dogs. Faulkner stopped attending Oxford High School midway through the 1914–1915 school year without completing the last grade. He returned the following fall, mostly to play football, but quit school at the end of the season. He had, however, been reading poetry with Phil Stone, an older friend who was important to Faulkner's development in these early years, and he had already begun showing his own poems to Stone.

Faulkner had several different jobs—ranging from bank clerk to postmaster at the University of Mississippi—during the long period before he established himself as a writer. In 1918, unable to meet height and weight requirements for the U.S. Army, he instead joined the Canadian branch of the Royal Air Force and went into training in Toronto. World War I came to an end, though, before he could take part. He received a discharge in early December and returned to Oxford, where his girlfriend, Estelle Oldham, had married Cornell Franklin, a local lawyer.

In 1919–1920, while attending the University of Mississippi as a spe-cial student, Faulkner had his first poems and sketches published, and in the early 1920s—after officially withdrawing from the university in November 1920—he wrote numerous poems, a few sketches, and a verse play, *The Marionettes*, which was performed in 1920 but not published until 1975. He went to New York, where he worked briefly as a bookstore clerk in 1921, and his first book, *The Marble Faun,* was published in Boston in 1924. That same year he met Sherwood Anderson in New Orleans, and for the first half of 1925, Faulkner lived in the Crescent City with the Andersons. The most formative year in Faulkner's development as an artist was 1925.

In this decisive year in Faulkner's career he made an almost complete transition from being a poet to becoming a fiction writer, publishing several pieces of experimental prose in the *New Orleans Times-Picayune* (most of them collected in *Mirrors of Chartres Street* in 1953; all of them in *New Orleans Sketches,* 1958). Faulkner sailed for Europe aboard the *West Ivis* in July 1925 and traveled in Italy, Switzerland, France, and England before returning to the States in December. Some of his early stories are set in postwar Europe, and his travels also paid off in his later fiction. His first novel, *Soldiers' Pay,* was published in February 1926, apparently on Anderson's recommendation. In the same year he wrote *Mosquitoes* (1927) in addition to minor works such as the novelette *Mayday* (1976) and poems for Helen Baird, whom he courted at this time, posthumously published as *Helen: A Courtship* (1984).

In 1927, dividing his time between Oxford and Pascagoula, Mississippi, Faulkner wrote *Flags in the Dust,* which was accepted only after his friend Ben Wasson cut it severely; it was published as *Sartoris* in 1929 (the original version was published in 1974). As he struggled against reluctant publishers, bad reviews, and low sales, Faulkner discovered his own "postage stamp of native soil," the basis for his fictional Yoknapatawpha County. With *The Sound and the Fury* (1929) a complete transition seems to have occurred. While his earlier novels are flawed by his almost narcissistic self-involvement and lack of distance from his characters, in *The Sound and the Fury* he has complete control of material and of narrative strategies. In his private life important events also took place: Estelle divorced her husband and married Faulkner on June 20, 1929. In 1930 they bought an old house, naming it Rowan Oak, and Faulkner began making money from the sale of short stories to the national magazines.

The years between 1928 and 1933 are in all respects the major years in Faulkner's career. In addition to *The Sound and the Fury* he produced three more novels—*As I Lay Dying* (1930), *Sanctuary* (1931), and *Light in August* (1932)—and his short story production was enormous. Safely established in the center of the world he chronicled, he was hard at work in Oxford for most of this period and would continue to live in the center of the world whose chronicler he became. He could not make enough money on his novels nor on the short stories he sold to the well-paying magazines, so he spent time in Hollywood as a screenwriter. He went there for the first time in 1932 and went back numerous times. After a sustained but unsuccessful attempt at making enough money on short stories ten years later, he spent a long time in California from 1942 on, but he only reached financial security and freedom when he sold the movie rights to *Intruder in the Dust* (1949)—then, of course, he received the Nobel Prize in 1950.

As Nobel laureate, Faulkner became a public figure and traveled widely on State Department missions. He spoke to his fellow southerners on racial issues, for the first time in his career publishing articles and essays more often than he published stories, and he responded to his incredible popularity in Japan by visiting there in 1955. Starting in 1957 he was writer in residence at the University of Virginia in Charlottesville, where he purchased a house and settled with his wife, Estelle (their daughter, Jill, had married in 1954). In 1957 and 1959 *The Town* and *The Mansion* were published, drawing heavily on material he had published before. This is also true for *The Reivers,* his last novel.

In Charlottesville Faulkner took up horseback riding on a regular basis and was injured in several falls. His final injury came in Oxford, Mississippi, however, on June 17, 1962; the connection between his injuries and the heart attack from which he died is by no means obvious, but he was taken to a sanatorium on July 5 and died the following day. He was buried in St. Peter's Cemetery, Oxford, near the graves of most of the Falkners.

The biographical facts of a writer's life and career cannot explain how the works were written or what made it possible to write them. Faulkner's craftsmanship came slowly, and he learned it through practice and stubborn dedication. He was willing to sacrifice most things to get his work done, and he was never in doubt as to the importance of the artist and his work. Faulkner was unwilling to compromise, and he had set a high standard for himself early on. Accordingly, his life never became simple or easy. His was a complex nature, so he had a complicated life. All his books have been examined thoroughly, but the man who wrote them is still an enigma, despite the assiduous detective work of numerous biographies.

# PART 1

# William Faulkner and the Short Story

# Introduction

The first part of this book—"William Faulkner and the Short Story"—consists of four chapters. They deal with Faulkner's short story achievement from a number of different perspectives. The first chapter is devoted to Faulkner's short story career. There I mention all his stories briefly and describe the circumstances surrounding their composition, revision, publication, and collection. Chapter 2 gives a broad outline of the study of Faulkner's short fiction. Chapter 3 deals with the short story genre and Faulkner's contribution to it. Consideration of his use of formulaic stories as well as his attempts to write experimental and more "literary" stories can help one understand why the great modernist novelist seems to have remained fairly traditional when he turned to short story writing. In the fourth and final chapter of the first part, I set forth my reasons for choosing twelve stories as Faulkner's best.

Part 1 is meant to function as an introduction to the reading of individual stories in part 2. It enables the reader to place each story in the context of Faulkner's career and to view it in relation to the short story genre. The concept of genre must be taken more seriously in the study of Faulkner's short fiction than has usually been the case; *genre* is therefore a key term in all of the chapters in part 1. Accordingly, even if part 1 is preparatory for part 2 of this study, it can also be read and studied on its own as a separate contribution to the study of Faulkner's short fiction.

# Chapter 1

# Faulkner's Short Story Career

Faulkner's best stories are outstanding, and there are more than enough of them to secure him a place as a major writer in the genre. His stories do not completely follow any of the formulas of conventional short fiction, although they were influenced by their time and place and the market for which they were written. The narrative control in his stories varies significantly from text to text—from cold objectivity to heart-shattering closeness—but above and beneath it all is the consciousness of the craftsman and born storyteller, whose voice can be heard from time to time. Faulkner's lifelong interest, as he once stated in a discussion at the University of Virginia, was in "all man's behavior with no judgment whatever": "You write a story to tell about people, man in his constant struggle with his own heart, with the hearts of others, or with his environment. It's man in the ageless, eternal struggle which we inherit and we go through as though they'd never happened before, shown for a moment in a dramatic instant of the furious motion of being alive, that's all any story is. You catch the fluidity which is human life and you focus a light on it and you stop it long enough for people to see it" (Gwynn and Blotner 1959). To render man in his ageless struggle and arrest motion for a moment, Faulkner explored the limits of storytelling techniques, but since the stories always have a solid kernel of substance he succeeded in keeping the precarious balance between content and presentation. His searching curiosity and willingness to try over and over again to improve a story, to find the right angle from which to tell it in order to catch the exact atmosphere, led to the creation of one of the most impressive bodies of short fiction in American literature.

But William Faulkner was first and foremost a novelist, and much of his achievement in the short story is closely related to his accomplishments in the longer form. This does not necessarily imply that his short stories are second to his novels in all respects but indicates how difficult it is to distinguish between Faulkner as novelist and as story writer. As a novelist Faulkner was innovative, experimental, and influential, whereas his contribution to the short story form is less significant. Yet one would do Faulkner's short fiction a serious injustice by regarding it as inferior. Compared to his novels the short stories may appear less impressive; compared to most other short story writers, though, Faulkner is a major practitioner of the form. His best stories, in fact, may be said to transcend the borders of the genre as we traditionally think of it. This does not happen often, but often enough to enable us to choose half a dozen stories that are his very best, to which we may add an equal number of stories that show a master storyteller's command of "old tales and talking" and in which he relies on "the best of gossip" to give us vivid images of man in motion and of people trying to find their place in an ever-changing and troublesome world. Yet we should not forget that the good stories are exceptions in Faulkner's career. He wrote some 120 stories altogether; thus in this study I have chosen only one out of ten stories as his best.

Faulkner wrote stories throughout his literary career, but he concentrated on the genre most during those periods when he had no new novels underway. Faulkner regarded the short story highly, deeming it the most demanding form after poetry. He worked consistently and conscientiously to perfect his stories—not to suit the needs of a particular market but to satisfy his own artistic demands. This is demonstrated in his arduous work on his collections, most notably *These 13* (1931) and *Collected Stories* (1950), in which he tried to superimpose a design or a structure upon the otherwise disparate short stories. He was a dedicated craftsman in all his work, and the seriousness of his story writing is demonstrated in the many different manuscripts and typescripts for individual stories as well as in his correspondence with magazine editors and agents.

Many of Faulkner's short stories may be regarded as a concentration of material later developed in novels. This does not imply that the shorter form was not the right one for the material. An immense array of strange local characters, hunting stories, tall tales, and the southern legacy, including the lost cause, slavery, and aristocratic families—all of which Faulkner drew from for his material—often seemed to require the longer form. Yet some of Faulkner's novels appear to have been conceived as a single image, a central episode, material fit for a short story: Lena Grove, barefoot and pregnant, getting around in the world; Caddy Compson in the tree; the idiot Snopes and the cow in the long summer days of Yoknapatawpha. Faulkner's desire to penetrate as deeply as possible to see why and how people react, his unrelenting scrutiny and unflagging search for understanding, forced him to link episode to episode to see whether new evidence could be found, new insights achieved. Thus stories might grow into novels, or related stories might be combined into unified works of greater length; but short stories could also be self-contained and independent, even in cases where they gained support from other stories and novels in the larger framework of Faulkner's Yoknapatawpha fiction.

The need that Faulkner apparently felt for supplying background information and adding atmosphere to many of his stories accounts for the length of some of them. One of his methods for creating suspense is to pause in his narration to provide capsule stories that include important information. Faulkner writes about the country and the village, about the South, and about the people living there: the Indians who originally owned the land, the blacks who slave on it, and the poor whites who barely eke out a living, as well as the well-to-do businessmen and plantation owners. Race relations is one of his subjects; war is another; and sexuality may well be said to be a third, although that topic is interlinked with others. In accordance with Faulkner's statements about the writer's proper material, his short stories deal with love, compassion, pride, pity, and sacrifice. The historical dimension cannot be overlooked. Broadly speaking, the stories take place in three major chronological periods: the remote past, which includes the early days of the Indian tribes, the Civil War years, and the undisturbed and apparently changeless rural history of Yoknapatawpha; the recent past—World War I and the years immediately following; and the immediate past—Yoknapatawpha and the world beyond it in the 1920s, 1930s, and 1940s.

## EARLY AND FORMATIVE YEARS—NEW ORLEANS SKETCHES

Faulkner published his first short story, a brief prose sketch called "Landing in Luck," in the *Mississippian,* the University of Mississippi's student paper, on November 26, 1919; it was collected in *Early Prose and Poetry* (1962). Drawing on Faulkner's experience during aviation training in Toronto in 1918, the story is about a young cadet's first solo flight. It displays humor and technical skill and has some interest as the author's first sketch about flyers and flying.

The second prose sketch to be published, "The Hill" (*Mississippian,* March 10, 1922; collected in *Early Prose and Poetry*), has been hailed by critics as Faulkner's most important early short story. It shows an author in complete control of his material and foreshadows many narrative techniques and themes in his later fiction. "The Hill" is an artful prose version of a poem Faulkner had written earlier. A nameless figure climbs a hill after a day of hard work and sits immobile, then slowly descends again. Mostly a detailed description of the view from the hill-top, the story gives a succinct picture of man's struggles and dreams.

In the early 1920s Faulkner also wrote intricate and overworked stories. "Moonlight" (first published in *Uncollected Stories*, 1979) and "Love" (*William Faulkner's Manuscripts*, 1986–87) were probably written before "The Hill." Another story from these early years is "Adolescence." This story about young love misinterpreted by the adult world foreshadows Faulkner's later use of local backgrounds and exploits themes he would return to some years later. "Adolescence" was first published in *Uncollected Stories*.

Those five stories are apparently the only ones Faulkner wrote before his sojourn to New Orleans in 1925, with the possible exception of "Nympholepsy" (*Mississippi Quarterly*, Summer 1973; in *Uncollected Stories*), an expansion of "The Hill." In this version a young hill climber's dreams are of a more sexual nature.

These sketches, influenced by Sherwood Anderson and Faulkner's close contact with literary bohemia in New Orleans at that time, gave Faulkner useful practical experience, particularly in the handling of narrative and the presentation of character. The sketches are uneven, and the hand of the apprentice can be clearly seen. They do not follow any fixed formula, but Faulkner seems to be most interested in sketching characters. He presents his characters from varying points of view, either through a first-person narrator or with distinct detachment. "New Orleans" (*Double Dealer*, January–February 1924; in *New Orleans Sketches*) is a composite of eleven subnarratives. Most of the sketches Faulkner published in 1925 appeared in the Sunday magazine section of the *New Orleans Times-Picayune*. For some of the sketches the *Times-Picayune* used a running head to indicate that this was a series: "Another 'Mirror of Chartres Street.'" Not all the New Orleans sketches were published in 1925. Completed sketches that survived in typescript— "Peter," "Don Giovanni," and "The Priest"—were not published until much later. ("The Priest" appeared in the *Mississippi Quarterly*, Summer 1976, and was collected in *Uncollected Stories;* the two other texts were first published in *Uncollected Stories*).

Closely related to the New Orleans material is an untitled short story, an expansion of one of the subplots in "New Orleans." This rather competent story was published with the title "Frankie and Johnny" (*Mississippi Quarterly*, Summer 1978; in *Uncollected Stories*). In 1926 Faulkner revised "New Orleans," presenting it in a handmade booklet, which he called "Royal Street," to Estelle Oldham Franklin, his future wife.

Few of the New Orleans sketches are extended narratives, although "The Liar" and "Yo Ho and Two Bottles of Rum" may be considered short stories. The former is rooted in the backcountry of Yoknapatawpha; the latter has an international setting and cast of characters. Each text points to a distinctly different type of stories that Faulkner would write in the near future.

Faulkner's experimentation in the New Orleans period seldom went further than an imitation of Joseph Conrad and Sherwood Anderson, but in the variety of narrative methods these stories anticipate the technical brilliance of *The Sound and the Fury*. Thematically they may be said to emphasize the individual's alienation from the natural world but also his search for communal ties, participation, and sharing.

After Faulkner published *Soldiers' Pay* he wrote several short stories in 1926 and 1927. Most of the stories from these years were later revised and appeared in print only after 1930. One story that found its final form in 1926 was *Mayday*, an allegorical tale about Sir Galwyn, who travels through life accompanied by the shadowy figures of Hunger and Pain and who finally finds peace in death by water. Faulkner made the hand-lettered, illustrated, and beautifully bound booklet for Helen Baird in 1926; the University of Notre Dame Press brought out a facsimilie edition in 1976. Similarly, Faulkner typed *The Wishing Tree* himself and bound at least one copy by hand as a present for one of Estelle Franklin's children in February 1927. Faulkner's only story for children, it employs the conventional framework of a fairy tale and gives comical treatment to numerous themes that occur in much of Faulkner's later writing. It was published in 1967. *Mayday* and *The Wishing Tree* were important steps toward Faulkner's conception of *The Sound and the Fury*. The unfinished "And Now What's To Do" (*Mississippi Quarterly*, Summer 1973) uses autobiographical elements to a degree not found in Faulkner's writing till a quarter of a century later, when he wrote "Mississippi" (*Holiday*, April 1954; in *Essays, Speeches & Public Letters*, 1966). For fun he also wrote a brief and humorous sketch, "Music—Sweeter Than the Angels Sing" (*Southern Review*, October 1976), while his long struggle with a novel called *Elmer* (published in fragmentary form in 1983) resulted in the short story "A Portrait of Elmer" (*Georgia Review*, Fall 1979; in *Uncollected Stories*). This complicated story about a young artist was never successfully completed and is not representative of Faulkner's capacity at the time he wrote it. "Two Dollar Wife" (*College Life*, January 1936; in *Uncollected Stories*), one of the worst stories Faulkner ever wrote, may be the same story as "The Devil Beats His Wife," written in 1926 and later revised as "Christmas Tree," which finally became "Two Dollar Wife." A much better and more ambitious story written in this period is *Father Abraham* (1984), the germ of the Snopes trilogy and Faulkner's first attempt to work with material that he would return to over and over again in the years ahead until he brought the many loose ends together in *The Hamlet* (1940).

## THE MAJOR YEARS (1928–1933)—*THESE 13*

The Europe of the post-World War I years and Faulkner's own "lost generation" sentiments may have combined to strengthen his feeling of despair and certainly added colors and contours to his bleak picture of the world as a wasteland in many of the stories that he began in 1926 and 1927. These stories demonstrate the outrage of a potential believer; the criticism of a stale and stifling social life is harsh. Faulkner's narrators lament the loss of traditional values and criticize the materialistic, ephemeral values that have replaced them. Novel writing took most of his time in the late 1920s, but when he had finished typing *The Sound and the Fury* in October 1928 he began his first serious effort to write and market short stories. His story-writing activity reached a peak in the early 1930s. Faulkner recorded his endeavors in the form of a story-sending schedule, as well as through his correspondence with editors and agents. The twenty-month period between January 1930 (when he finished *As I Lay Dying*) and August 1931 (when he began *Light in August*) were the most productive in terms of short fiction. On January 20, 1930, he recorded his first sale to a national magazine: *Forum* bought "A Rose for Emily" (April 1930; in *These 13*), which encouraged him to continue his story writing for the profitable American slick-magazine market of the 1930s. From the time "A Rose for Emily" was accepted until he began work on *Light in August,* Faulkner submitted more than twenty stories to various magazines. Altogether he sent off more than seventy submissions during this period, earning enough in the process to buy Rowan Oak in April 1930; the Faulkner family moved there in June. The purchase led to a chronic shortage of money, and in May 1932 Faulkner had to leave for Hollywood to find a steady income. His story writing then came to a sudden halt, and only for brief intervals later in his career would he concentrate on short fiction, never with more than moderate success. At home his first daughter, Alabama, died a few days after her birth in 1931, and Jill was born in 1933.

The more than forty short stories that Faulkner wrote in the late 1920s and early 1930s are his most autonomous and "pure" short stories. With a few exceptions they do not stand in any close relationship to his novels. Ten of these stories, published in the early 1930s or not published at all in Faulkner's lifetime, are known to have existed before 1930: "Ad Astra," from 1927; "Mistral," "Pennsylvania Station," "The Leg," the two-part "'Once Aboard the Lugger—,'" "Spotted Horses," and *Miss Zilphia Gant* from 1928; and "Elly," "There Was a Queen," and "A Rose for Emily" from 1929. Some of the stories had different titles in their original versions, and some were so much revised as to become virtually new stories before they were published.

The Memphis and Gavin Blount stories are among those that never saw publication. They consist of two pairs of stories: "The Big Shot" and a substantial revision of it, named "Dull Tale," both from 1930; and "Rose of Lebanon" (1930) and "A Return" (1938). With the exception of "Rose of Lebanon" these stories were published in *Uncollected Stories of William Faulkner.* "Rose of Lebanon" was finally, in 1995, published in the *Oxford American,* and was included in *New Stories from the South 1996.* Twenty-one new stories have been dated to 1930, including the separately published *Idyll in the Desert.* In 1931 Faulkner submitted five new stories for publication. In addition he used three short stories that he apparently never submitted to magazines in *These 13:* "Victory," "Crevasse," and "Carcassonne." Only two stories can be dated to 1932: "Turn About" and, possibly, "With Caution and Dispatch."

In the stories from this period—by far the most productive and significant in Faulkner's career—certain recurrent patterns can be established as to how characters react to a situation that has become untenable or simply to the changing world. The narrating voice, often someone beyond or above the story who communicates with the readers behind the back of protagonists and other characters, invariably sides with the loners who fight losing battles against a rigid, nonpermissive society. Progress is shown as a threat to human values, and man's misuse of man for selfish ends is part of a recurrent motif in these stories, as is man's destruction of nature, understood as physical nature as well as the natural qualities in man. Faulkner did not always think highly of individual human beings, but his belief in humanity seems to have grown stronger over the years. And among the basic qualities which are required for man to live peacefully in an ordered and civilized society are endurance, love, compassion, and sharing, values to which the stories always return.

Faulkner's narrative method is more varied and heterogeneous in the major period than it is later on. It is abundantly clear that he had no privileged approach but used all conceivable strategies in order to get a story told. He maneuvers first- and third-person narration with great ease, so that the distance from characters and events becomes more of a question of attitude and language than of technical skill, although the narrator (especially when we have a personal narrator, perhaps even a child narrator) always commands our attention and interest. Faulkner's use of the first-person plural narrator, representing a community conscience or consensus, is typical for the many stories located in Jefferson, where social control is fairly rigid. The village stories differ considerably from the stories placed in the countryside, not least because of the stronger group pressure and the better-defined role expectations in the small town.

During the spring of 1931 Faulkner put together his first short story collection. He then had some forty stories from which to choose. One can only guess his motives for selecting the thirteen stories he included in the book, but the resulting volume presents a rather coherent and convincing picture of the world as a wasteland filled with dust and dreams, hopes and frustrations, nonlife and death.

*These 13* has three main sections. The first one includes four World War I stories: "Victory," "Ad Astra," "All the Dead Pilots," and "Crevasse." In section 2 six stories about Yoknapatawpha are grouped together: "Red Leaves," "A Rose for Emily," "A Justice," "Hair," "That Evening Sun," and "Dry September." The final section includes three stories: "Mistral," "Divorce in Naples," and "Carcassonne," all dealing with Americans abroad and with experiences far removed from Yoknapatawpha in all respects. Faulkner took great care in structuring this collection to achieve unity, moving toward a definite finale.

"Victory" opens the collection. Extensive in terms of its scope and time span, it deals with World War I and its aftermath. A God-fearing young Scot, Alec Gray, is one of the many losers who faces years of unemployment after the war. He rose to the officer class through bravery, but his downfall after the war is as rapid as his rise. The generalizations in the other World War I stories about the sad and undeserved fate of the soldiers who served their countries are made concrete in the description of Gray's destiny. "Victory" is in some respects Faulkner's most successful World War I story, not the least because its length allows room for Gray's story to develop. (See chapter 14 for a reading of "Victory.") "Ad Astra" (originally published in *American Caravan,* 1931), on the other hand, is a concentrated, almost painful, portrayal of loss and decay, and of the futility and waste of war. Soldiers drink, talk, quarrel, and fight on the night of Armistice Day in 1918, and an Indian subahdar voices the opinion that those who survived the war are also dead. Those who died in battle may in fact be better off. Rather vague "lost generation" sentiments slip into this story, as they also do in the companion piece, "All the Dead Pilots" (previously unpublished). A frame narrator looks back upon the war and describes the plight of the pilots who have had to live on after their short time of bravery and vitality. They are all "dead" now, because they survived the war and must adjust to a quiet bourgeois life. The dreams of bravery and glory could only be realized by dying a hero's death. How heroic life on the battlefield might really be is then shown in "Crevasse" (originally a part of

"Victory"), in which a small infantry patrol marching over a dead-looking and ominous landscape suddenly disappears when the earth begins to move. The trapped soldiers dig desperately to find a way out. War is here shown as demoralizing and brutalizing. "Crevasse" demonstrates what kind of reality the soldiers' dreams had to be tested against. Even though humor may be found in these war stories, the ultimate impression is one of darkness and despair.

"Red Leaves" (originally published in *Saturday Evening Post,* October 25, 1930), a story about the Indians of Yoknapatawpha County and one of Faulkner's three or four best stories, is placed first in section 2 of *These 13.* This story is structured around a burial ritual which holds that the body servant of the dead Indian chief must also die. The black servant runs away, however, and must be hunted down before the corpse of the chief starts decomposing. The story is discussed in chapter 11 of the present book.

"A Rose for Emily," Faulkner's most widely read, criticized, and anthologized short story, begins with the announcement of the death of Miss Emily Grierson, who has lived so long she has become an anachronism. A corporate narrator recounts Emily's life—a life of loneliness and poverty because her father drove away her suitors and little was left for her when he died. Critics have found in "A Rose for Emily" a description of a whole society that lives with a dead but unburied past, and much energy has been expended in attempts to establish the chronology of events in the story. "A Rose for Emily" is not Faulkner's best story, but it may well be regarded as the central one in his short story career. A reading of "A Rose for Emily" is given in chapter 12.

Quentin Compson is the unreliable narrator of the second Indian story in *These 13,* "A Justice" (previously unpublished). An innocent child, he does not grasp what his story is really about. "A Justice" is amusing, even though it deals with the tragedy of the Indians' inability to adjust to new situations. In this story, which shows a development over a long period, important links between the past and present of Yoknapatawpha are established.

"A Justice" is followed by "Hair" (first published in *American Mercury,* May 1931), the weakest story in the collection. It is a story of stubborn patience, loyalty, and endurance beyond the grasp of the townspeople, told by a fallible narrator. Quentin takes over the narration again in the next story, "That Evening Sun" (*American Mercury,* March 1931), and the tragedy inherent in the story is seldom surpassed in Faulkner's short fiction. (See chapter 14 for an extended discussion of this story.) His accomplishment was perhaps equaled later, but hardly surpassed, in such small-scale masterpieces as "Barn Burning" (first published in *Harper's,* June 1939) and in one or two of the short stories later revised and included in *Go Down, Moses* (1942). One of the most inexhaustible of Faulkner's short stories, and a favorite among critics, "That Evening Sun" tells about the black servant Nancy and her irrational fear of being killed by her husband, Jesus. Quentin tells the story some fifteen years after the events took place, juxtaposing the white Compson household with Nancy and her world. By implication, "That Evening Sun" becomes a story about the general human plight: despair, guilt, and lack of love. The uses of local history and racial injustice are combined with individual frustration and fear in a story with broad significance.

"Dry September" (first published in *Scribner's,* January 1931), another of Faulkner's best stories (see chapter 7 for an analysis of this story). Often called classical in its tragic intensity, it describes a town's ritualistic enactment of the scapegoat pattern to achieve redemption. The story is a superb example of how the description of landscape and climate can be used to set and amplify tone. After many rainless days the men in town are restless, and Minnie Cooper, barren and dry in her empty life, initiates the action when she accuses a black man of rape. The brutal story of evil and injustice develops rapidly; the violent, tragic events have been interpreted differently by the many critics who have taken an active interest in this story. "Dry September" concludes the middle part of *These 13* on a note of stillness, death, and hostility.

The final group of stories is enigmatic. The three stories (all previously unpublished) are experimental departures from the rest of the volume. "Mistral" may be overwritten and too long, but its intricate presentation of passion and murder through the outsider experience of two young men who happen to travel through town foreshadows narrative techniques Faulkner used later. "Divorce in Naples" tells about a homosexual "marriage" and divorce and is in some respects more genuinely Faulknerian than "Mistral." The grim but understanding humor and the rich use of similes and metaphors in pure, lyrical passages leave Faulkner's stamp on this story. "Carcassonne" is one of the most abstract of Faulkner's stories. Its protagonist endures suffering because he has a dream of performing something, of negating death's ultimate effect, which is to make one lie still. "Carcassonne" also reflects Faulkner's preoccupation with the agony and fear an artist has to face in order to create. The story is considered in chapter 6 of this study.

Faulkner's first collection received more laudatory reviews than any of his novels before 1931, although many critics complained that the volume was uneven. *These 13* still holds an important position in Faulkner's long career, although his *Collected Stories* may be said to have reduced the importance of the earlier volume since the stories reappear in a new context there.

*Idyll in the Desert* was published as a book in 1931, and in 1932 the Book Club of Texas published *Miss Zilphia Gant* (both appear in *Uncollected Stories*). *Miss Zilphia Gant* deals with overprotection and rebellion and is not too different from many other stories from this period in which females are shown as frustrated and deprived. *Idyll in the Desert* shows Faulkner's mastery of oral storytelling techniques and gives one version of his theme of endurance and love lasting beyond death.

## THE MIDDLE PERIOD—*DOCTOR MARTINO,* *THE UNVANQUISHED, GO DOWN, MOSES*

Faulkner continued publishing short stories after 1932, although his writing of new stories declined drastically. Still, by the time of *Doctor Martino and Other Stories* (1934) he had an ample supply of stories from which to select for inclusion. Whereas *These 13* includes seven previously unpublished stories, *Doctor Martino* only includes two: "Black Music" and "The Leg." Unlike the earlier collection, there seems to be no internal organization of this volume.

There is a clear shift from the preoccupation with war, wilderness, and town life in *These 13* to a focus on sex, death, and loss in *Doctor Martino.* The title story (*Harper's,* November 1931) presents a love triangle of a peculiar kind; usurpation and manipulation for private ends create an emotional parasitism. (This story reappears in the "Middle Ground" section of *Collected Stories,* together with five other stories from *Doctor Martino:* "Wash," "Honor," "Fox Hunt," "There Was a Queen," and "A Mountain Victory.") Although all the stories in *Doctor Martino* are competent, only "Wash" and "A Mountain Victory" show Faulkner at his best. "Wash" (*Harper's,* February 1934) is a taut and forceful narrative of almost apocalyptic horror, reused by Faulkner in *Absalom, Absalom!* (1936). "A Mountain Victory" (*Saturday Evening Post,* December 3, 1932), like "Wash," is set in the years after the Civil War. Here one sees the tragic development of a conflict arising suddenly and inevitably from what should have been a normal encounter between strangers. The movement toward disaster is implacable, and brutal death comes at the end. A deeply felt humanity pervades this story, which clearly transcends interpretation as just another tale about the Civil War and its human effects. "Mountain Victory" is discussed in chapter 9 and "Wash" in chapter 16 of the present study.

"Death Drag" (*Scribner's,* January 1932) and "Elly" (*Story,* February 1934) are the only two stories in *Doctor Martino* that are set in "the village." The young title character in "Elly" resembles Miss Emily in her reaction against overprotection and conformity. "Death Drag" deals with stunt flying and wing walking, although the way people lived and behaved in the years after World War I is at the center of the story, as it is in "Honor" (*American Mercury*, July 1930). "Honor" is another of Faulkner's stories about a strange love triangle with a tragic outcome. "Turn About" (*Saturday Evening Post*, March 5, 1932) is the only full-fledged World War I story in the collection. It differs from earlier such stories in that it is set in England and depicts an unusual brand of courage. "The Hound" (*Harper's*, August 1931)—one of the strongest stories in the volume—was reused in the Mink Snopes section of *The Hamlet*, although it was not originally a Snopes story. This story is discussed in chapter 8. "Smoke" (*Harper's*, April 1932) is Faulkner's first story of detection, but it is decidedly one of the weakest of his whodunits. It opens his 1949 collection of detective stories, *Knight's Gambit*.

The final three stories in *Doctor Martino* are all strange so-called "beyond" stories: tales of the supernatural or the fantastic. The story titled "Beyond" (*Harper's*, September 1933) was the only one of these that found periodical publication; "Black Music" and "The Leg" (called simply "Leg" in *Doctor Martino*) are the other two.

*Doctor Martino* elicited fewer reviews than *These 13*, and those critics that did respond stressed too heavily the decline in quality of the individual stories and of the collection as a whole. Yet most Faulkner scholars consider *Doctor Martino* inferior to *These 13*.

In addition to the stories Faulkner included in his first two collections or published as separate books, there are many stories that have other functions in his canon. "Spotted Horses" (*Scribner's*, June 1931) and "Lizards in Jamshyd's Courtyard" (*Saturday Evening Post*, February 27, 1932) were later reused in *The Hamlet*. "Spotted Horses" is analyzed in chapter 8. Together with "The Hound" and "Fool about a Horse" (*Scribner's*, August 1936), these "Snopes stories" are collected in *Uncollected Stories*. "Centaur in Brass" (*American Mercury*, February 1932) was reused in *The Town* (1957) but had by then already appeared in *Collected Stories*. Three more autonomous stories, any of which might easily have been included in one of the two early collections, remained uncollected till 1950, when they appeared in the "Middle Ground" section of *Collected Stories*: "Artist at Home" (*Story*, August 1933), "The Brooch" (*Scribner's*, January 1936), and "Pennsylvania Station" (*American Mercury*, February 1934).

Most of the previously unpublished stories from the early 1930s are included in *Uncollected Stories*. These include "Thrift" (*Saturday Evening Post*, September 6, 1930)—a humorous World War I story about a proverbial Scotsman who makes a profit from his participation in somebody else's war, the first Faulkner story published in the *Post* and hence a first encounter with this writer for thousands of readers—and "'Once aboard the Lugger'" (*Contempo*, February 1932), a story from the "prohibition industry," the second part of which first appeared in *Uncollected Stories*. Finally, "Evangeline" (*Atlantic*, November 1979; in *Uncollected Stories*) deserves mention. A long story, it is closely related to the Sutpen family's life and mores, and it was absorbed into *Absalom, Absalom!*

With a few exceptions Faulkner's best short stories, and many of his good stories, were written in the early 1930s. Moreso than the stories which preceded or followed, they are short stories in their own right: conceived, executed, and published as such. Only in a few instances can they be seen as by-products of Faulkner's novels. The richness and diversity of themes and techniques were unsurpassed in the years to come. Nevertheless, Faulkner continued to write short stories from time to time during the late 1930s and early 1940s—some of them almost formulaic, others serious and of high literary merit.

Still, Faulkner's output of short fiction declined sharply after 1932, when financial problems forced him to go to Hollywood and write for the screen. His Hollywood experience left him better off financially, and after 1933 he turned his attention almost exclusively to novel writing. Also, the Snopeses were beginning to occupy the author's mind, resulting in an occasional short story before he finally joined together material he had worked on for more than ten years in the episodic novel *The Hamlet*. In 1942 Faulkner returned to story writing for a brief but concentrated period with only moderate success, and near the end of that decade he started planning for publication of his collected stories, which finally resulted in two very different volumes: *Knight's Gambit* and *Collected Stories*.

The stories Faulkner wrote from 1933 until his last attempt to write stories for a living in 1942 fall roughly into four major categories. Miscellaneous stories, some reused in novels, others collected in *Collected Stories*, make up the first group. The second category comprises the stories that were later considerably revised and used in *The Unvanquished* (1938). The stories for *Go Down, Moses* form a third group, and finally there are the detective stories collected in *Knight's Gambit*. In the first group, "Lo!" (*Story*, November 1934; in *Collected Stories*), written in 1933, is Faulkner's third Indian story, a wildly exaggerated and extremely funny tale about an Indian chief's visit to Washington. "A Bear Hunt" (*Saturday Evening Post*, February 10, 1934; in *Collected Stories*), also written in 1933, is another story in the humorous vein; in the tradition of oral tales, it relies on elements of superstition, exaggeration, and comic effects. "Mule in the Yard" (*Scribner's*, August 1934; in *Collected Stories* and reused in *The Town*) is a Snopes story, hilarious and well deserving of its inclusion in the major collection despite Faulkner's use of it in *The Town*. His work on the Snopes material also yielded "Barn Burning" (*Harper's,* June 1939; in *Collected Stories*), which many critics and readers hold to be Faulkner's best short story. It was originally written as the opening chapter of *The Hamlet* and then excised from the typescript; only scattered minor fragments of the story can be found in the book. "Barn Burning" draws its interest, quality, and aura of deep personal suffering from its relationship with *The Hamlet,* a marvelous novel about the infestation of Yoknapatawpha by the Snopeses and on a deeper level about how myths are created. "Barn Burning" is a superb story in its own right; yet Faulkner was capable of fusing so many elements in this story because of his lasting interest in the Snopeses and because of the longer work in progress. This short story is discussed at length in chapter 5. The novel *Pylon* grew out of an unpublished, uncollected story, "This Kind of Courage," written in 1934 and revised when Faulkner began to expand it for the novel.

In 1934 Faulkner also wrote the first six stories in *The Unvanquished,* and in December 1935 "Lion," the germ of *Go Down, Moses,* was published in *Harper's* (collected in *Uncollected Stories*). He set his second story of ratiocination, "Monk" (*Scribner's,* May 1937; in *Knight's Gambit*), in the backwoods of Yoknapatawpha, again using his detective-lawyer Gavin Stevens as protagonist. In 1939, 1940, and 1941 Faulkner wrote most of the short stories he later revised for use in *Go Down, Moses,* and he also wrote three more detective stories. During some hectic months from spring to autumn 1934, the first six stories featuring the characters of Bayard and Ringo were written: "Ambuscade," "Retreat," "Raid," "The Unvanquished" (later titled "Riposte in Tertio"), "Vendée," and "Skirmish at Sartoris" (the Drusilla story). The first three stories were published in 1934, "Skirmish at Sartoris" in 1935, and "Vendée" and "The Unvanquished" late in 1936. A seventh story, "An Odor of Verbena," was written in order to complete *The Unvanquished,* although Faulkner also made unsuccessful attempts to sell it to the magazine market. Faulkner had to revise the stories for *The Unvanquished,* some of them substantially. He considered his Civil War stories, including these, "trash," and in a letter to Morton Goldman (August 1934) he stated that "As far as I am concerned, while I have to write trash, I don't care who buys it, as long as they pay the best price I can get." He felt that he sacrificed more important work by writing his romanticized tales about heroic Southern action during the Civil War, but when he undertook the work of revising and transforming the stories into a unified book, more of his genuine concerns were included. The original magazine stories are now all available in *Uncollected Stories* with the exception of "An Odor of Verbena," of which only the version printed in *The Unvanquished* exists. With his revisions Faulkner carefully brought the thematic content of the earliest stories in line with the serious direction of the later stories, adding a mature narrator who could give a more clearly retrospective view of the incidents and cruelties of war. The issue of race also became more significant. Faulkner proved that he could make a unified and serious novel out of short fiction he had described as trash. *The Unvanquished* is certainly not a mere collection of short stories.

Like Faulkner's first six Civil War stories, the stories for *Go Down, Moses* were all written over a relatively short span of time with almost no other story-writing activity intervening. One may thus say that this continuous process resembles the writing of a novel; and it is a critical commonplace today that *Go Down, Moses* is a novel and not a collection, although by some editorial mistake it was originally published as *Go Down, Moses and Other Stories*. Of course, the chapters of the book were written as short stories and, when accepted by magazines, published as such. "Lion" was greatly expanded and revised for chapter 5 of *Go Down, Moses,* becoming the well-known long story "The Bear" (a version of which appeared in the *Saturday Evening Post,* May 9, 1942). "The Old People" was written in 1939, while "A Point of Law," "Gold Is Not Always," "The Fire on the Hearth," "Pantaloon in Black," "Was," "Go Down, Moses," and "Delta Autumn" were all composed in 1940. With the exception of "The Fire on the Hearth" and "Was" (of which only the version used in the book exists), *Uncollected Stories* includes all the original stories that Faulkner developed into *Go Down, Moses.* The *Post* version of "The Bear" is also included there.

*Go Down, Moses* is one of Faulkner's most convincing artistic creations, a unified volume with emotional impact far greater than that of any of the individual stories, though it is possible to discuss them independently. "Was" is the opening section of *Go Down, Moses,* while three other stories form the second section, called "The Fire and the Hearth." Here a revised version of "A Point of Law" is used as the first chapter, and an extensively reworked "Gold Is Not Always" is incorporated as chapter 2 of section 2. The previously unpublished "The Fire on the Hearth" concludes this section. The entire section may be considered a single long story, one of Faulkner's finest. Centering on the scheming and cheating Lucas Beauchamp, it is a light, comic collection of anecdotes concerning among other topics moonshining and "planted" gold coins. Lucas and his wife, Molly, appear as stereotyped blacks, but "The Fire on the Hearth" softens and modifies the work in both characterization and tone. The central symbol of the fire burning on the hearth is strengthened, and Faulkner barely avoids melancholy and pathos in the description of the old woman's plight. Molly becomes the embodiment of all the virtues cherished in her society.

"Pantaloon in Black" (*Harper's*, October 1940) is the story of a giant black man whose wife dies. He buries her and then does everything possible in an attempt to provoke his own lynching. His delicate feelings are contrasted with the rude understanding that white characters show. In *Go Down, Moses* "Pantaloon in Black" intervenes between what may be regarded as the two main parts of the book: the story of Beauchamp and the story of Isaac McCaslin in "The Old People," "The Bear," and "Delta Autumn." "Pantaloon in Black" is analyzed in chapter 10 of the present study.

Ike McCaslin only gradually assumes central place in these stories; Quentin Compson was the central character in the early version of "The Old People" (*Harper's*, September 1940). The ritualistic hunt in that story points forward to "The Bear," and "The Old People" to an unusual degree provides links with the past of Yoknapatawpha and with other stories. The revised story devotes much attention to Ike's formative years in order to explain where he got his knowledge of "the old people" and his deep respect for the untamed wilderness. Sam Fathers, an Indian of mixed ancestry, has been Ike's substitute father and mentor. Ike's renunciation of his inheritance later in life and most of his subsequent behavior may be considered as acts of sacrifice and expiation, but they may also be viewed as acts of weakness and escape. Many of the elements that make Ike believable are found in "The Bear," one of the great hunting stories in world literature and one of the truly great stories in Faulkner's career. The book version has often been anthologized, although without the long fourth part (a practice begun by Malcolm Cowley in his *Portable Faulkner*, 1946).

Ike's three-part saga ends with "Delta Autumn" (*Story*, May–June 1942), set in a wilderness that is slowly being destroyed by civilization. "Delta Autumn" is a moving and penetrating story. Human beings in conflict with nature and with themselves are presented in a web of ideas and thoughts about race, history, morality, and love. Ike McCaslin is portrayed as an old man, "uncle to half a country and father to no one."

The story "Go Down, Moses" (*Collier's*, January 1941) depicts Molly Beauchamp's struggle to get her dead grandson back home to be buried where he belongs. It opens onto a larger world beyond the plantation, beyond Yoknapatawpha, and is thus a fitting conclusion to *Go Down, Moses* as a novel.

## LATE STORIES—*KNIGHT'S GAMBIT, COLLECTED STORIES*

In "Smoke," written circa 1930, Faulkner introduced Gavin Stevens, a lawyer who puts his skills as a detective to use in the investigation of mysteries within the borders of Yoknapatawpha County. The second whodunit, "Monk," was not written until 1937. Stonewall Jackson "Monk" Odletrop lives in an isolated area of the county populated by clannish people who "made whiskey and shot at all strangers from behind log barns and snake fences." To a large degree the story is really about his physical and mental isolation, and Gavin is only in the background, uncovering the truth about the deception of Monk by a fellow convict in prison. Gavin functions much more prominently as a detective in "Hand upon the Waters" (*Saturday Evening Post,* November 4, 1939), perhaps because he shares so much with the story's central character, Louis Grenier (Lonnie Grinnup). Gavin and Lonnie are the only surviving offspring from the three original founding fathers of the county. Still, the ratiocinative work, the solving of the murder of Grinnup, is more important here than the crime and its ramifications. Young Chick Mallison works with his Uncle Gavin in solving some crimes, and in "Tomorrow" (*Saturday Evening Post,* November 23, 1940) their ingenious detection leads to insights into human nature and teaches Chick a moral lesson. "An Error in Chemistry," written in 1940, is the only story in *Knight's Gambit* that was originally published where it rightfully belonged, in a sense: it appeared in the June 1946 issue of *Ellery Queen's Mystery Magazine,* having won second prize in a competition. The story is pure detection, but the detective work is so simple that even the boy narrator, Chick, draws the inevitable conclusion and deduces who the killer is. The last of Faulkner's detective stories, "Knight's Gambit," was written in 1942. Unable to sell the story, Faulkner expanded it into a novella to make his collection of detective fiction large enough for publication in book form in 1949. The short, early version of "Knight's Gambit" has never been published.

*Knight's Gambit* is closer in form to *The Unvanquished* and *Go Down, Moses* than to ordinary collections because it has a central figure and central themes: detection, justice, and the relation between outsiders and the community. Still, *Knight's Gambit* is less of a unified work; Faulkner simply collected his detective stories in the chronology of their periodical publication. The volume received little critical attention, although critics treated it with modest respect. *Knight's Gambit* still has a minor, perhaps even underappreciated, place in Faulkner's total oeuvre.

The short version of "Knight's Gambit" was the first work in Faulkner's 1942 burst of story activity. He hoped to earn enough money on the sale of these stories to avoid another journey to Hollywood. With the exception of "Knight's Gambit" and "Snow" (first published in *Uncollected Stories*), all the stories from this time are in *Collected Stories*. In "Two Soldiers" (*Saturday Evening Post,* March 28, 1942) a nine-year-old boy narrates a patriotic story about loyalty and endurance.

In "Shall Not Perish" (*Story*, July–August 1943), a sequel to "Two Soldiers," the young narrator tells about receiving word of his brother Pete's death and about the family's reaction. Another soldier, the son of wealthy parents, has also been killed in the war, and in the course of the narrative the boy slowly grasps that he is part of a larger community and that love for one's country may necessitate sacrificing one's life. "Shall Not Perish" is one of Faulkner's most emotional stories, but the sense of personal grief and tragedy gives it deeper significance, so that it appears less sentimental than its companion piece, "Two Soldiers." Yet it is almost a relief when, in "Shingles for the Lord" (*Saturday Evening Post*, February 13, 1943), readers meet members of the same stricken family again in a humorous, almost incredible story. "My Grandmother Millard and General Bedford Forrest and the Battle of Harrykin Creek" (*Story*, March–April 1943) is closely related to central elements in *The Unvanquished*, but the story is by no means serious; it was written with the sole purpose of evoking laughter and succeeds in doing so. Another humorous story, "A Courtship" (*Sewanee Review*, October 1948), is about courtship and a competition between a white man, David Hogganbeck, and the Indian Ikkemotubbe. The competition is of marathon proportions, and Faulkner quotes from Homer as well as from Lord Byron in his description of the girl in the story.

With *Collected Stories* in 1950, Faulkner further solidified his reputation in the world of letters. The Nobel Prize for literature in 1949, awarded to Faulkner in Stockholm in December 1950, was the ultimate proof of his success and achievement. *Collected Stories* is, of course, Faulkner's major collection, a milestone marking the culmination of a long and varied career and including almost all of Faulkner's previously published stories that do not stand in close relationship to his novels. Faulkner had suggested this collection as early as 1939 but did not begin considering it seriously until 1948. According to lists that Faulkner made, he planned to include only previously uncollected short stories, including the Gavin Stevens stories, in the new book. He then decided, however, to leave out the detective stories and collect them in a separate volume. According to a November 11, 1948, letter to Robert K. Haas, Faulkner intended the *Collected Stories* to be "comprehensive of all my short pieces except those previously allotted to other complete volumes in the future." Although the collection is not really comprehensive, it may be said to include the forty-two stories Faulkner wanted to represent his achievement as a short story writer. The book contains most of Faulkner's independent stories but not all of them, and those stories not collected in the volume also deserve attention.

Twenty-five of the forty-two stories had been collected before in *These 13* and *Doctor Martino*, while seventeen stories were previously uncollected. Some of them date back to 1930, and most of them were written before 1940. Planning his collection, Faulkner wrote to Malcolm Cowley on November 1, 1948, that "even to a collection of short stories, form, integration, is as important as to a novel—an entity of its own, single, set for one pitch, contrapuntal in integration, toward one end, one finale." He organized *Collected Stories* with such principles in mind, although the criteria for arrangement are often difficult to determine. There are six sections in the book. The first section, "The Country," includes six stories, none of them previously collected and all written between 1938 and 1942, beginning with "Barn Burning" and ending with "Two Soldiers" and "Shall Not Perish." These six stories deal with the people of the Yoknapatawpha countryside, black, white, and Indian, rich and poor, brave and foolish. The conflicts between black and white, and between established families and foreigners to the region, are accompanied by broader conflicts inherent in loyalty and endurance, finding one's place in the world, identity, and self-assertion. "Barn Burning" establishes themes that recur throughout the volume. The first section has a high degree of unity, which is not true for all sections in the volume. Section 2, "The Village," includes ten stories, all written before 1935, with the four village stories from *These 13* at the core. These stories show a great variety in mood and narrative handling, although the community is central in all of them. Major themes in Faulkner's writing—individual versus community, isolation versus involvement, and escape versus endurance—are displayed here. Jefferson, a village in Yoknapatawpha County, comes to life in these narratives. The sense of place is strong, and the village functions to measure the effects of change and progression, since the people of a town such as Jefferson often struggle to keep up with improvements and changes in the larger, outside world.

Section 3, "The Wilderness," includes four Indian stories—two of them from *These 13* together with the later "Lo!" and "A Courtship." Tragedy and comedy are thus found within the same section. In section 4, "The Wasteland," there is no place for humor or comedy. The four World War I stories from *These 13* make up this section, together with "Turn About" from *Doctor Martino*. It may be worth noting that Faulkner's war stories from the early part of his career are included in this section, while the war stories from the 1940s are included in the first section of the book. Antiwar sentiment seems to have been replaced by questions of loyalty, duty, and endurance in the more mature writer.

Section 5, "The Middle Ground," comprises eleven stories, six of them from *Doctor Martino* and five previously uncollected stories from the first half of the 1930s. Bereavement, loss, suffering, and death—both symbolic and violently real—are central in them all. Rootless, searching characters try to find their place in life and ascertain their identity. In contrast to the country people, many of these characters are uprooted or alienated. Although this section includes stories that criticize contemporary life, some of the stories (such as "There Was a Queen" and "A Mountain Victory") deal with tradition and with problems more aesthetic than social.

"Beyond," section 6 in *Collected Stories,* includes the three supernatural stories from *Doctor Martino* and, to conclude the whole volume, "Mistral," "Divorce in Naples," and "Carcassonne," the stories that make up the final section of *These 13.* The collection thus moves from the cohesive and stable life in the countryside of Yoknapatawpha to an artist's dream of creation. In "Carcassonne" the artist goes "beyond" the bareness of his environment to live within the world of his imagination. But to live within the walls of one's "Carcassonne" is not necessarily a dream come true: anguish accompanies the artist in his struggle "to create out of the materials of the human spirit something which did not exist before."

*Collected Stories* was reviewed widely, and not one reviewer was clearly hostile or negative. Instead critics stressed the practicality and usefulness of the volume as an introduction to Faulkner's rich fictional world. *Collected Stories* thus marked another important step forward in the general acknowledgment of Faulkner's total achievement. Many reviewers stated or implied on the basis of the richness of the *Collected Stories* that recognition of Faulkner as the leading American novelist of his generation would soon become commonplace. The collection was chosen by the Book-of-the-Month Club as an alternate fiction selection for September 1950 and received the National Book Award that same year.

After the publication of *Collected Stories* Faulkner published few stories of importance. With few exceptions they derive their significance from their relationship to his longer fiction. *Notes on a Horsethief* (conceived as early as 1940 but not published until 1951) was an early precursor of Faulkner's *A Fable* (1954). It was revised before being incorporated into the novel. The narrative prologue for act 1 of Faulkner's play *Requiem for a Nun* (1951) is a revised version of "A Name for the City," a story published in the October 1950 issue of *Harper's.* "By the People" (*Mademoiselle,* October 1955) is a lighthearted Snopes story about a political rally, and it became chapter 23 of *The Mansion;* "Hog Pawn," which Faulkner tried to sell to the magazine market in 1955, remained unpublished as a short story until it appeared in *Uncollected Stories.* This is an early version of what later became chapter 14 of *The Mansion,* also known as the Meadowfill episode. The last short fiction to be published in Faulkner's lifetime, "Hell Creek Crossing" (*Saturday*

*Evening Post,* March 31, 1962), is hardly a short story in its own right but rather an excerpt from *The Reivers* (1962).

In addition to these stories, with their close relationship to longer works, two independent stories were written and published during this time. "Race at Morning" (*Saturday Evening Post,* March 5, 1955) is Faulkner's most successful story from his later years. His last hunting story, it is a tribute to the wilderness. A slightly revised version of this story was incorporated into *Big Woods* (1955) and reprinted in *Uncollected Stories.* The second independent short story is "Mr. Acarius" (written circa 1953, published in the October 9, 1965, issue of the *Saturday Evening Post,* and included in *Uncollected Stories*), a story about alcohol abuse and personal conflicts.

Preparations for the publication of Faulkner's hunting stories in *Big Woods* included revising and borrowing from previously published works and adding linking material between various stories. The volume is of a secondary nature and includes no new material of any special significance.

## CONCLUDING NOTE

Time and again Faulkner despaired over his inability to succeed as a writer of short stories, especially when they were turned down by magazines. He deemed his stories his most marketable merchandise, the product he could sell at the highest price in the American magazine and book market in the late 1920s and 1930s. His lasting and unflagging attempts to sell his stories demonstrate not the despair of a failed short story writer but the confidence of a storyteller who knew the worth of his material. Accordingly, he also knew when he produced for the market, as was the case with the stories that became *The Unvanquished.* There is ample evidence in his correspondence and public statements to show that Faulkner regarded very highly the short story as a literary form; more easily than in the case of his novels, however, he accepted revisions, simplified narrative structure, and even rewrote whole stories in the attempt to sell a story that proved particularly difficult to place anywhere. And as he grew older and committed himself more exclusively to novel writing, the short narratives he wrote and published separately very often were the result of early and tentative work on what would finally become a novel. Faulkner wrote short stories for money, as he wrote novels too to make a living, and by and large it is fair to say that despite his willingness to comply with editors' wishes in a few cases, he revised and rewrote his stories not to suit the needs of a market but in order to satisfy himself and his own artistic demands.

Faulkner's short stories show man in his ageless struggle and may be described as universal in their thematic implications. But his stories do not only deal with the "ageless, eternal struggles," even if he may have thought that the episodes and incidents he recorded were part of some basic, unchanging way of being alive in the world. His stories are very much the stories of the people, customs, and mores of a specific historical time. Even so, Faulkner claimed time and again that there are old, unchanging verities of the human heart. Perhaps he is closest to a portrayal of these verities in stories about the illiterate and poor people of Yoknapatawpha, who seem somehow to live their lives as if under ancient laws whereby myths are still believed in and destiny cannot be chosen or changed. This is only part of Faulkner's world, however; all in all change must be considered one of the key terms in a description of his achievement as a writer, almost the same way as time is a central concern. The conflicts of the human heart may well be ageless and eternal, yet Faulkner's stories show that man must change with an ever-changing world and that adjustment to new situations is required, despite the pain it may cause. To record the minute changes that add up to real changes only over years, Faulkner might have chosen a few key moments and episodes, minimal stories with great impact and significance, instead of a wide array of disparate tales. Faulkner's interest was with people, and he loved a good story; thus only in a few cases did he write a short story in which almost nothing happens, but in which the passing of a world and an age is still felt. Faulkner preferred to tell more stories, longer stories, but he told them in such a way that they serve as records of these minimal and almost invisible changes in a social group. He succeeded in making his stories reflect the passing of a way of life and of an era. His was a rich heritage of a heroic past, a sense of history which included defeat and defiance, a strong sense of belonging to a stable, well-ordered albeit somewhat rigid community. What he had inherited could not be changed quickly, but he saw the changes and became their chronicler in stories and novels of lasting value. Even if the short story, almost by definition, cannot be as polyphonic and dialogic as the novel, a dozen of Faulkner's best short stories most certainly serve to give a vivid, colorful, and diverse impression of his writing, of his fictional world, of his limitless probing and searching in order to see and understand. More than anything else, they show the generosity of the human spirit in some of its richest and fullest moments.

# Chapter 2

# The Study of Faulkner's Short Fiction

When I first began my study of William Faulkner's short fiction some twenty years ago, very little scholarly work had been done. Michael Millgate had written a detailed, informed, and useful chapter on the short stories in his *The Achievement of William Faulkner* (1966), and James B. Meriwether had published a number of bibliographical studies that also included the short fiction. Some of the books on Faulkner's novels also included chapters on the short stories, notably studies by Irving Howe (1952), William Van O'Connor (1959), Hyatt H. Waggoner (1959), and Joseph W. Reed, Jr. (1973). Numerous articles had been published in journals and magazines, but in general the field was wide open for research. Indeed, so little was done, and what was done was so tentative or unreliable, that contrary to what I had planned I had to establish the facts of his career as accurately as I was capable. The textual and bibliographical study published as *William Faulkner: The Short Story Career* in 1981 was the first book-length study of Faulkner's short fiction, although quite a number of doctoral theses had been written at American universities. I then used the textual and bibliographical information as a starting point for an analysis of Faulkner's short fiction and tried to present brief interpretations of each individual story seen in the context of periods, collections, and cycles. *William Faulkner: The Novelist as Short Story Writer* included all of Faulkner's short stories, even the marginal ones that today I probably would exclude from discussion, such as "Mississippi" or "Sepulture South: Gaslight." The next book on the short fiction was published the same year as my second book, based on a dissertation that had proved helpful in my own study—James B. Carothers's *William Faulkner's Short Stories* (1985).

This means that it was probably still correct a decade ago to maintain that Faulkner's short fiction had not received the attention it deserved; today we should not hide behind such commonplaces. We have finally reached the point in Faulkner scholarship where the stories are studied for their own merit and not because of the interesting and intriguing interdependency of novel and story, which has been the main reason that the stories have been considered in a number of competent studies of one or more of Faulkner's novels.

In *William Faulkner: The Novelist as Short Story Writer* I stated that "Faulkner's short fiction is still the most neglected area in Faulkner studies" (9). It was true at the time, and although much has been written on the stories since then, there is still a lot to be done. Too often critics still seem to wrestle with a set of fundamental questions: Are the stories really worthy of extended treatment? Are they in general inferior to his achievement as a novelist? Can the study of the stories be defended only if it is helpful to the explication of the complex questions that the novels raise? More and more scholars have found that the study of Faulkner's short fiction is well worth the effort, whether they are studied in their own right or for their relationship with particular novels. I set forth my understanding of the value of Faulkner's short fiction without reservation in *William Faulkner: The Novelist as Short Story Writer:*

> Faulkner's short stories form an important part of his complete *oeuvre,* and there is no reason whatsoever to give them only cursory treatment or mention them as interesting when or if they have any bearing upon his novels. (15)

The same sentiments are expressed in two other book-length studies of Faulkner's short fiction; James B. Carothers's *William Faulkner's Short Stories* and James Ferguson's *Faulkner's Short Fiction* (1991). Carothers argues convincingly for the high quality of Faulkner's stories and claims that they accordingly should be treated on a par with his novels:

> Faulkner's short stories are considerably more than rough drafts or minor footnotes to his novels; they deserve serious study in their own right and are of sufficient merit to assure Faulkner's place in the first rank of twentieth-century writers, even had he never written novels. (xv)

Ferguson begins his book by stating that there is no reason to complain that Faulkner's works have been neglected by scholars and critics, although he apparently feels that he too has to apologize for writing on the stories and not the novels. His use of "neglect," however, is necessarily more qualified than it had to be in Carothers's and my own studies:

> And yet there have been, until quite recently, curious lacunae, strangely neglected areas on which little important work has been done. The most obvious of these gaps, until about 1980, has been the short fiction. (1)

Ferguson also notes that certain individual stories have been neglected by critics, despite the fact that they are among Faulkner's best. "Mountain Victory" is his leading example of this neglect, which may be a result of understandable concentration by a few scholars on Faulkner's complete story-writing career and on his achievement in the genre rather than on interpretations of individual stories. Some stories, notably "A Rose for Emily" and "That Evening Sun," have received more than their fair share of attention, and the time may well have come for new readings, in new contexts, of other stories, though not necessarily of all of them. Perhaps a concentration on the best stories—even if some of them have already been extensively discussed—is one way of demonstrating Faulkner's mastery of the genre.

In 1992 *Faulkner and the Short Story: Faulkner and Yoknapatawpha, 1990,* a collection of papers from the 1990 University of Mississippi Faulkner conference, was published. Neither the conference itself nor the volume that resulted did what one would have expected it to do, despite a number of very competent papers and interesting readings of individual stories. *Faulkner and the Short Story* should have contributed to the understanding of the special quality of Faulkner's story writing in a more general sense. The conference raised important questions but gave them only slight or cursory treatment: questions of genre, for example, storytelling techniques, thematic concerns, and differences and similarities between stories for different markets or between story and novel. Very often the intricate stories themselves and their complex relationship with novels—as in *Go Down, Moses*—receive undue attention and emphasis when Faulkner's short fiction is up for discussion, at times to the exclusion of other texts which do not relate directly to a particular novel.

In the *Reader's Guide to the Short Stories* series, Diane Brown Jones has written a volume on Faulkner's short fiction (1994). The choice of stories presented and discussed in the book is governed by two concerns, extrinsic to the stories themselves: the size of the volume and the curious decision to deal with the *Collected Stories* alone. In other words the *Collected Stories* is preferred to all other possible choices, and since the forty-two stories in the collection could not be covered in one volume, all stories in "The Wasteland" and the "Beyond" sections are left out, leaving Jones with the still-formidable task of presenting thirty-one stories. Jones is right when she claims that the *Collected Stories* is "the most significant gathering of Faulkner's short pieces." But she clearly puts too much emphasis on "the master's selection"; it is impossible to laud Faulkner's wish to have a collection that was comprehensive and then leave out eleven stories from that collection. Knowing that so many good Faulkner stories found their place in other "collections" such as *Go Down, Moses* and *The Hamlet* or simply were not collected at all, the selection in this volume cannot be explained, excused, or defended with anything but pragmatic reasons.

Jones's treatment of the stories is fair enough, straightforward, to the point, and informative. But it is almost completely derivative in the sense that she draws on research done by other scholars, and even if the presentation and evaluation of interpretation and criticism are central tasks for her, very little new is added to what has previously been written.

Another anthology of seminar papers on Faulkner's short fiction must be mentioned, since I have had the opportunity to use the material in this volume in the preparation of the present book, even if it was not published then: *William Faulkner's Short Fiction: An International Symposium* (1997). Being myself editor of the volume, which is based on a conference in Oslo, I am obviously in no position to give a critical evaluation of this volume. Accordingly, let me offer just a few remarks to give an impression of it.

The symposium did not concentrate on Faulkner's short fiction in order to right a wrong, fill a lacuna, or close a gap. The conference papers demonstrate this clearly. They deal with the short story achievement because the stories deserve to be taken seriously. The collection includes numerous discussions of the interdependency of stories and novels, the relationship of individual stories to one particular novel, and the transition from short stories to longer fiction, among other topics. A few papers discuss a single story or a group of related stories, and in combination with questions of genre, theoretical discussions, and fresh methodological approaches, these contributions are no less important than the others. New looks at potential contexts (textual or cultural) have also produced readings of what might be considered Faulkner's worst stories. The conference was not organized to cover that which had not been done before, and a multiplicity of approaches is accordingly found in the volume.

In addition to the books mentioned, hundreds of essays and articles on Faulkner's short stories—most of them dealing with one story only—have been written, a critical interest that began very early in Faulkner scholarship. It would be a serious misunderstanding not to read and use the best of these articles in one's future studies of Faulkner's short story writing, a point which Diane Jones demonstrates very clearly in her volume. Together with the books mentioned above, there is absolutely no reason to talk about neglect, but there is certainly also no reason to apologize for writing on the short fiction. Instead we should concentrate on what has not been done well enough, what can be improved on, and what can be explained and analyzed more satisfactorily. We should not haggle over borderlines between different but closely related genres but discuss the various versions of stories without any prejudiced hierarchical understanding of their relative inherent worth. We do not need deconstructionist reading of each and every Faulkner short story, nor do we need to place them all in a cultural or postcolonial context. Textual and intertextual studies should be kept within the sensible and reasonable, and the study of Faulkner's short fictions should little by little profit more from the important developments in literary theory in general than it has done so far.

# Chapter 3

# The Short Story Genre and Faulkner's Contribution to It

William Faulkner despaired of his own failure to write short stories and sell them, asserting that he had no feeling for short stories and at one point even claiming that "I never wrote a short story I liked."[1] He complained that story writing took time and energy away from the writing of novels. Nevertheless, there is little doubt that Faulkner held the short story in high esteem, ranking it second only to poetry, although his statements to this effect came late in life when he no longer despaired over failures any more. "In the novel you can be careless but in the short story you can't. I mean by that good stories like Chekhov wrote. That's why I rate that second—it's because it demands a nearer absolute exactitude."[2]

This apparent paradox is typical of a writer who was divided in his loyalties, who always seemed to wish for more than he could have, and who set standards for himself that he could not match. He regarded himself as a failed poet and perhaps also as a failed short story writer who had to turn to the novel, which offered opportunities for "the most splendid failure." In spite of his thinking about the hierarchies of literary forms, in his own literary practice—which must be understood as the most revealing commentary on his literary ambitions—the novel was always the preferred genre. Clearly, a high number of his short stories would not have been written were it not for the market and the money, whereas on the other hand, more stories—and, most likely, more "literary" stories of high quality—would have been written had he not had the novelistic tendency to sacrifice stories, anecdotes, fragments, and drafts and subsume them in longer narratives which would be published as novels. Even if this is particularly true for the episodic novels—*The Unvanquished, The Hamlet, Go Down, Moses*—it may also be true in a more interesting and revealing way for the non-episodic novels, as

Michael Millgate has shown.[3] The only way to resolve the paradox is probably to emphasize the novel's unlimited capacity to include all sorts of narrative units, its ability to integrate and transform and combine episodes and incidents into the larger framework of its dialogic structure. If Faulkner succeeded as a short story writer only in a few of his best stories, we may on the other hand say that he succeeded also as a short story writer in his novels, episodic as well as unified ones, which may also be true of the failed poet who retained so much of his poetical language in his novels. This means that even if Faulkner experienced a sense of failure as a short story writer, we should not automatically accept this judgement. We should rather look at the longer form, which he quickly moved on to after much poetry and short fiction in the 1920s and then spent most of his career trying to perfect, always making good use of his experience as well as his material as a failed poet and largely unsuccessful short story writer.

Malcolm Cowley claimed that Faulkner was not primarily a novelist, and that he was at his best in individual long stories (Cowley 1946, 18). Michael Millgate at an early point also argued that Faulkner "is perhaps most consistently at his best in short stories than he is in novels" (Millgate 1961, 65). Critical consensus has since then rightfully established Faulkner as primarily a novelist, and his novels have received wide critical attention, whereas the stories by and large have been discussed chiefly because of their relationship to particular novels. His contribution to the short story genre has been described as slight or of minor importance by some critics. He has accordingly been read and analyzed as a born storyteller who had few other concerns than to get his stories told, so that the readers were allowed to listen to old tales and talking and to the best of gossip, presented as directly and simply as possible.[4] By and large the art of Faulkner's short fiction is not much different from that found in a strong American tradition, where most fiction writers have worked within both genres, without specializing in one of them. And since the stories relate so significantly to so many of the author's great novels, they have often been used to help in the analysis of a novel, with the result that only a few stories have been extensively discussed in their own right. It is of course no surprise that Faulkner's shorter narratives have been regarded as inferior to his longer works, if only tacitly or implicitly; in this respect his short fiction shares the fate of the short story form itself in literary history and scholarship. The study of the relationship between novel and short story is a valid and important one in itself, but it also tends to blur significant distinctions between two related but different forms of narrative. In Faulkner's case one important question may be whether his stories are so dependent on his novels and so closely interlinked with novels that questions regarding genre in a general sense are of no interest.

It has been maintained that generic concepts are of little interest in a study of Faulkner's short fiction, not because of the uneven quality of the stories or the relatively few experiments in the short narrative Faulkner made but because his use and reuse of material in novels and short stories implies the upheaval of the borderlines between long and short narrative. In Faulkner's work, the German critic Ruth Kilchenmann says, "Unterscheidungen nach Genres [haben] keine Bedeutung" (Divisions according to genres are of no significance) (Kilchenmann 1967, 149). But to see in the dense intertextuality of Faulkner's work a transcendence of the traditional boundaries between types of literature so that generic concepts are of little interest is perhaps to rely too heavily on the obvious and superficial.[5] The reuse of material, the reappearance of characters, the echoing of phrases and the propensity for talking and for proverbial wisdom, the linking of episodes in order to create loosely connected novels or cycles of stories that have the ultimate impact of a novel all suggest the need to emphasize the functions of literature and not the borderlines between related genres.

Modern generic studies are descriptive, seeming to recommend a position somewhere between Croce, on the one hand, who has written in favor of doing away with all generic divisions and the many rigid taxonomies wherein all texts can be pigeonholed once and for all. We should focus on the function of literature, not on the borderlines between texts, which is of course also what modern text theory insists on.[6] All the same, we cannot rid ourselves of the idea of forms of literature. It remains a fact that generic concepts still exert a strong influence in literary studies and on authors, so it would not be wise to underestimate their role in most of our interpretive work.

The basic question when we discuss the genre of the short story, which inadvertently seems to imply a discussion of the novel if only for simple comparison, is whether the difference between the two forms of fiction is one of length only or whether it is a difference in kind. Let us look briefly at some of the genre problems before discussing a few characteristics of Faulkner's short stories. Numerous critics, beginning with Brander Matthews almost a hundred years ago, have insisted that the difference between the short story (which does not have *short* in its name in most languages) has something to do with the difference in length but also that the brevity of the short story has structural consequences. In Matthews's understanding the difference is even more profound:

> . . . the difference between a Novel and a Short-story is a difference of kind. A true Short-story is something other and something more than a mere story which is short. A true Short-story differs from the Novel chiefly in its essential unity of impression. In a far more

exact and precise use of the word, a Short-story has unity as a Novel cannot have it. . . . [7]

"Shortness" or "brevity" opens up comparisons with the novel that go beyond mere quantitaive measures to aesthetic properties such as condensation, compression, unity, and synthesis. Shortness can obviously only be understood in relation to something else that is not short—specifically, the novel. There is obviously no way to describe a genre without making reference to other genres. But as Mary Louise Pratt convincingly has shown, relations between genres do not have to be symmetrical: "The relation between the novel and the short story is a highly assymetrical one . . . Their relation is not one of contrasting equivalents in a system (separate but equal), but a hierarchical one with the novel on top and the short story dependent" (Pratt 1981, 180). Pratt states that facts about the novel are necessary to explain facts about the short story, but the reverse is not so. Long and short would correspond to such relations as major to minor, greater to lesser, even "mature" to "infant." If this description is correct, it helps explain why the short story seems to have become a "marginal" genre, especially well suited to render experiences of marginality, oppression, and loneliness—in short, experiences which are not of the open, daylight kind and which sometimes may be deemed more profound. The Freudian concept of the "uncanny" has been used to describe some of the special qualities of the material for which the short story is better suited than the novel, with its broader perspective, its depiction of society and life in a given community at a certain time. The novel can incorporate almost anything and still remain within its genre, but thinking in terms like these may get us somewhat closer to the characteristic traits that have become trademarks of the literary short story and which today may appear not to be genre characteristics but literary conventions associated with the short story. In this sense, both Frank O'Connor (1962), referring to traditional and even old short stories, and Charles May (1984), trying to define and conceptualize the "modern short story," may be right in putting heavy emphasis on estrangement, human loneliness, and existential experience of an almost religious kind as part of the reader's experience in a literary short story of our day and time. I shall return to the concept of the modern short story below.

One of the chief characteristics of the short story, whether told to an audience or written, seems to be its orientation toward an end. In a sense the structure of the short story implies that it will be completed at its conclusion; tensions are resolved, crises have passed and led to happiness or grief, characters have gone through decisive experiences and lost or won; and all this has been implied from the very beginning of the story because of its structure, its tradition, and the coercive concept of "short story" itself. Edgar Allan Poe's definition of the story, with its insistence on "a certain unique or single *effect*"[8] to which everything in the story contributes, has been very influential and must be seen as vital in establishing some of the most lasting conventions of the story as well as some of the expectations which readers bring to short stories as part of their overall literary competence. It may be wrong to maintain that the brevity of a short story is so significant in its structural consequences that Poe's definition is valid for literary short stories in the twentieth century. But if the story is short on time (the time it takes to tell it and to read it, but also in the sense that it brings in and treats time) and therefore cannot deal in any real sense with the passing of time or with temporality, it might be viewed as almost exemplary for momentary and revelatory if not epiphanic experiences.

The plotting of a short story leads intentionally to its conclusion, which in literary stories may well be an open ending, involving unresolved or contradictory tensions, or a kind of narrative mediation on an experience not quite grasped. The conclusion may be called a denouement, a turning point, a crisis that leads to revelation or insight, and it may engender many questions from the listener or reader who lives in a world where something always follows the ending of a story. Still the short story, to be a short story and not a scene, a summary, an episode, or an image, tends to give us a sense of an ending in the many possible interpretations of this term. The Russsian formalist Victor Shklovsky distinguishes between two basic types of motivation that give us this sense of finality: either we experience in the short story resolved opposition or revealed similarity. In both cases Shklovsky sees a kind of circular movement that links the ending with the beginning by comparison or by contrast, thus giving the feeling of wholeness or completeness.[9]

This orientation toward the ending and feeling of completion is peculiar to the short story, even if the novel certainly also may be described on the basis of its narrative desire toward the end. Yet more than the novel, the short story must keep within the limits established in its early parts and by the inherent motivations for the concluding parts discernible there. The novel, on the other hand, may conclude its main line of action long before the end and may then go on to tell new stories, reveal new destinies and new worlds, apparently in a way that would make it possible to extend a novel to any length. It is also possible to contend that the short story, despite its being a highly sophisticated literary form in the hands of its major practitioners, is susceptible to all kinds of experiments and never ceases to surprise in its inexhaustible resourcefulness, more closely related to oral storytelling than the modern novel is. Thus the narrative voice, which is often so pervasively "heard" or felt in many short stories even when they appear to have no explicit narrator and minimal narration, may be inherited from the original and genuine storytelling situation. The many narrators, overt or covert, obtrusively felt or minimally present in Faulkner's short fiction, are worth a close study, even if some of these narrators are shared with his longer fictions (for example, Ratliff).

In accordance with the discussion above, my reason for asking if Faulkner's stories may be said to go beyond genre has nothing to do with his use of the same stories in short and long narratives, nor does it imply that distinctions between types of literature are no longer valid. After all, to know when a story transcends the type or class of literature it belongs to, one has to have a fairly clear understanding of the *differentiae speci-ficae* of that class. What I want to discuss is whether it is reasonable to find in Faulkner's best stories a special kind of interest and a specific narrative mode that set them apart from most of his own stories and average stories by other authors. If this is so, we could say that the art of his short fiction transcends the limits of the traditional short story, even most of his own stories; and I think this is true for the stories in which an existential experience is described and reflected upon. Since I shall have to modify this statement later on, let me make it perfectly clear that most of Faulkner's stories still must be seen as a novelist's short stories and that they remain firmly placed within a storytelling tradition in which action and plot are key components. Often we may find that the momentary insights die quickly or that they only have a vague feeling which escapes the protagonists, an *epiphany manquée,* as in a number of the early sketches and story attempts, or a foreboding of knowledge which will be obtainable only later, as in the stories with the child Quentin Compson as protagonist.[10]

This description of the stories in which Faulkner presents existential experience seems to place these works very much within the genre, not beyond or outside it. Even if it complicates my argument, Charles E. May's fine essay on "The Nature of Knowledge in Short Fiction" (1984) should be mentioned here, not because it insists on the absolute difference between long and short narratives, which it does, but because it describes aspects of the modern short story which are clearly present in Faulkner's best stories.

According to May, "The short story is the most adequate form to confront us with reality as we perceive it in our most profound moments" (338). The idea of "our most profound moments" may here indicate just the kind of existential experience that I find in Faulkner's best short fiction, and the quotation obviously also supports the notion of a close link between the short story form and the special kind of experience presented in it. In comparison with the narrative long form—the novel—with its broader perspective and wider range, the brief narrative seems to be much more subtly adjusted to present our encounters with something beyond ourselves and everyday life; it is admirably suited to present existential experience and thus function as exemplary. The modern short story reflects a modern experience and conscience, an experience of loss and pain, of something broken and not mended, of strings and attachments gone, of uncertainties as to one's place in the world and in society.

This understanding should give an indication of the close affinity between existential experience and much, although certainly not all, short fiction. Heide Ziegler's very competent study, *Existentielles Erleben und kurzes Erzählen* (1977) investigates this affinity by looking at the comic, tragic, grotesque, and mythic in Faulkner's short fiction. Charles May's short story theory is based upon the alleged different experience and knowledge in the brief narrative. Yet contrary to Ziegler, who stresses that the combination of existential experience and short fiction cannot be understood as a necessary constituent of the genre (167), May insists that "short fiction, by its very length, demands both a subject matter and a set of artistic conventions that derive from and establish the primacy of an experience directly and emotionally created and encountered" (328). As mentioned, I am reluctant to define short fiction as narrowly as does May yet willing to insist upon the short story's unique ability to present a different reality in which we experience disruptions and dangers which we normally avoid in our protected lives. Since all short story definitions have stressed the intensity of vision and the focus on the climax of a situation, it is perhaps not very radical to claim that the short story is particularly suitable for presenting existential experience. If a choice involving an ethical value is at the center of the story, the text is free to make use of only the absolutely necessary elements to establish the crisis and the choice. Accordingly, the subject matter and thematic interest become responsible for the narrative strategy, resulting in the brevity of the story.

Many of Faulkner's brief narratives are of the kind that give confirmation, comfort, and safety, albeit that hyperbolic humor or a generous irony may be needed to abate some of the hardships and pain. In some texts tensions remain unresolved; characters are torn between conflicting forces and interests; oppressed and poor and weak, they fight to convince at least themselves that they exist, that they have a choice, or that some day they shall know more and be better off. Faulkner's best short stories often become a vehicle for expressing not only the protagonist's vague or misunderstood feeling of bereavement but also a description of and reflection on the very moment when opposing forces struggle for command of soul and body. That Faulkner's narrative principle for pre-

senting such central scenes is the "frozen moment" seems to be generally accepted by Faulkner scholars today,[11] but one should bear in mind
that to capture and isolate a split second from the everlasting flow of
time, halting time and showing man in his ageless struggle before sending him off again, is more than technique or habit. It shows man's plight
in an unappeasable temporality, and in the final analysis the effectiveness
of the frozen moments, of the tableaux, depends not on the tableaux
themselves—that is, the story components—but on the reflections which
are transmitted in a voice coming from a different place than the point
of view—a voice addressing questions of historicity and temporality. So
perhaps, after all, Faulkner's "time novels" have their equivalents in his
best short stories, if we look beneath the obvious surface meaning. One
must remain aware, too, that man is in motion, despite the key rhetorical device, and it may be more correct to describe the frozen moment as
dialectic in nature: we always encounter stasis *and* change, immobility
*and* motion, sound *and* silence.

Yet independent of our interpretation of the "frozen moment," its
central function in Faulkner's narrative strategy cannot be doubted, and
it is furthermore possible to suggest a close connection between this technical device and the special thematic concern which I have called existential. Man is viewed in midstride, stopped for a moment on his way to
some new foolishness, but he is also subjected to inevitable choices. The
choices are often of the kind that can only be made by individual man,
in situations where he is left completely alone. In the fictional accounts
of these crisis situations they often appear as ephiphanic moments of
clarity or possible insight. Whatever the outcome of the confrontation
with oneself, some sort of basic value, a personal ethos, is revealed or
reached. The existential crisis may easily be seen as exemplary because
of its apparent universality. When or if *conditio humana* is depicted in
Faulkner's short stories, we are inclined to interpret such texts less in
relation to a particular situation for one human being than in relation to
the common plight of mankind. This tendency to generalize in humanis-
tic terms seems to be something inherent in the short story form itself
when explored and exploited to its fullest.[12]

From these remarks on problems of genre in general and on the significance of the existential mode of experience in short fiction, it is time
to become more pragmatic. So let me present a few more observations
about the nature of the short story before I resist all theory.

The short story at its most characteristic is placed in a world different from the social world with its civilized life in most novels, and it
seems to put our accepted knowledge of the world and our fellow men
in jeopardy. The short story, as Frank O'Connor says, "remains . . .
remote from the community" and gives "an intense awareness of human

loneliness." In William Faulkner's short story world we find a number of "outlawed figures wandering about the fringes of society" (19–21), but we also find numerous lonely, estranged, lost souls in the midst of organized life in a community of men. Although we may discuss the lonely outsiders in stories such as "The Hill," "Barn Burning," "That Evening Sun," "Red Leaves," and "A Justice," the strange but not so surprising fact is that existential crises occur more frequently in Faulkner's "Middle Ground" stories; that is, in the short stories in which "mainstream America" and middle-class values, rules, and regulations are presented and scrutinized through the fate of an outsider: "Uncle Willy," "There Was a Queen," "Golden Land." The loneliest figures in Faulkner's short fiction are lonely in the company of men. And because they try to keep their integrity and some pride and self-esteem in the midst of social deterioration, their estrangement is the result of a society which has forgotten all these important values, which Faulkner's narrators refer to as the old verities of the heart. These truths are compassionately defended in some of the short stories from World War I, notably in "All the Dead Pilots," and they are preached as if they were the gospel in the World War II stories, notably in "The Tall Men" and "Shall Not Perish." These sentiments seem to have been an inevitable and almost inadvertent part of the rhetoric in stories about a collective crisis and are of little interest here. More important are the "Beyond" stories, which present man as essentially alone in critical situations and which also have a philosophy of life to discuss, in some cases even with comments on the artist's special kind of lonely life in the never-ending struggle with elusive words.

The existential mode of experience is not found in Faulkner's short fiction all through his career. As he grew older and perhaps even wiser, more and more stories were located in the countryside regions of Yoknapatawpha, and the loyal, courageous, and hardworking people there were used to demonstrate ways of being which other characters in earlier stories fought hard to achieve. As readers we are left uncertain in the early open-ended stories.[13] The potential for freedom, even to choose one's own ethical value, in a world apparently devoid of meaning, requires open texts and demands a technique that allows the hero to reflect. Hence the frozen moment's significance in these stories and the use of narrated monologues that somehow give access to the consciousness of the protagonist and the existential situation he experiences. Faulkner's "old verities" may in relation to a character's particular experience be seen as an unchanging anthropologic value, a universal ideal, which may lead the character toward the discovery of a personal ethos.

In Faulkner's fiction many characters are often so degraded and poor that they fight hard to convince themselves that they exist, repeating insistently to themselves *I am;* but they have to prove this through their existence. Perhaps we as readers are so accustomed to subtleties and high tragedy that we do not see the existential experience of such characters as very important, because it happens on a small scale, in familiar settings, and with few of the overtones modernistic literature has prepared us to look for. Yet the struggle for a personal ethical value and a recognition of self in one's own eyes and those of the world is at the center of the existential experience in Faulkner's short fiction, although I would not say that it is in the foreground of most stories. The values are often so traditional and basic that they may escape our attention, but they are also so basic that without them life would not be worth living. Numerous narrators and characters lend their voices to statements of this sort, or they may express one of the proverbial truths that are echoed so often in Faulkner's stories that we are tempted to ascribe them to a different voice, a voice above, behind, or beyond the narrators and characters. It is a troubled voice, yet always in good faith, characteristic of the author's most prominent quality: his generous acceptance of man's folly and man's greatness.

# Chapter 4

# Choosing Faulkner's Best Stories

When choosing twelve as the best of Faulkner's more than one hundred short stories, I have encountered numerous problems, but fewer than I had expected. It would have been more difficult to choose, say, thirty stories, and it would have been easier to choose six. Picking twelve stories has given me the opportunity to include those that by unanimous critical consent must be regarded as Faulkner's best, almost irrespective of the criteria on which the evaluation is based; the problem has been to choose the additional stories on the basis of literary (aesthetic) qualities alone, which has been my guiding principle. None of the stories have been chosen in order to broaden the critical perspective and make the selection more representative of Faulkner's short story achievement as such. Representativeness of a story in relation to historical time, area, race, theme, or narrative technique has not been one of my criteria, although it would have been difficult if I had found none of Faulkner's war stories good enough for inclusion among his twelve best, or if all of his best stories were found to belong in the same section of *Collected Stories*. They do not; some of them are not included in this major collection.

In selecting Faulkner's best stories I have not limited myself in any way to autonomous stories, and I have chosen among all of Faulkner's short stories, whether collected in his time or not. Stories later revised and integrated in novels have not been left out of consideration, including those totally reworked and completely appropriated by longer texts such as *Absalom, Absalom!*, *A Fable*, and *The Reivers*. Obviously the stories that live on as integrated but still separate units in *The Hamlet* must be included among Faulkner's short stories, and, even more obviously, so must the stories that make up *The Unvanquished* and *Go*

*Down, Moses.* The textual problems that arise in choosing from among these stories were put aside to be dealt with later, since I did not want such "minor" problems to be decisive in any way. In only one case— "The Bear"—did the textual problems prove to be so difficult that instead of making what I consider an impossible choice among story versions and a novel chapter I chose not to include "The Bear" at all; "The Bear" in the end proved to be only one of many possible stories to fill the last two or three places on my list.

As a starting point I had all of Faulkner's stories to choose from, many of them in different versions, many of them with a final and canonized place as a section or chapter in a novel. Taking a close look at each of the four periods into which I divided Faulkner's stories in *William Faulkner: The Short Story Career,* I quickly determined even before making my criteria clear that no stories from his apprentice years would rank among his best. Some of the stories from the major period were most certainly written in one or more versions in this early period. Still, Faulkner's first "successful" story in many respects (also because it was his first sale to a national magazine) was "A Rose for Emily," a masterpiece on a small scale, one of the author's more novelistic stories, and by far the most famous, most widely anthologized, and most criticized of all his stories. From the point of view of his entire career, it was fairly obvious to me that my choices would be made from stories between 1928 and 1942, which is not to limit the search very much since Faulkner's short story writing consisted of brief sketches and uneven attempts before that period and dwindled to almost nothing afterward.

Leaving the career perspective aside, there is little doubt that Faulkner scholarship in general and short story studies in particular, the consensus regarding those few stories considered to be his best, and some attempts to reevaluate stories that have received little treatment have been a significant influence on my choices. This does not mean that I have necessarily followed tradition or that I am afraid of new and radical departures from the critical norm. It simply means that scholars and critics over the years, through their readings and interpretations of certain stories, have argued convincingly and demonstrated the richness, complexity, profundity, and the disturbing uncertainty and subliminal fear of a story such as "That Evening Sun," and that I basically find them to be right: the story is undeniably among Faulkner's best. Saying this, I have also introduced some of my criteria for finding a text to be of high quality, good literature, or even one of the best. For some of the very good short stories there is often a strange feeling of something unnameable, indescribable, intangible; a blurred quality of vision, a tone below hearing, an unsettling uncertainty that is hard to find words for. More often than not I think this quality is what Freud referred to as "das

Unheimliche"—the uncanny—and it is precisely the presence of this almost extraliterary quality that leads me to conclude in a few instances that certain stories are his best. Indeed, this quality may well be found only in his very best stories, and we shall have to rely more on reader response theory to find ways of describing this "affective response" than on any other textual and aesthetic criteria. I shall return to the question of the reader's part in analyzing Faulkner's short stories in the interpretive chapters in part 2 of this book.

The strength of Faulkner's best short stories is their combination of detailed descriptions of the realistic, everyday world, and the sudden, at times epiphanic, experience of the self in a much larger context, often implying a choice of values that through symbolic language and imagery may be interpreted as more general than the individual's experience of the crisis which led up to it. His best stories cannot be grouped together on the basis of subject matter, and they do not share similar narrative presentations, symbolic or allegorical structures, or tropological modes. They may all make use of some preconceived pattern, be it mythological or simply anecdotal, but they hide this more abstract pattern under descriptions of conflict and confrontation which are linked to a specific time and place.

Yet Faulkner's best stories do more than present conflicts of the human heart in critical situations which somehow must lead to a resolution or a revelation. They do more than add to their interpretive richness by referring to a tragic or comic substructure. They transcend their own apparent limitations of time and place, and they often gain additional significance through a narrator or a narrative voice above and beyond story events, a voice troubled and insecure, on the brink of grasping some deeper meaning but forced to an acceptance of his and our predicament. The texts flaunt most conventions of storytelling, often reflecting different characters' behavior and attitude in relation to conformity and adjustment to a reality which is debilitating and destructive to those who expect and demand more from life than simply staying alive. Faulkner may be right when he claimed that he wrote about man in his ageless and eternal conflicts, but he did so by telling stories about people he "knew" from his fictional world, Yoknapatawpha, and locating them firmly and securely in situations he controlled but which his narrative power and poetic language lifted out of time and place so that the conflicts and their meaning grew much larger than the mold in which they were originally cast. All in all, some of these stories—not as many as twelve but certainly three or four—go beyond the short story as it is commonly described and defined, and they do so thematically as well as formally, since the formal aspects are thematized. They present experiences, episodes, and critical situations which are not of the everyday type, which are not controlled and tempered by society's rules and conventions, which somehow elude us in normal daily life but which may be seen as more basic, more primitive, and perhaps more genuine than the experience relayed in stories of action and event in a society of men and women, at a given time and in a specific place, from which the stories never take off. I have called these experiences "existential"; I might instead have referred to them as experiences of the mythic, religious, or sacred or perhaps of the uncanny. The literary short story's most prominent feature is its particular emphasis on aloneness, meaninglessness, anxiety, emptiness, freedom, and choice, presented in narrative structures that also insist on freedom from conventions and rules. This is true in Faulkner's case, even if his stories on the surface may appear to be fairly traditional. And even if references to questions of genre have been given above, it should be fairly obvious that a story's compliance with or adherence to some abstract or general genre concept cannot be used in an evaluation of that story's quality as a literary text.

Having thus shown what, in a general sense, I find to be the narrative and thematic characteristics of Faulkner's best short stories, we are prepared for a brief discussion of the actual choices I have made. There is little reason to comment on each and every story at length or in great detail since they will all be discussed extensively later on.

With reference to sound Faulkner scholarship and a general consensus, and also in complete accord with the criteria mentioned above, I chose the following stories without hesitation: "Barn Burning," "Dry September," "Red Leaves," and "That Evening Sun." I had also initially included "A Justice," another brilliant initiation story with Quentin Compson as a child narrating an experience he does not quite grasp, on my list. Yet my decisions to include "Red Leaves" and "That Evening Sun" inevitably and subconsciously must have worked against "A Justice," which was eventually dropped. The sublime inevitability of the tragic development in "Mountain Victory," a story about the Civil War and its aftermath, made this story another one of my obvious choices.

The same argument is valid for "The Hound," a taut, almost claustrophobic narrative about a poor farmer who shoots and kills his neighbor to defend his so-called rights and stumbles blindly about in the undergrowth of the river bottom and of his mind. The story's place in *The Hamlet,* its centrality in the rise and fall of Flem Snopes with Mink Snopes replacing Ernest Cotton of the original story, does not reduce its significance as a short story in its own right. Also reused in *The Hamlet,* with important changes in the narrative handling and thematic emphasis, the magazine story "Spotted Horses" nevertheless must be ranked as one of Faulkner's best and deserves inclusion in the present book. The superb balancing of the comic and the tragic, the quiet despair of the women and the stupid ignorance of the men, the irresistible temptation of the Texas ponies all combine to create one of Faulkner's most humorous and convincing short tales. In "Spotted Horses" the author allows himself almost anything, and the hyperbolic and fantastic events are convincing because of the narrator's total familiarity with the world and people of the story.

"Carcassonne" is one of the strange Faulkner stories—its elusive qualities make it something close to a long prose poem—for which I do not hesitate to cite personal preference as a reason for choosing it. It is by far the most interesting of those stories Faulkner placed in the "Beyond" section of *Collected Stories,* a story from beyond the realm of ordinary experience, even from beyond the gate of death.

When choosing Faulkner's best stories, numerous conflicts and problems inevitably arise. One of the real difficulties of choice, and even (though not so much) a difficulty when it comes to explaining the choice afterwards, has to do with those most widely read and anthologized stories that may not necessarily belong among his best. "A Rose for Emily" and "The Bear" are cases in point here. As mentioned, I have omitted "The Bear" for many reasons, the most important being that the best and complete version is a chapter in a novel and not a story, whereas the magazine version is so much inferior to the chapter in *Go Down, Moses* that I do not consider it to be among Faulkner's best stories. The many uses of other versions of this text (without the most important section of the book chapter) must be deemed anomalies and could not be considered for use here.

"A Rose for Emily" is in my opinion by no means Faulkner's best story, but I still think it fair to include it among his dozen best, even if I should be able to leave all other considerations than literary quality out, which, of course, I am not. The story is clearly inferior to "Dry September," for example, and it lacks the deep emotional impact and feeling of abiding tragedy of "That Evening Sun." But poor Emily's story is deftly handled, and the communal point of view used with easy mastery. Change and resistance to change, the passing of time and the attempt to halt it add to the thematic significance of a story the surprise ending and shocking revelation of which should not mislead us to place it among the cheap and slick magazine stories. I see no reason to exclude it because it has received much more than its fair share of attention, not only in separate articles but even in casebooks.

Having decided to leave "The Bear" out, I still felt that one of the stories from *Go Down, Moses* deserved inclusion, not only because this novel is made up of (revised) short stories of unusually high and even quality but because the best among these stories most certainly belongs among Faulkner's twelve best. One of my favorites among the stories that combine to make *Go Down, Moses* a superb novel is "Delta Autumn." Unfortunately, in the end I had to exclude it as well. The story is intimately related to the whole story of the McCaslins and to intricate developments in history as well as in white and black families, and I therefore think it deserves to be discussed in the context of its place in the whole of the novel rather than as an autonomous short story. I therefore settled for "Pantaloon in Black," which according to many critics is the least integrated of all stories in *Go Down, Moses* and even has been said to damage the overall structure of the book. Critics generally agree that "Pantaloon in Black" is one of Faulkner's supreme performances within the short story genre, and I obviously also hold this text in high esteem.

Having thus explained my choices of ten stories, let me mention some of the other stories that I considered seriously for inclusion but for various reasons had to leave out. "Mule in the Yard" and "Shingles for the Lord" are definitely among Faulkner's funniest stories, and their narrative tone and mild irony show an author generous enough to offer overbearing portraits even of characters who are at a loss in most situations because of serious flaws in their character. I also had "Uncle Willy" on my list for a long time but reached the conclusion that the long-winded story about a dope addict who in the child narrator's view is the finest man he has ever known was too heavy-handed in its fairly shallow criticism of life in Jefferson, even if the narrative itself is convincing. So laughter and fun and social criticism, even when told in highly competent narratives, were not enough to compete with "Wash," the penultimate choice among Faulkner's twelve best although it clearly ranks higher than number eleven in terms of overall quality.

The story about Wash Jones and Thomas Sutpen is undisputedly one of Faulkner's most forceful short narratives, self-contained despite its close relationship to *Absalom, Absalom!* It is a story of unmitigated horror, told in retrospective glances with remarkable narrative control. We follow the line of action from sunrise to sunset, entering a pervasive darkness of evil and horror. But we also glimpse Wash's almost epiphanic insight when he suddenly understands who Sutpen really is.

With its implicit commentary on the evil that comes from the experience of war, breeding ever more aggression and, in Sutpen's case, an arrogant and violent behavior which is completely misunderstood by Wash, "Wash" is not only Faulkner's best story about the Civil War; it is closely related to his stories from World War I. Faulkner worked hard on these stories, and even if he did not succeed in having many of them published in periodicals, he gave them a section of their own in *These 13* and also in *Collected Stories,* where they are grouped under the rubric "The Wasteland." Having chosen eleven stories of the highest literary

quality, I still felt that Faulkner's war stories are of such cental importance to his short story career that I decided to take a look at them once
more to see if one of them could reasonably be included if also judged by
its literary quality. I felt that it was deplorable that none of Faulkner's
war stories had been selected; but the stories about World War II are
among the worst he wrote, and the World War I stories are rather static, limited in their outlook, and at times awkward in their narrative
structure. "Turnabout" would have been a possible choice, or
"Crevasse," a competent story which is tight, grim, and universal in its
anonymity and can thus be compared to "Wash." "Crevasse" was,
apparently for a long time, a section in early typescripts for "Victory";
and so I decided that if a war story were to be included it would have to
be "Victory," well aware that the few critics who have commented on it
find it to be too long, inconsistent in its development and portrayal of
character, and all in all of little merit. Yet this short story, in its almost
novelistic slow movement and long timespan, deals with *Kriegserlebnis*
in new and interesting ways; it demonstrates how destructive the sin of
pride can be and how the positive value of endurance can be perverted
to its opposite. It also shows a writer who is incredibly insistent and
momomaniacal in his beliefs and thus points to shaping forces behind
most of Faulkner's best short story writing.

My choice of twelve Faulkner stories is, as far as it has been possible, based on my understanding of their quality as literary texts, with
emphasis on narrative handling as well as language and thematic impact;
and then only minimally, and very deliberately, have I made some con-
cessions to representativeness or the career aspect. The twelve stories
should convey an impression of the richness and variety of Faulkner's
short fiction and also demonstrate his consummate artistic ability and
integrity as well as his lifelong dedication to creating something out of
the anguish of the human spirit which was not there before. All of the
stories chosen were written in the middle part of Faulkner's career, during a period of not more than ten years. More than half of them were
collected in *These 13* in 1931. The twelve stories thus do not represent
Faulkner's short story achievement at all stages of his career, nor do they
represent all his subjects, interests, attitudes, or idiosyncrasies. Among
the late stories, only "Race at Morning" seems to me to be on a par with
Faulkner's better hunting stories, and the stories of detection, interesting
as they may be in themselves, cannot possibly compete in quality with
the stories selected.

Literary quality has been my guideline, then. The selection of stories
would have been a completely different one if I had wanted my selection
to be representative of the long career, or to include examples of all subjects, themes, or narrators. It might be a good idea to make such a selec-

tion truly representative of Faulkner's range as a writer of short fiction and of his continued interest in the form. I have, however, chosen what I find to be his twelve best stories, and even if some explanations always seem to be afterthoughts, I do not feel that I might as well have flipped coins. But it is well worth remembering that for each story chosen there are nine or ten left out, and despite the uneven quality of his stories, readers will find interest in many more of them than those discussed in part 2 of the present book.

*PART 2*

# Reading Twelve Short Stories

# Introduction

Part 2 consists of twelve chapters, one on each story, in alphabetical order. The relative place of the stories in Faulkner's career is of little importance in this study, since each story is read and discussed as a self-contained, autonomous text. Nevertheless, in each chapter rather extensive textual information and publication history are provided first, accompanied by brief comments on the story's place in the Faulkner canon and its relationship to other works; then I give a reading of the story. The readings vary from text to text, but they all follow the text instead of being responses after having followed the text. My readings are obviously indebted to previous criticism and interpretations of each individual story, but given the availability of guides, handbooks, and bibliographies related to Faulkner's fiction, I have seen no need to give surveys of criticism.

For textual information I rely on my first book on Faulkner and the short story, *William Faulkner: The Short Story Career,* supplemented with new information which has become available since its publication. Criticism and interpretations of the stories have been referred to in the text and notes only when it is actually and actively used. Much that has been written on Faulkner's short stories deals with particular aspects of a single story, or the story is read within specific contexts. My purpose has been to present readings of the twelve selected stories that address as many aspects of the text as possible and to avoid specific and special contextualization until after the reading. My purpose has been to remain close to the text and explain or explicate it as a literary text. Still, the readings represent my understanding of how and what the text signifies, and I make no attempts whatsoever to present "objective" or "innocent" readings. They are, moreover, often open readings in which I reach no closure but rather point to other possible approaches and contexts to make the rich and ambiguous texts signify even more.

# Chapter 5

# Barn Burning

## TEXTUAL INFORMATION AND PUBLICATION HISTORY

Any description of the textual history of "Barn Burning" must take into account its early place as the opening chapter of *The Hamlet*. The textual history of the excised, autonomous short story itself is simple, but its origin in the Snopes material and Faulkner's "pulling together" of it is complicated. Despite dates found in the manuscript and recorded by Faulkner's literary agent, Harold Ober, the exact time of composition is still unclear.

Faulkner began the composition of *The Hamlet* some time in 1938, but hardly as late as the date November 7, 1938, in the left-hand margin of a manuscript with the heading "BOOK ONE / Chapter One" and with the deleted title "Barn Burning."[1] "One" for chapter numeration is also deleted and substituted with the roman-numeral I. This is really the manuscript for what became the short story "Barn Burning," of which there is also a typescript with the heading "Chapter One." Both manuscript and typescript are likely to have been written before the date on the manuscript, which presumably records when Faulkner began the work on the novel in earnest and had decided to use the barn-burning episode as its first chapter. The seventeen-page manuscript is complete, and it seems likely that it was removed from the rest of the manuscript for the novel only after a typescript of the first chapter was finished. How far Faulkner had gotten in his manuscript when he decided to remove "Barn Burning" is difficult to say, but the manuscript indicates that he may have finished the new first chapter earlier, opting to let the marvelous description of Frenchman's Bend's geography and topography as well as its past and present open the novel. Page numbers have been deleted and substituted with new lower numbers in correspondence with the seventeen removed pages. The first pages of the new second chapter have no deletions, and those that appear later come as a result of many changes in the chronology of events and episodes. The pagination of the typescript for the setting copy of *The Hamlet* also shows that "Barn Burning" not only bore the heading "Chapter One" but also in typescript form for a time was the opening chapter of the book. There is a typescript page among the many rejected versions of page 1 which has the editorial note "Rec'd 3/20/39," and this page is close to the published opening page of the novel. By this time, then, Faulkner had made his decision, but since the story was sold quickly and published in *Harper's Monthly*[2] for June, the decision may have been made well in advance of this date. Acceptance by the magazine came too late to be a possible reason behind Faulkner's decision, and we also know that he normally felt free to use previously published stories in new novels. The description of Frenchman's Bend's past and present which he had already written as chapter 2, combined with the autonomy of the "Barn Burning" story, may have shown Faulkner that he had given undue emphasis to characters of minor significance in the story he was about to tell. He needed to introduce Ab Snopes to the world of Frenchman's Bend less obviously and to pit him against one of the representatives of this region, more than telling a story of his past which made everything almost too clear and transparent. The fact that another of the manuscript pages has the deleted heading "Chapter Two" and recounts the first encounter between Jody Varner and Ab Snopes supports this argument; this opening *in medias res* also had to be relinquished, and the wide and sweeping generalizations about the region finally came to stand as the novel's effective opening.

In a long and leisurely letter to Robert K. Haas received on December 15, 1938, Faulkner gives an outline of his plans for the Snopes trilogy. One small point is of interest to his short stories and relates directly to "Barn Burning": "his [Flem's] youngest brother tries to keep his father from setting fire to his landlord's barn, believes he had caused the father to be shot, and runs away from home. . . ."[3] This is an inaccurate summary of what Sarty Snopes does and believes in the story as we know it, and as Faulkner should have known it if he had just finished writing it! Faulkner's short stories are often uncertain as to a character's possible death; since we are aware of Ab's continued role in *The Hamlet,* we know more than Sartoris Snopes, whose fear of having contributed to his father's being killed may be one of the simpler reasons why he is running away. Obviously, we must accept that the text does not exactly correspond to what the author had in his imagination at various times in its composition and that it is vague or ambiguous at decisive points. Faulkner had certainly revised and rewritten the opening chapter and hence what would become the story when typing it on the basis of the seventeen-page manuscript. Numerous alterations can be found; they may be significant details in themselves, but basically they are well within the normal reworking procedures that Faulkner followed—even if he typed a new version on the basis of an earlier (rejected) typescript.

"Barn Burning" was received by Ober on November 19, 1938 (Skei 1981, 93). It should be fair to say based on the manuscripts and typescripts to which we now have access, of stories as well as of novels, that there is little reason to think that Faulkner wrote the story in the ten days or so following the pencilled date on the manuscript and then quickly sent the typescript version off to Ober (Jones 1994, 4). What is abundantly clear from the text of the story is that Faulkner knew exactly what he had taken out of the novel and that he had also discovered why he had to do so: not because he had a good, self-contained story which he could sell at a good price, which alone would not have kept him from using the same text (or a version of it) as the opening chapter of a novel. Despite numerous attempts at starting the novel, Faulkner returned to his original conception of the Snopes material as it is found in *Father Abraham* (Creighton 1977, 21) and realized that much more sweeping generalizations about the region's geography and people were needed instead of a dramatic and vivid *in medias res* beginning. But there seem to me to be reasons of creativity, character use, and dramatic confrontations that led to Faulkner's decision not only to find a new opening but virtually to leave all marks of the story out of the text except as hearsay, rumor, and vague statements about the little one who disappeared. For one thing he saw a different use for Ab Snopes, much more in keeping with the Ab he had created in earlier texts and which we witness in Ratliff's tale in *The Hamlet* in which he depicts Ab as a fool about a horse. Also, the older son soon comes out from the shadows and leaves the mule and plow lines in the field, and his rapid rise seems much more powerful and believable than it would have if he were to replace his father as narrative focus and center of interest.

"Barn Burning" establishes family relationships among a mother, father, aunt, two pairs of sisters, an older brother, and ten-year-old Sarty. Most of all the story sets up an opposition between father and youngest son as well as conflict within Sarty. Furthermore, it establishes powerfully and vividly the absolute distinctions between classes, between those who own property and those who do not, and between races. The inhumanity and humiliation of the sharecropper system is captured in a few sentences, and the system of law enforcement is both taken seriously and set up for ridicule in the opening paragraph. All these elements of the story, to which more could have been added, are used economically and with a sense of tragic inevitability. But the same oppositions, down to small episodes and details, are also used in the novel from which the story was excised at a fairly early stage. Key conflicts and small dramatic scenes, used with great flexibility and unexpected twists to portray folly, misery, and inhumanity but also friendship and consideration, are used in both texts. Parallel to Ab Snopes and his sons outside the store in the short story, we find Eck and his little son outside the store in the novel, dividing the cheese, relaxing, as if everything were alright with the world.

All this simply indicates that despite the autonomy of the story, it is very much a story within and from the world of *The Hamlet,* and if, as some critics maintain, it is not only one of Faulkner's best stories but the best, this is a result of its coming out of a world he knew intimately from having created myriad stories about it and from having begun to pull it all together to form the last of his great books, *The Hamlet.* So even if we should be cautious not to read "Barn Burning" in the light of *The Hamlet,* we should not forget, since so many interpretations of the story emphasize conflicts of personality and morality, of loyalty and choice, that the economic theme and sociological questions are at the center of the longer work. Their presence is very much felt also in "Barn Burning."

## READING "BARN BURNING"

After more than ten years with Snopeses on his mind, using characters and incidents in novels and stories but never returning to the long fictional portrayal of them promised by *Father Abraham,* Faulkner was so absorbed in his subject, so completely familiar with everyone and everything in the world he had named Frenchman's Bend, that "Barn Burning" became a masterpiece—technically brilliant, thematically disturbing and convincing, emotionally complex, and without any of the sentimentality that destroys so many of his stories from around 1940 on. The child protagonist and narrator had added emotional impact and a depth of understanding in the Quentin Compson stories ("A Justice," "That Evening Sun"), but in "Barn Burning" narrative commentary and authorial intrusion allow for an active manipulation of sympathy and irony and let the reader experience the events from multiple perspectives and different points in time. Initiation, growth, and maturity thus become central questions in the story. James Ferguson (1991) is probably right when he holds that "the most important archetype in the works from 1932 to 1942 is initiation" (41). In "Barn Burning" this theme is further complicated by the tension that arises from having to choose between different forms of justice. The conflict is also one of loyalty to kinship and the ties of the blood as opposed to a vague understanding of decent behavior and the rights of others. We may call it a new and intu-

itively recognized set of moral imperatives. For a child the conflict is confusing, disturbing, and disastrous even if it may prove to be liberating in
the long run. The narrative method in "Barn Burning"—multiple perspectives but basically a third-person omniscient narrator in command of
the discourse—is probably better suited to present this kind of anguish
and despair than the first-person child narrator in other stories with similar or comparable conflicts ("That Evening Sun," "Two Soldiers,"
"Uncle Willy"). Joseph Reed (1973) argues that "a first-person solution
would have severely limited 'Barn Burning'; instead the third-person
with a strong point of view is combined with rhythmic interruptions of
objective narration and dramatic dialogue . . ." (43). But Reed also
asserts that there is no obvious difference in narrative distance between
first- and third-person narration, a vitally important premise to understanding how cold objectivity and close emotional involvement can be at
work in the same story and furthermore to understanding how sympathy is distributed and empathy created in "Barn Burning."

As readers we follow the story as it unwinds, from the first scene
with the Justice of the Peace holding court in a country store until we
watch Sarty move on down the hill, into the dawn of a spring morning,
cold and a little stiff, which walking and the coming sun will cure. As
readers we have been given the role that the listener or hearer had in relation to oral storytelling; we should be aware that even if we inadvertently
sum up, evaluate, and naturalize the story we have heard, the final
response is, at least for as long as the story lasts, less important than its
elements, the narrative units, the episodes and incidents, linked together
and given narrative form (plotting, sequence, chronology, cause and
effect) through the very act of narrating. We react and wonder, adjust
our reaction, readjust over and over again as new elements change our
understanding. The reactions from the listeners, not necessarily verbal
but expressed through facial expressions, body language, and gestures,
may force the teller to adjust, to redirect his narrative or add comments
to the narrative itself. In modern theories of reading we talk about the
transaction that takes place between text and reader, and our interpretation would have to elaborate on the limits for meaning set by the text
and hence also the extent of reader collaboration and contribution to
textual meaning. The reader is not free to fabricate textual meaning.
Faulkner's best short stories, "Barn Burning" included, are open to many
interpretations, full of lacunae and indeterminacy, yet overdetermined at
the same time in the sense that an event may be contextualized and interpreted in many ways and still remain within the sensible and reasonable
and, most importantly, within the text of the story. The challenge for the
reader is not to concentrate on a particular possible reading while reading the text but rather to let oneself be surprised by the narration itself

and by the many strange detours from the main road of the straightforward narrative it offers. We have to accept that the narrative in "Barn Burning" is the text at hand, for us to read and interpret, and that whatever is outside the text is not the text. This also means that whenever the narration is "strange" or deviates from our expectations, with their bases in our literary competence, we are not confronted with additions[4] to the text, in Ferguson's sense of the term, and certainly not deceptive tricks to add a significance to the story which it otherwise would not have.

The title of the story seems to point in two different directions: to the fact and symbol of a barn set on fire, which we hear about but never actually see in the story, and to the activity of burning barns, an activity well documented in literature and fact and in Faulkner's text clearly used as a means of revenge, of terror, and of proving one's own integrity and pride in a world where little else is left. It seems to indicate a primitive violence, but in relation to other people's property it simply represents the ultimate reaction when Ab Snopes feels that he has been seriously wronged. He owns nothing and is said to have "an inherent voracious prodigality with material not his own" (*Collected Stories,* 7).[5] The title is thus indicative of the class system, of the economic motif in the story, but it also points clearly to Abner Snopes as more central in the text than those who early claimed the story for Sarty were willing to admit.[6]

The story does, of course, describe the coming of age of Colonel Sartoris Snopes, and we are allowed to watch him closely, at times even witnessing events from his point of view and getting information about how he would have thought twenty years from the time of the story. The development of Sarty takes him from being an ordinary Snopes, submissive to "the old fierce pull of the blood" (*CS,* 3), through the story's denouement, where he lets down his father and runs to warn his enemy, to his running away from his kin and blood—the repetitive cycle of moving and burning and trial—into a society whose laws and regulations the boy intuitively seems to have not only accepted but come to trust.[7] Sarty almost unknowingly seems to have tired of being on the move, and when he senses a different world, symbolized not the least in the de Spain mansion, he is on the verge of a new understanding. Later he even considers the possibility of living in peace, unoffending, not suing, not burning, and so the reader sees a steady development toward an understanding of the need to live in society with one's fellow citizens, so that the final rebellion comes naturally and inevitably. In other words, the story centers on Sarty Snopes and his refusal to act out his father's wishes or become like his father. Sarty is torn between conflicting loyalties to his family on the one side and to his sense of justice and righteousness on the other. When his loyalties are put to a test, his "good" nature wins, but Sarty has no other option than to leave his family and escape into what he knows to be a hostile world ("ourn enemy"), although also a world that promises decency and perhaps even a stable life. Despite the central position of Sarty in the story, it may still be fair to say that Faulkner's ultimate concern is not with the boy. We reduce the value of the story if we only find an initiation rite played out or demonstrated in it or just an enactment of some old and universal moral dilemma. Faulkner's language may lead us to think that we have another instance of "the old verities of the human heart" and the age-old struggle, but in "Barn Burning" the framing of the internal fight is realistic and concrete and signifies much more than most critics tend to see when the eternal truths seem to take precedence. The point here is simply that the story is capable of fusing many levels of meaning and is coded so that our contextualization as readers is both an act of our own will, dependent on our literary competence, and imposed on us by the text itself.

Let us briefly look at the narrative structure of the story, with particular emphasis on the narrator and the triumphant use of internal monologues within a third-person narrative which shifts its focus freely and moves easily in time through analepses and prolepses, in a narrative which perforce is about past events but still gives the reader a sense of being present at something which happens here and now, with a quite unusual actuality and directness. "It seems almost as though Sarty is telling the story about himself," according to one critic (Franklin 1968, 191), which is a precise observation of what it seems or feels like at times but which is also completely wrong when it comes to the question of who narrates the story. Having learned to distinguish between narrative point of view (or even split this into different focuses) and narrative voice, we may easily see that an extradiegetic narrator, omniscient in his knowledge[8] and never manifest in the text, tells the whole story and that he tells it as an adult narrator about the childhood experience of another adult—Sarty Snopes—at least twenty years after the events narrated in "Barn Burning." The opening paragraph demonstrates very clearly how the text makes use of different levels of awareness, different points of view, and different sensational details. The superb, almost unnoticed, sliding perception prepares the reader for similarly abrupt changes in style, diction, and focus and for movements even in time from the present of the story to points much closer to the present of the narration. Through long, winding sentences that shift focus numerous times we come closer to critical points in the plot and in the narrative, and the overall structure of the story corresponds to the structure of the family and situation in which Sarty finds himself, which very aptly has been described by Joseph Reed as the "cycle of burning-trial-moving-offense-burning" (47). The story opens as follows:

The store in which the Justice of the Peace's court was sitting smelled of cheese. The boy, crouched on his nail keg at the back of the crowded room, knew he smelled cheese, and more: from where he sat he could see the ranked shelves close-packed with the solid, squat, dynamic shapes of tin cans whose labels his stomach read, not from the lettering which meant nothing to his mind but from the scarlet devils and the silver curve fish—this, the cheese which he knew he smelled and the hermetic meat which his intestines believed he smelled coming in intermittent gusts momentary and brief between the other constant one, the smell and sense just a little of fear because mostly of despair and grief, the old fierce pull of blood. (CS, 3)

It is important to notice that the story begins in a synesthesia of hunger (Reed 1973, 43) and that numerous levels of awareness (Carothers 1985, 60) are implied here. What strikes the reader is also the smooth introduction of numerous realistic details, which not only serve to create an illusion of reality but project a world by mentioning important elements of that world that through metonymic representation introduce the central concerns of the story we are about to be told. First there is the store, crowded with people. It is not the only store, and we shall be allowed to enter another one before long. The store is at the center of the hamlet's society; everyone in the area is tied to the store, where they buy all their necessities against the next crop. Despite the fact that the first piece of information we get is that the Justice of the Peace's court is sitting in the store, our initial experience of the setting comes from a welter of sensations—smell, vision, and hearing—which the boy *thinks* he feels: the smell of cheese is real, the smell of meat is not, and the boy reads the contents of the tin cans on the shelves with his stomach, because he knows (we suppose) the symbols (if not icons) on the tins: the devils and the curved fish. The smells, real and imagined, come at intervals and mingle with a different smell—of fear, of grief, and of despair. We, the readers, could hardly get closer to Sarty than through the numerous feelings that he senses, none of which he can express, and we are tempted to think that he concentrates on the tin cans to distract himself from the proceedings going on in the store, which he cannot see from where he is sitting in the back of the room. Also, the narrator, through the varied and detailed description of the boy's hunger, despair, and grief, has created a "real" world with a boy character in serious trouble. Sarty feels hunger and fear and grief; he is illiterate but has some knowledge of the products in the store, where he crouches on a nail keg among strangers whom he is trained to think of as enemies. As we read on we understand that the "old fierce pull of blood" refers to his father and to the court's dealings. For a brief moment we get inside the boy's mind, but his thoughts come to us indirectly, reported by the narrator in parentheses and italics: "(*our enemy* he thought in that despair; *ourn! mine and hisn both! He's my father!*)" (*CS*, 3).

The story moves on to direct speech, rendering the discussion between Mr. Harris, from whom Ab Snopes has rented land on a share-cropper's contract, and the Justice. Harris's barn has burnt down, and he knows Snopes is the arsonist but cannot produce proof. He therefore wants to bring the little boy to testify before the Judge. Sarty thus has to walk the aisle between the grim faces, feeling no floor under his feet, up to where the Justice sits. He knows that he encounters the enemy again, and he feels the "fear and despair and the old grief of blood" (*CS*, 5), but the text subtly tells that something, perhaps unnoticed and unseen but still heard, happens to the boy. He gives his name, in a whisper, as Colonel Sartoris Snopes, and the Justice, almost jokingly, says, "I reckon anybody named for Colonel Sartoris in this country can't help but tell the truth, can they?" (*CS*, 4). The Justice's face is described as "kindly" and his voice as "troubled," and even if the boy is in emotional uproar he knows that he has been saved from something, "had been caught in a prolonged instant of mesmerized gravity, weightless in time" (*CS*, 5). The boy does not have to answer, and the "pull of blood" and the old fears perhaps subside a little because of what the Judge said to him and because he does not have to resolve the two opposing expectations of him. He knows his father wants him to lie, and he has heard that the Justice thought it impossible for him not to tell the truth. Beneath it all he knows what his father did to Harris's barn, and still he fights the first boy who says "Barn Burner!" as they walk away from the store.

I have dwelled at some length on this opening scene, not only because it introduces the basic conflicts of the story but also because it introduces a recurrent pattern, an almost cyclical movement from one landowner to the next, with the same conflicts starting over again in each new place. We have not yet met the Snopes family, except the two boys and their father, and so far the story has remained within the established time frame and narrative pattern so that the discourse presents story elements in chronological order, telling of something that once happened with the immediacy of quoted speech and indirect rendering of internal monologues.

As the story proceeds we watch the family move on in the wagon to their new, dilapidated two-room house, where they move in and settle down before the father pays a visit to the landlord. He takes the boy with him. There are important elements for an understanding of the story in the description of the family as such, and of Ab in particular. Even if the narrator chooses to stay close to Sarty and tell the story more or less from his point of view, seeing the world through his eyes and at times even attempting to render events in his diction and vocabulary, we need to understand Ab and his reactions to understand Sarty—perhaps even to understand the forces of the society in which they both live and of which to a certain extent they are products, despite all the rhetorical language about blood and heritage.

Who is the Ab Snopes we meet in this story? What is abundantly clear is that he is a person who sees no option but to turn to violence whenever he believes that he has been threatened. Violence has become second nature for him; he flings his wife savagely into the wall, beats the young boy, and is a stern father, unwilling to listen to anyone. We know more about his background and his past than Sarty does both within the time of the story and afterwards, and even if this information does not explain or excuse his violent ways it helps explain Ab's nature and behavior. The first description we get of Ab is related to his stiff leg. He is "walking a little stiffly from where a Confederate provost's man's musket ball had taken him in the heel on a stolen horse thirty years ago" (CS, 5); Sarty does not know this, however, and near the end of the story, when he is running away, he cries out, "He was brave! . . . He was in the war! He was in Colonel Sartoris' cav'ry!" (CS, 24). The narrator adds coldly that his father went to war "for booty—it meant nothing and less than nothing to him if it were enemy booty or his own" (CS, 25). The boy does not know this either, but he listens to a story his father tells about having been a professional horsetrader[9] in one of the rare moments when his father seems to relax and behave in a pleasant and friendly manner.[10] Sarty's father may be an evil person, even equipped with a foot and a walk which are suggestive of the Devil; yet the narrator finds something admirable in him and thinks he knows exactly why Ab is a barn burner.

The most important description of Ab in "Barn Burning" may well be related to the fires he made whenever the family stopped for a night. The fire was "neat, niggard almost, a shrewd fire; such fires were his father's habit and custom always in freezing weather." Typically, though, the fire is made by using "a rail lifted from a nearby fence and cut into lengths" (CS, 7). The narrator speculates about what the boy, when he was older, might have thought about his father's habit and explains the habit with reference to his experience as a Civil War fugitive. But the narrator also gives us the "true" reason in an explicit judgment of Ab's character and behavior: "the element of fire spoke to some deep mainspring of his father's being, as . . . the one weapon for the preservation of his integrity . . ." (CS, 7–8). It is important to notice that this is not something the older Sarty has come to understand; the narrator speculates that the boy *might have* come to understand,[11] whereas in other asides we are told what Sarty "was to tell himself" (*CS*, 8). The boy's understanding grows as he develops and matures, although his knowledge about his father apparently remains the same.

Sarty's ignorance is not the reader's, a decisive distinction for the interpretation of the story. We are given a series of descriptions and witness dramatic actions, as well as receiving background information and explicit judgment. As readers we have to balance our sympathetic understanding of the small boy with the irony created by his ignorance. When we as readers, even near the conclusion of the story, learn how wrong Sarty is in his assessment of his father, the text seems to question the readers' understanding which it has helped create. There is no doubt that "explicit judgment"[12] is an important part of the narrative technique of the story, but it complicates rather than simplifies the interpretive work on the part of the reader.

In our speculations about Ab, with his "wolflike independence and even courage when the advantage was at least neutral" (*CS*, 7), we have paused and gone back and forth in the text of the short story as a whole. We shall have to return to where we left the text and follow it toward its conclusion, and we rejoin the Snopeses in the wagon on the road to the next sharecropper's house.

The description of the wagon, loaded with the family's belongings, with two hulking sisters and a crying mother, is indicative of what sort of life Ab Snopes has created for the family from which he expects total loyalty. It is also indicative of an unfair agricultural system that keeps people in bondage. A choice between imprisonment and freedom may well be another way of looking at Sarty's internal struggle, a struggle of which the other family members seem to be totally unaware, beaten and subdued as they are, perhaps with the exception of the older brother. He remains utterly quiet, loyal, and nondesdcript, except for the inevitable tobacco, and if we read him in the light of *The Hamlet* we know that he has other plans and that the barn burning rumor is a part of his scheme.

Reading the descriptions of the family's belongings and watching their work, the trained reader of Faulkner discovers "pure Faulkner." Among the broken furniture there is a "clock inlaid with mother-of-pearl, which would not run, stopped at some fourteen minutes past two o'clock of a dead and forgotten day and time" (*CS*, 6); this is one of the relatively few references to time in the story, to a past that is forgotten, perhaps with good reason. More importantly in our attempt to understand Sarty and his troubles is the fact that the clock had been his mother's dowry, since the story specifies character traits that Sarty may have inherited from her and not from his father. The mother-of-pearl may be the last heirloom of Sarty's mother's family, the only remaining object of beauty that had been appreciated and bequeathed to her; broken and stopped, the clock is totally out of time and place in the barren, violent world of which it now almost stubbornly is an anachronistic part.

At the center of the story is Ab's dealings with his new landlord, Major de Spain. It follows the established pattern: Ab pays a visit to de Spain and on purpose smears the major's French rug with horse manure he has intentionally stepped in. When de Spain furiously sends the carpet to be cleaned by the Snopes family, Ab deliberately destroys it. De Spain decides to have him pay ten bushels of corn for the ruined carpet; in response Ab acts completely within his nature as the narrator explicitly has described it and sues the landowner. Another court session takes place, in a new country store, and Ab is fined half as many bushels as de Spain had originally demanded. The court proceeding is followed by the leisurely Saturday afternoon we have already considered and then by the preparations to set fire to de Spain's barn.

Sarty's role in all this is central, not only in the narrative sense that we observe and watch everything from his perspective but because his father has seen what he might have done in the first trial and now puts him to a test, demanding absolute loyalty to his blood and kin "or you ain't going to have any blood to stick to you" (CS, 8). Accordingly, he has to accompany his father to the de Spain mansion and responds with awe and an emotional joy that he is said to be too young to put into words. But the house itself and the life it symbolizes contribute to Sarty's development: he thinks that finally his father deals with people out of his reach, safe from him, in their shaded peace and dignity. The boy is wrong, of course, and later, in the fields with the rich soil "shearing cool and damp against his bare ankles" (CS, 17), he has an almost epiphanic moment closely related to that which he felt upon first seeing the de Spain mansion: "*Maybe he even won't collect the twenty bushels. Maybe it will all add up and balance and vanish—corn, rug, fire; the terror and grief, the being pulled two ways like between two teams of horses—gone, done with for ever and ever*" (CS, 17). Sarty has become painfully aware of the returning, never-ending conflicts that result in violence and fire. He seems to hope that what he felt when he saw the big house would have changed his father also, so that opposites finally could be reconciled; the young boy, however, carries Colonel Sartoris's name, and his understanding of his father is based in part on the mistaken belief that he participated in the Colonel's cavalry. For complex reasons beyond the scope of this discussion and perhaps beyond the short story's reach as well, Ab is pure Snopes, if we still think that the opposition between Snopes and Sartoris makes any sense. To quote Carothers, "Ab is what he is, while Sarty is in the process of becoming" (Carothers 1985, 63).

Confused and bewildered, but with a vain hope of reconciliation and decent life, Sartoris reacts violently when he is told to help out with his father's plan to set fire to the barn. He has tried to establish an under-standing with his father about the fine they are to pay when October comes, but everything he has hoped for suddenly collapses. So he is left behind when Ab and the older son leave to take their revenge upon de Spain, and even if he is not tied up[13] he is left in the custody of his moth-er who is told to hold him. Ab knows that Sarty may tell on him, and we may wonder why he does not follow his older son's advice and really tie the boy up. Sartoris gets loose from his mother, who is afraid of the con-sequences, and his aunt advises her sister to let Sarty go, although she too tries to grasp him when he breaks loose. De Spain is thus forewarned and rides desperately to stop the barn burners. Following Sartoris as he runs again, this time to warn his father, we hear one shot and then another and are left uncertain as to the fate of Ab and his older son. Realizing he cannot go home again, Sartoris runs on, sobbing "'Father! Father!'" (CS, 24), until he finds himself completely alone on the crest of a hill in the middle of a dark woods at midnight. We see him beneath the slow con-stellations that "wheeled on" (CS, 25), and recognizing that the stroke of midnight marks the beginning of a new day, the reader knows that Sarty has moved from chaos to cosmos, from imprisonment to freedom, from darkness to possible light. He still has a long, strenuous way to go, but we have the narrator's many comments from later in Sarty's life, and know that he has looked back, from the perspective of later years. While he may not be proud of what he did, he comes to understand why he had to do it.

Two minor aspects of "Barn Burning," which so far have only been touched upon, deserve further mention. One is related to Sarty's under-standing of a decent and peaceful life in a society of men, and his intuitive trust in the customs and rules that regulate this society. The opposition between nature and culture is thus also present in the story, but it is by no means a simple opposition. In "Barn Burning" Sarty may well be found to have some in-born human qualities—a sense of justice, a feeling of what is right and wrong—but he is contrasted with his father, whose animal-like character and brutal behavior might also be described as natural. On the other hand, de Spain and his mansion do not only rep-resent negative qualities, despite Ab's correct association of the black man's sweat with the construction of the mansion, despite the strong class hatred it understandably elicits within him. In Sarty the mansion awakens a dream of a better life and comes to represent the positive val-ues of a tempered, cultivated nature.

Finally, Ab Snopes shares his problem—and to a certain extent also his violent solutions to it—with Wash Jones in the short story "Wash," later incorporated in *Absalom, Absalom!* The problem is there called "all the living Sutpens"—with that family representing people of de Spain's class and character. "Barn Burning" is some thirty years later in historical time than "Wash," yet it shows that in Faulkner's fictional world the Sutpens are still alive and vital and that the situation has not changed much for the poor people of Yoknapatawpha. This is, however, only a minor element in "Barn Burning," since the story centers on Sarty Snopes and his refusal to act out his father's wishes or to become like his father. "Barn Burning" is a rich story, and the complexity of its narrative pattern contributes significantly to that richness and to its openness to different emphases and hence different interpretations. I have suggested different possible interpretations and tried out a few approaches. And even if I have presented my preferred reading of the story, I have not pursued it to a final resolution or revelation. The story is one of Faulkner's best not because of its treatment of the age-old truths or its development of one or more abstract themes. It is a superb story because it narrates the response of a sensitive and brave young boy to a very difficult situation. The boy is torn between forces of which he is vaguely aware but comes closer to understanding as the story develops, and these forces should not only been seen as blood and kinship but as social and economic forces. These forces contribute significantly to the feeling of almost tragic inevitability as the story develops.

# Chapter 6

# Carcassonne

## TEXTUAL INFORMATION AND PUBLICATION HISTORY

Most of the stories which Faulkner included in *These 13* can be found on his short story sending schedule (Meriwether 1971, 157–80; Skei 1981, 36–37), although seven of the thirteen stories appeared in print for the first time in the collection. This indicates the trouble Faulkner had when trying to sell his stories, but also that he did not necessarily collect stories that had been published. Even those that had been rejected a number of times found a place in his first—and best—story collection, and he also included stories of which no trace can be found on his schedule or in his correspondence with editors and agents. "Carcassonne" is one of the stories that turns up for the first time in *These 13,* and the earliest date we can be certain that the story existed is some time prior to June 18, 1931, when the typescripts for the collection were sent to the printer.[1] Naturally the story would have been written at least some weeks or months before this date, yet it is hard to believe that "Carcassonne" was not written much earlier, and not much later than 1926. There are numerous connections between this story and stories that were composed much earlier than 1931, and Joseph Blotner for one assumes that "Carcassonne" was written in the first months of 1926, as he believes that "Black Music" was (Blotner 1974, I: 501–2). Based on the internal evidence it seems to me very reasonable to think of these two stories as companion pieces from approximately the same time in Faulkner's career. A "Mrs. Widdrington" figures in both stories, as does the Latin-American port of Rincon. In the earliest typescript of "Carcassonne," Mrs. Maurier, a character in *Mosquitoes,* is a woman who owns everything, even the darkness. In both the extant typescripts of the story, the protagonist is named David, which is a name that recurs

with a number of characters early in Faulkner's career. The most interesting parallel is perhaps that David is the first-person narrator of "The
Leg" (written not later than 1928 but unpublished until *Doctor Martino*
in 1934), or that a character named David appears and disappears in the
New Orleans sketch "Out of Nazareth."

Two typescripts of "Carcassonne" are extant; both are seven pages
long, and even though they do not settle the question of when the story
was composed, they definitely indicate a pre-1930 composition. They
also show that Faulkner had worked on and off with the text and that
the technique of free association was deliberate, handled with the utmost
care and with an ear for rhythm that clearly identifies the text as a loosely defined, modernistic prose poem. A closer look at the discursive practice in "Carcassonne" also demonstrates the elaborate, sophisticated
stylistic and rhetorical devices employed in this very brief short story,[2]
which would place the origin of the text with Faulkner's literary strategies of 1926 and 1927—certainly before *The Sound and the Fury*. There
is, on the other hand, reason to think that the final version was revised
and polished not long before Faulkner selected and arranged the stories
for *These 13*, although the changes are not sufficient to place the text as
a coda or finale, its changes resulting from, produced by, the other texts
in the volume and thus testifying to the writer's "tragic vision of life."[3]

Of the two typescripts, the earlier one is corrected in ink in a few
instances while the other one has no such corrections. The corrections
are minor; the change from Mrs. Maurier in the earlier version to Mrs.
Widdrington (!) in the later typescript is of some significance, as is the
fact that the protagonist has a name: David. The published version of the
text is a slightly different—and probably much later—version of the
story. But in relation to the starting point for some of the interpretations
of the story, it should be absolutely clear that we are still talking about
the same story, cast in the same mold, executed in the same fashion, with
no changes substantial enough to alter its characteristics. The unnamed
character adds to the story's abstractness, but other realistic effects are
kept unchanged, and there are so many references to Christianity and to
Christ that a character named David would not have changed the story
much. There is no indication of a plan to italicize parts of the text in the
typescripts, which is how some (not all) of the poet-dreamer's direct
speech appears in the printed text.

Before trying to explicate and interpret the story, let me just state
that in my reading I find very little in the changes from the early typescripts to the published version intended to evoke a description of the
world as wasteland, the tragic view of life, or the outrage of the potential believer. "Carcassonne" remains the same text—about the artist's
need for a Carcassonne so that his reach may exceed his grasp, and about
the despair of never getting to see Carcassonne.

## READING "CARCASSONNE"

The most extensive and detailed interpretation of this story—the first perhaps to read it seriously as something more than an allegory of the poet's plight (Polk 1984)—interprets the story almost exclusively in the context of the collection; and although the critic finds numerous intertexts, there are other contexts as important and as meaningful as the one he chooses. Contextualization does not come by itself; it is an act of the will, yet one has to measure a choice of context against other options. I am convinced that Faulkner did not write "Carcassonne" as a conclusion to his first volume of stories. I do not doubt that he revised the story (minimally) and that he deliberately chose to end the volume with it. Its position in the volume is significant, but, after all, it is one short text among others, and its possible intertextual and contextual relationships to other stories are not dramatic or special. I doubt strongly that the imagery and language, narrative handling and vision are so consistent within the first twelve different stories that a thirteenth in a sense sums them all up; I prefer to read the text as the technically brilliant and thematically problematic short story and prose poem that it is, and to indicate a few reasonable contexts for the story when the work of explicating the text is done. The most significant readings of the story will also be discussed briefly then, for they all inevitably contribute to my reading and interpretation of the story, even if only inadvertently in some cases.

"Carcassonne" is a text about the necessity of dreams and about reality threatening to destroy them although we cling desperately in a never-ending attempt to keep them alive. The dualism, the conflict, is not solved within the frame of the text, and for the tramp-poet of "Carcassonne" no resolution is possible. The very text of the story is proof that art and literature in their modernist expressions do not reflect or represent the "real," objective world. So how then may one reach a solution, how can one live as if writing poetry could possibly be integrated into normal life? We shall return to these and related problems in our interpretation of the story. I shall attempt a reading of the text as if it had not already disappeared under the dust of scholarly commentary— textual, biographical, intertextual, contextual. Less has been written on this story than on most of Faulkner's short stories, which is perhaps surprising, but the significance attached to this story seems nevertheless more than it can carry. Interpretations of "Carcassonne" come close to representing the critic's dream of his own Carcassonne; they seem to represent a vainglorious vision of finally getting inside the mind of the man who wrote the text. The biographical approach will not be pursued here.[4]

The text of "Carcassonne" is open to many interpretations, and the unresolved tensions and contradictions in the strange dialogue between "he and his skeleton" should perhaps not be reduced to the kind of harmonization critics have been almost too eager to find. Perhaps meaning is always deferred in this text because its message is precisely deferment and difference; perhaps the only reading is an aporetic one. The story resists naturalization to a high degree, and if we insist on translating every problematic phrase in accordance with some general code or system to make it intelligible, we risk doing serious injustice to the story as a literary text.

"Carcassonne" is a prose poem but also a brief prose narrative: a short short story. It does not have much of a plot. The basic situation remains fairly stable if not static throughout the text, yet there is minimal development: a conversation takes place, to be followed by dreams and by brave words spoken silently into a void, and even if the structure of the text is close to being circular, the perspective is enlarged to become external and cosmic instead of being internal and claustrophobic, as when the text begins. Initial despair gives way to something else—to hopes expressed in a dream of performing something or to an easy escape by avoiding the real and slipping peacefully away through sleep, perhaps even death. Whether the young man in "Carcassonne" just dreams empty dreams in order to escape the pressure from the real world or whether he—on the basis of defeat, shortcomings, poverty, and exile—builds mansions in eternity, which in Faulkner's language would be to commit a "splendid failure," is a question any interpretation must address, although the answer may well be an ambiguous one. If the fantasy of the protagonist is a postmortal flight of consciousness, if he is on the brink of dying or already dead, he has "escaped" without performing anything of value. If, on the other hand, the dreamer is imagining his body lying on the floor of the sea, the very power and richness of the death imagery indicate that he is capable of feats of creativity. Turning to the text itself now, we should keep this question in mind: Is the dreamer in "Carcassonne" someone who has failed completely in what he has aspired to, who has escaped from all responsibilities, demands, and ambitions into his dreams, to finally end up unnoticed, "lying still?" Or is he a poet who dreams of grand and impossible creations, an artist who knows that his ambitions should be greater than his capabilities and who in failure nevertheless has accomplished more than those who never tried for more than the ordinary and average?

"Carcassonne" as a title signals a story different from its companion texts in *These 13* and *Collected Stories*. Even if the reader knows that it is the name of a medieval French walled city and recognizes that Faulkner uses the name also in *Absalom, Absalom!* (on p. 160, when Miss Rosa describes Sutpen as talking "with the bombast of a madman who creates within his very coffin walls his fabulous immeasurable

Camelots and Carcassonnes") and has commented on it elsewhere (see below), the reading of "Carcassonne" begins with this uncertainty as to what kind of text it is, where it will take us, what to make of it. The story opens dramatically, in the midst of a flight of imagination, a vision of the speaker on horseback in what we tentatively must judge to be a fantasy:

> *And me on a buckskin pony with eyes like blue electricity and a mane like tangled fire, galloping up the hill and right off into the high heaven of the world.* (CS, 895)

This is clearly part of a dream, an epic fantasy in which the dreamer and his horse, with all its special features, seem to be performing an act of heroism, soaring above everyday life, leaving reality behind. The name of Carcassone and this first italicized paragraph of the story places the rider within a medieval world of knights and crusades, of fighting for the causes you believe in, but also within the epic or visionary literature describing these phenomena; *The Song of Roland* may be the most important among those intertextual references. The name of a medieval city, chosen perhaps also because of its sound, and elements from heroic poetry are accordingly two factors behind the production of the text we read: The story's direction, even when it seems to move on through free and fairly random associations, is set by such instances of intertextuality. If we listen to the strange rambling of the ego-figure or to the more controlled and discursive presentation of the third-person narrator, it does not make much of a difference. "Carcassonne" develops according to a pattern established in the title of the story and does not deviate seriously from it. In this respect "Carcassonne" is also an implicit comment on the interdependency of texts, since Faulkner makes little effort to mask what he is doing. Thinking along these lines, the reader may also wonder as to the identity of the "me" of the first line of the story: it is fair to assume that "poet" is a better guess than "dreamer."

From the world of the imagination, with its vision of the protagonist performing some unknown deed, the text quickly brings us back to "the real." The transition from what is so obviously a fantasy to the real world is not less dramatic than the opening, for there is nothing in the text to prepare us for it: "His skeleton lay still" (CS, 895). As readers we expect to come down from the lofty opening, and we may be both surprised and pleased that the transition to something which appears to be simple and intelligible occurs so quickly. "Skeleton" is a little awkward in combination with "lay still"—because of the mild surprise of this word we have to relate it to what we have already read, and we are led to understand that while part of him that is not the skeleton has been on a flight of fantasy to "the high heaven of the world," the rest of him, represented by his metonymous skeleton, remains still. Perhaps the normal expectation of the reader would next be to get information as to the whereabouts of the skeleton, but instead we get another mild surprise. The skeleton is probably lying still because it is thinking! Thinking about what? "This." Which may refer back to its lying still or to its lying still while the rest of him went on wild and fanciful travels beyond its boundaries. The skeleton groans but does not speak, and "he" admits that "*a little quiet is . . . pleasant*," implying that the skeleton normally is dissatisfied and complaining and that the relationship is a problematic one. Most significant is the opposition between "him" and "his skeleton" thus established. It is further developed in the rest of the second paragraph but becomes explicit only in the third, in which the dualism or dichotomy between "he" and "his skeleton," between spirit and flesh, mind and body, and dream and reality is elaborated through an outside narrator whose perspective is close to the protagonist's. The skeleton, in addition to being one of two halves in a simple dichotomy applied here, represents the certainty of death and the fact that we live in a real, objective world.[5] The description in the third paragraph is basic to everything that follows in the story, because it presents the two spheres, the two worlds, and adds background and color to them. Are they contrapuntal? Are they mutually exclusive? Does one of them function as a symbol of the modern world, perhaps even of the world as wasteland, while the other one is an escape that is either legitimate because it signifies creation or empty and futile because it leads to nothing but daydreaming?

As we read on through the following paragraphs of a story so short that we must look very closely at every surprising or unexpected turn it takes, we learn that the protagonist, a male character of unknown age but probably relatively young, is lying "beneath an unrolled strip of tarred roofing made of paper" (*CS*, 895), which is his blanket.[6] He is completely covered by the tarred roofing paper, except for the part we have met in the opening paragraph, the part which now, by the narrator's less dramatic description, "galloped unflagging on the destinationless pony, up a piled silver hill of cumulae . . ." (*CS*, 895).

Dreams and fantasies seem to be a product of the night: they come out of the dark and are related to "the mother of sleep." This explains perhaps the textual dwelling on the procedures of going to bed and getting up, "the mechanics of sleeping, of denning up for the night" (*CS*, 895). This is an important part of the story as a narrative structure, because we cannot claim that the story is "an artistically arrested moment right in the crack between living and dying" (Polk 1984, 38). The story has an onward progression, a motion, which is toward the protagonist as he imagines himself either dead or dying, but the story is also about the living character and the life he leads—and apparently has

led for some time. The iterative "each morning" is used to tell how the
bed rolled back (*CS*, 895), and the spectacles into which he transforms
his tarred paper bed are used "nightly" (*CS*, 896) for dreaming. The text
also includes a description of how "at times" he used to watch the rats
when daylight "slanted grayly along the ruined pitch of the eaves" (*CS*,
898). The phrases "each morning," "nightly," and "at times" seem to
place the dreams and fantasies within a framework of "normal activity"
that has lasted for some time, and other realistic descriptions of Luis in
the cantina and how Mrs. Widdrington expects her guests to behave
clearly indicate a stay of some length in Rincon; the narrator thus greatly expands the time dimension of the story. This particular night that we
listen to his garbled thoughts, then, is not so dramatic or drastic that it
by necessity leads to his death in the dark. Within the narrative structure
of the story, the soundless words of the protagonist must perforce be
given meaning by the narrator. Yet with the closeness between the two,
narrator and character, there is no need to investigate the coloring of
reported speech in this text.

Following the descriptions of the "mechanics of sleeping" is the first
mention of the place where he lives, the Latin-American port of Rincon.
The contrast between "him" and "his skeleton" is thus reinforced and
expanded to become one between the "real" world of the port, where
people own everything from oil and the air one breathes to other people,
and an inner world of a young poet's imagination.[7] This dream world
may be seen as a way of coping, a means of escape from a too-harsh reality for someone who does not want to adjust.

The description of Rincon is in a poet's language, the modernist
imagery borrowed from T. S. Eliot ("Prufrock" more than "The Waste
Land" here) and typical also in the verbal painting of the urban scene:
"Rincon followed its fatal, secret, nightly pursuits" (*CS*, 895–96); but
after the sounds and noises, silence breathes again and dreams can be
pursued.

The story opens on lines from a dream or a fantasy; when we return
to the dreams again, they are described from the outside, hidden from us
within the dreamer's imagination. The long passage describing the horse
that still gallops is kept in the present tense, and this is repeated when
horse and rider appear again in the ultimate paragraph of the story:
"steed and rider thunder on" (*CS*, 900). When the protagonist nightly
peruses the fabric of dreams (*CS*, 896), he is watching the horse but not
riding it. This is significant. It is not that the rider is now under the horse,
as one might infer since he can see the "saddlegirth and the soles of the
rider's feet in the stirrups" (*CS*, 896); we are told that he is perusing the
fabric of dreams. In the darkness of the night he has visions of horses and
riders and battles long ago, of those who charged and fought and fell in

the sacred dust. This is reported speech, or rather thoughts put into words by the narrator, and not flights of fancy or imagination only. The poet-dreamer thinks of the Norman steed, cut in half and still galloping, perhaps unaware of the parallel to his own divided self; but to the reader parallels and contrasts have by now become recognized features in the text. Repetition and echoes, allusions and intertextual references account for more and more of the text as it develops. "It was dark" is used five times, filling the text with a pervasive darkness, like the oncoming night. Darkness and night add to an atmosphere of something almost impenetrable, yet not threatening, because there are the "twin transparencies" to look through, there are the dreams for comfort and for escape.

The poet-dreamer lives in a garret with a ruined ceiling which slants down to the eaves. "Ruined" is used twice in almost identical descriptions of the room. He sleeps on a hardwood floor, under his tarred-paper blanket. Under these conditions, in spite of them and not because of them, the dreamer becomes a poet, who can see not only the valiant crusaders of old but also see himself from the outside:

> It was dark, and the body consciousness, assuming the office of vision, shaped in his mind's eye his motionless body grown phosphorescent with that steady decay which had set up within his body on the day of his birth. *The flesh is dead living on itself subsisting consuming itself thriftily in its own renewal will never die for I am the Resurrection and the Life. . . .* (CS, 896–97)

The dreamer has clearly a special quality of vision, capable of forming and shaping "in his mind's eye" even his own situation, here seen in relation to the fact that he is mortal and that the skeleton's cynicism in the long run is a "correct" attitude: The end of life *is* lying still. But the quarrel with his skeleton comes a little later, near the end of the text. The reader encounters a number of difficult passages and paragraphs, but they seem to become a little easier to handle if we are aware of the narrative situation and if we follow the text closely instead of relating it to other texts.

We follow the thoughts of the dreamer-poet in the narrator's voice. From speculations about wood and comparisons of it to "any other skeletons" (CS, 897), the text introduces sea imagery for the first time. It is related to the horse and rider imagery that have dominated earlier, and from wood, to skeleton, to bones the associations seem simple enough. The thought of bones lying under the sea is no greater surprise than the buckskin pony in the opening line. It seems as if the poet's mind is capable of spanning heaven and earth, reaching from the bottoms of the seas to the dying stars far away in the sky, if only his horse is willing to take him there.

The bones that lie under the sea could be bones of horses long dead, now cursing their inferior riders and thinking of the deeds they could have accomplished with first-rate riders up. "But somebody always crucified the first-rate riders" (CS, 897). So they are dead, too, and so the horses might as well accept their fate: it is better to lie at the bottom of the sea if there are no first-rate riders to lead them to success or victory.

This is an ambiguous part of the text. It is likely to represent a dream of peace and quiet with the motion of falling tides, especially if the only other choice is the sense of inferiority evoked by the horses' bones, a life of hopes deferred and dreams not fulfilled. The passage says one thing, and means something else, but its chief quality as text is its poetic appreciation of the simple beauty of language, in which recurrent images and repetitive sounds echo through the whole paragraph, making it more of a poem than any other part of this prose text, this minimal narrative.

As we read on we leave the realm of imagination, of the beyond, of the fear of a mediocre life but also of dying, for the world of the skeleton, the world of the real. The dreams continue, but the description turns to the outside world: of Luis, who runs the cantina downstairs and lets him sleep in the garret. But we are told that the Standard Oil Company (and its "wife," Mrs. Widdrington) owns everything, including the darkness. And the question of the protagonist being a poet seems to arise as much from the narrator's portrait of Mrs. Widdrington as it comes from the poetic quality of the dreams and fantasies of "him":

> She'd make a poet of you too, if you did not work anywhere. She believed that, if a reason for breathing were not acceptable to her, it was no reason. With her, if you were white and did not work, you were either a tramp or a poet. Maybe you were. (CS, 897–98)

The fact that Mrs. Widdrington has made a poet of the protagonist does not mean that he is not naturally a poet; it does not set aside the poetic quality of the small performances to which we listen, nor does it make him an inferior or would-be poet who does not have the endurance and courage to put words to paper. We simply do not know more about these matters. What we are told by this halfway realistic and critical description of a society where some people own everything and others have nothing is that the protagonist has serious problems in adjusting and accepting the conditions under which he lives. This is true for the "real" life of the skeleton as well as for the nightly life he spends in the imaginary realms of battles long ago. Like Childe Roland of old who to the dark tower came, he has experienced nightmares and imagines that his own whitening bones may soon be knocking together "in the caverns and the grottoes of the sea" (CS, 897).

We read on. It is still dark, and the darkness is now filled with "a fairy pattering of small feet" (*CS*, 898), rats "in whispering arpeggios of minute sound" (*CS*, 898). Similar descriptions of rats can be found in Faulkner's writings before and after "Carcassonne," but I do not think we should exaggerate the importance of the rats in this text. They add to the description of sordidness and poverty, of life in the garret and in the dark, and they are part of the kind of life at the bottom which the dreamer leads in Rincon, a neglected or wasted corner of the world.[8] The only difference between poet and rat seems to be that the rats do not have to earn their use of Mrs. Widdrington's darkness by writing poetry; this thought leads the poet to associate the rats with Byron ("Something of the rat about Byron" [*CS*, 898]). A passage of italicized text follows, eloquent and intricately intertextual, with references to King Agamemnon as well as to Prince Hamlet (Brooks 1978b; Polk 1984).

The text returns to the dreamer-poet's original vision, but this time less dramatically. This time his words are spoken, given to us within quotation marks: "'I would like to perform something'" (*CS*, 898). Soundless, the wish is a modest one, as if all passion is spent, but the horse again fills his head. This time the narrator's description may include a key to the protagonist's own situation, his emotional strain, his despair. When he thinks of the Norman steed, he thinks of a horse bred to bear iron mail "in the slow, damp green valleys of England" and who is now "maddened with heat and thirst and hopeless horizons filled with shimmering nothingness" (*CS*, 898). It thunders along in two halves, with obvious parallels to the poet-dreamer's dilemma, his inability to live at once in the two worlds of body and mind and also his acceptance of the illusion that these worlds must be made one and whole. The reader has waited for the dialogue between the poet and his skeleton to continue, and since the skeleton must help the poet with "bits of trivial information" (*CS*, 899), a significant conversation begins. Critics have with good reason attached much importance to this dialogue because it seems to be decisive for an interpretation of who is right and who is wrong, skeleton or "he himself," about life's meaning, the end of life, and other very big questions. But it is also worth noticing that the dialogue covers only about half a page of the story, and its significance should not be overemphasized. The story is not a body-soul dialogue: the dialogue is but a part of the total conflict in the story. The dialogue is, of course, framed by bits and pieces of poetic language, and his mind wanders off into areas of the imagination, until he lies peacefully "in the windless gardens of the sea."

"Caracassonne" has the quality of a dream, as the poet repeatedly lapses into escapist fantasies of final quietude and solitude, the result of the despair that accompanies his dream of performing something—perhaps even a dream of artistic creation. He dreams of a less barren soil from which to feed his imagination, and his skeleton moans in dissatisfaction with the wooden floor. It provides him with the wisdom that "the end of life is lying still" (*CS*, 899), a wisdom not agreed upon by the spiritual "he." The conclusion of the dialogue shows that the poet accepts that somebody must give him advice, but he then qualifies his assent: "At least it looks like it" (*CS*, 899), implying perhaps that the trivial things the skeleton can feel and understand ought to be unnecessary. It does not look like it, however: withdrawn, isolated, in a corner of the world, the world is still very much with him, with bits of trivial information, with the oil company, with the intruding texts of heroic literature. The skeleton is there, the outside world is there, but the dream is also there, the dream of heroism and of creation, or perhaps only the dream of being alive and finding something meaningful in life:

> I want to perform something bold and tragical and austere . . . me on a buckskin pony with eyes like blue electricity and a mane like tangled fire, galloping up the hill and right off into the high heaven of the world. (*CS*, 899)

And so be it: steed and rider thunder on, becoming "a dying star upon the immensity of darkness and of silence." But the earth abideth, "the dark and tragic figure of the Earth, his mother" (*CS*, 900). Steed and rider, like the riderless Norman horse, have galloped all through the text in the imagination of the protagonist. He has seen them through his imaginary spectacles, and we have read his soundless words as reported by the narrator. There is no reason that the final report should not also be another dream, of greater magnitude and more certain failure perhaps but still a dream, which lets us see the maker of fantasies and dreams in a cosmic perspective but still bound to the earth.

"Carcassonne" is a poetic narrative about the dilemma of poetic creation, and its central problem seems to me to be in understanding the material from which literature is made. The twin inspirations in reality and in fantasy or imagination seem to me to be the real opponents in the story, and the conflict that is vaguely described on many levels, most notably as a (medieval) dichotomy between skeleton and spirit, seems to represent the struggle between opposing and apparently incompatible wishes in the artist's search for his material. Thus I am convinced that in addition to being the beautifully arranged prose poem which moves readers by its grandiloquence, in addition to being a text replete with echoes and images and symbols from the other stories in *These 13*, in addition to being an extraordinarily literary text in its intertextual dependence, "Carcassonne" also depicts the modernist understanding of the world and of art, an exploration of art in relation to life and of the need for art to transcend the real. But it is also a text about the function of the real in art, about art's distortions and its creation of difference. David Minter (1992) thinks that the particular strength of "Carcassonne" is that two actions he finds in the story, "one of easy surrender to the real, the other of failed yet grand defiance" (90), are not resolved. He goes on to say:

> What we have in "Carcassonne" is an oscillation, a going back and forth, between particulars of the real and visions-dreams-nightmares of the bizarre, that poses the same kind of question [a question without answer] and then leaves it unresolved. In "Carcassonne," furthermore, this going back and forth is not only between heaven and earth, imagination and reality, art and life, nor merely between grand gestures of empty dreams and deeds done. It is also between Faulkner's own divided response to the evocations of the far and the strange and the presence of the near and familiar. (90–91)

This is about as far as I want to go with trying to explicate and analyze "Carcassonne" without bringing in more than the normal number of quotations and comparisons that are an integral part of a shared literary competence. Thus far I have relied on previous criticism, which at its best is very sophisticated and very good, even if the theoretical basis for some of the readings may be debatable; now it is time to bring in a couple of statements about the story from the author himself. Authors are notoriously unreliable when it comes to their own texts, and it is high time that Faulkner scholarship reduces the importance and value attached to the voice of the master and concentrates on the meaning of the texts he made. Nevertheless, this is what he said about "Carcassonne" when asked about it at the University of Virginia:

> That was—I was still writing about a young man in conflict with his environment. I—it seemed to me that fantasy was the best way to tell that story. To have told it in terms of simple realism would have lost something, in my opinion. To use fantasy was the best, and that's a piece that I've always liked because there was the poet again. I wanted to be a poet, and I think of myself now as a failed poet, not as a novelist at all but a failed poet who had to take up what he could do.[9]

In my reading of the story, this statement might have been useful, since one of the problems is whether the protagonist is a poet or not. We have tried to show the text's implications and indications, and I see no problem in letting him be both a poet and dreamer, even a failed poet of less-er magnitude than those failures Faulkner used to talk about. To insist on one indivisible meaning of the phrase "there was the poet again," namely that Faulkner referred to himself and not to the character in the text, makes little sense. The text was written by a poet and bears all marks of this, but there is within the story a dream of performance, the creation of poetic discourse, the transformation of a bleak and barren world into fantastic stories of horses and battles and rides transcending all barriers. To some people our dreamer is a poet, within the frames of the narrative, which is all we have access to.

Let us bring in another reference to "Carcassonne" given by Faulkner when he was asked about the revival of Southern literature: "I myself am inclined to think that it was because of the bareness of the Southerner's life, that he had to resort to his own imagination, to create his own Carcassonne."[10] This clearly supports an understanding of "Carcassonne" as a text about the artist's struggle to create in spite of his background, although literature may be seen as an attempt to work through grief and loss, to create something in the absence of other things, and finally perhaps to find that real and unreal, near and far, literary and popular may be balanced to create convincing fictions. Michael Millgate (1966) says that "Carcassonne" "perhaps represents an attempt to cap-ture in words the anguish and ecstasy of the creative experience, or at least of the creative ambition: . . . 'Carcassonne' should perhaps best be regarded as expressing a commitment to an ultimately tragic vision of life" (261). Our reading seems to confirm the validity of this early assess-ment of a difficult Faulkner text.

Many critics have felt that they must deal with "Carcassonne" at length because of the extra significance it gains from being the final story in *These 13* as well as in *Collected Stories,* and they quote Faulkner's thoughts about the demands of a short story collection in a letter to Malcolm Cowley: "even to a collection of short stories, form, integra-tion, is as important as to a novel—an entity of its own, single, set for one pitch, contrapuntal in integration, toward one end, one finale."[11] Faulkner wrote this when planning *Collected Stories,* and one should not exaggerate the importance of it for a collection assembled almost twen-ty years earlier.[12] Reading "Carcassonne" in the light of *These 13* is bound to be a reading much more of *These 13* than of the short story, even though the story contributes to the collection's bleak picture of the world as a wasteland.[13]

I have tried to follow the text of "Carcassonne," looking at it from different possible contexts. And still the story is very much the same to me as it has always been—a poetic fable of the artist's plight. It is an evo-cation of the imaginary realms the creative spirit can reach in spite of the strange and hostile world surrounding it. In the last resort "Carcas-sonne" negates that "the end of life is lying still" by being one more scratch on the wall against oblivion.

"Carcassonne" is an elusive and dreamlike story about an artist's struggle to create. The problematic nature of artistic creation is central in the story, but it is contemplated only in very general terms. The dream is one of creation, so that the text presenting the dream indicates the validity of this kind of experience as a way of coping with the world and at the same time contributing to an understanding of it. The text is proof that the dream is valid: it produces the literary text in spite of the bareness of the surrounding world. The story shows that the poetic spirit may transcend all such matter, so that it becomes possible to "create out of the materials of the human spirit something which did not exist before."[14]

# Chapter 7

# Dry September

## TEXTUAL INFORMATION AND PUBLICATION HISTORY

According to his story-sending schedule Faulkner mailed a story called "Drouth" to the American Mercury on February 8, 1930. After the American Mercury rejected the story Faulkner sent it to Forum on March 7 and then to Scribner's on April 21. The story was returned from Scribner's "without having been read at all," according to a letter of April 28.[1] Faulkner must have been very quick in sending out another copy, since the next entry in his sending schedule is May 1. This last date is encircled, which was Faulkner's customary practice to indicate that the story had been accepted: he was paid two hundred dollars by Scribner's, which published "Dry September" in the January 1931 issue (Skei 1981, 59–60). We have no information as to who changed the title or when it was done. We do know, however, that the editors at Scribner's discussed the titles of other Faulkner stories with him (for example, the story published as "Spotted Horses") and came up with suggestions for improved titles. "Dry September" was included in *These 13* later that year and also in *Collected Stories*. It has always been one of the most anthologized of Faulkner's short stories and a favorite among his critics.

Two pre-publication versions of "Dry September," both complete, are extant. This is an eight-page manuscript and a nineteen-page carbon typescript. James Ferguson (1991) discusses the minor yet significant corrections in the manuscript itself (122–23)—not only the changes from manuscript to typescript, which is what is usually done if textual criticism is attempted at all. Knowledge of some of these changes could have been helpful for numerous critics who have found individuals or groups of individuals, and not the community in a larger sense, to be responsible for the lynching in the story. Faulkner's revisions point in the direction of greater emphasis on the shared responsibility of a civilized community. The carbon typescript is probably a copy of the typescript from which the setting for the magazine was done.[2] Accordingly, changes from manuscript to typescript here also mean changes from manuscript to published text. These changes are of great significance, whereas the changes from magazine text to the text in *These 13* are minor.[3] The changes from manuscript to typescript demonstrate Faulkner's growing craftsmanship and are well worth looking at more closely.

In the manuscript Faulkner made a nearly complete draft of the story, but the sequence of the first and second parts is the opposite of what it became in the printed versions. By this transposition of the first two parts Faulkner improved the short story immensely. The story now begins *in medias res*, with a quick description of "the bloody September twilight, aftermath of sixty-two rainless days" (*CS*, 169), followed by the rumor about the rape in the first paragraph of the text. This gives a much greater impact than the descriptive beginning in which Minnie's story is told. The deletion of a few paragraphs at the beginning of the third section—a description of the town in which Minnie lives—is also a great improvement. Millgate (1966) notes that the "advantages gained through omitting the paragraphs are obvious, since their abstract statements were presented powerfully and concretely elsewhere in the story in terms of the lives of the people involved in the action" (263).[4] Millgate finds an even more striking example of the impact of such editing in "A Rose for Emily." Indeed, it seems to have been Faulkner's practice to delete general statements about "how women are," prejudiced opinions based on vague notions about what is typically female, and instead he gave his female characters individual lives and related their destinies to their environment. Faulkner's narrators often know how women are, but the author must have felt that there were too many unwarranted and unmotivated negative descriptions of female characters in his short stories. Accordingly, as is the case with "Dry September," he left them out when revising. This is seen even more clearly in the revisions of "Mountain Victory" and "Beyond."[5]

A curious fact about the manuscript of "Drouth" is that it is divided into numbered parts or sections, a practice Faulkner seldom followed. This may indicate that Faulkner was confident with his material and knew exactly where to take the story from the beginning. There is less reason to guess that the manuscript is based on an earlier draft or extensive notes, although this may of course have been the case. Except for the transposition of the first two parts, the story did not change substantially from manuscript to typescript, but this does not necessarily suggest that it was written in one burst of inspiration. The structural movement of the story is so deliberate and obvious as to be almost natural and inevitable. Furthermore, symbols, parallels, and juxtapositions of elements are all handled with care and easy mastery. "Dry September" is probably one of those texts for which the inspiration was sudden and strong, but it also took a lot of hard work get the original idea written down and structured to satisfaction.

What do the textual study and the publication information tell us that may be helpful in an interpretation of this story? First of all, "Dry September" gives a superb example of Faulkner's growing awareness of the importance of structure, in a period when his creative powers reached an all-time high and four or five of his best short stories were written, revised, and finalized. The opening of a short story is of particular significance: within a brief narrative the tone must be established and the direction set immediately. "Dry September" opens on one of the strongest, most concentrated symbolic images of Faulkner's entire career. We can see the advantage of the transposition of the two first parts of the story: point of view and the pace of narration have changed from a descriptive and narrated background story of Minnie's life (the past) to a present scene, allowing for immediacy, speed, and action. Faulkner uses psycho-physical parallelism, in the sense that a description of climate doubles as a symbol to reinforce the feeling of strong emotions, boredom, violence, and even doom.

## READING "DRY SEPTEMBER"

"Dry September" is a problematic story to read and interpret, not because of its violent subject matter and the traumatic situations it describes nor because it is a story about which critics disagree openly and directly. The problem is rather that the text seems to bring forth entrenched attitudes and prejudices in its readers, so that we shall have to be extremely cautious in studying Faulkner's handling of the narrative and the rhetoric of this text. My understanding is that the text distributes sympathies and antipathies fairly obviously, even if the justness and fairness of this may be questioned or undercut through small ironies in the text. Yet even if we discover that the text "sides with" Minnie and sees her as a victim, it is still possible to see McLendon as a victim as well; and in both cases we still have to face the question of the causes and forces which shape the lives of these people. Our readings would differ almost completely if, on the one hand, we read the story in terms of individual psychology, with an emphasis on female sexuality and hysteria, or on the other hand, we read it in terms of sociology or social psychology, looking at the role given to women of Minnie's class and background in the particular time and place Faulkner describes. Questions about guilt and responsibility for the terrible events of the story must be addressed, which means that I am not much in favor of interpretations that read "Dry September" as the acting out of a myth, be it ritualized through the sacrificial scapegoat ceremony or not. I am also rather doubtful about interpretations which concentrate on individual psychology.

"Dry September" opens on a description of drought, violence, and death that is summed up in the words "the bloody September twilight," through which "the rumor, the story, whatever it was" (*CS*, 169) about Miss Minnie Cooper and a Negro has spread. The dry weather has lasted for sixty-two days and seems to have created an unrest bordering on despair. So when the rumor reaches the audience in the barbershop, it is like fire being set to the grass. None of the men in the barbershop "knew exactly what had happened" (*CS*, 169), but they are nevertheless "attacked, insulted, frightened." The men seem more than willing to accept the rumor as true, although the text clearly informs us that it is only a rumor or a story and indeed not much to rely on. The men in the barbershop are so ready and willing to accept the story that their readiness must somehow be related to the season of drought, to an unease and a tension that has been building up for a long time; but the real basis of the immediate reactions of the most active of the customers is obviously their racial prejudices, their absolute conviction that the Negro is inferior, or at least that the social order they have created and maintained takes "a white woman's word before a nigger's" (*CS*, 169). The psychosexual basis of racial bigotry is abundantly demonstrated in the text, although Faulkner's analysis goes in many directions, linking the readiness to act with "this durn weather" (*CS*, 170) and also showing that one strong man alone can end all talk about right and wrong and persuade people to follow him. It is clear that there is a basic level beneath all actions here. At this level we have a collective fantasy that is taken to be truer than factual evidence, even if someone bothers to look for evidence. John Matthews (1992) thinks that it is only natural and reasonable that "the community grants greater authority to 'the rumor, the story, whatever it was' as an image that now must be entertained than to the particular history of any individual" (23).

As readers, we are allowed to listen in to the ensuing conversation in the barbershop, given in direct speech but organized so that the narration almost resembles a series of stage directions. Faulkner has set the scene with deliberate consideration, arranging it so that the focus is on a barber (as if he were the only barber in the shop), described as a "man of middle age; a thin, sand-colored man with a mild face" (*CS*, 169) but not named until later on. His first comment seems to be in response to a question from a customer to whom he is giving a shave. This is a client from out of town, who has good reason to ask questions, being a stranger. It is important to notice that even if McLendon is the most active in the vigilante band of men from the barbershop in Jefferson, he arrives in the shop only later, having heard the rumor somewhere else. There is no indication before he arrives that the men in the shop would have gone from verbal expressions of their racial hatred to actually doing anything. Some of them are eager, others are willing to wait for the sheriff and the facts, but the "drummer and stranger" (CS, 170) in the chair is never in doubt as to what must be done. He even claims to speak on behalf of the South—presumably in defense of all white Southern womanhood—but his aim is clearly to get the "hulking youth in a sweat-stained silk shirt" (CS, 169) to act upon beliefs he is not even capable of finding words for.

We learn details regarding the rumor—the Negro's name, Will Mayes, is mentioned. The barber, whose name is Hawkshaw,[6] knows Will and knows that he is a good person. He knows Minnie as well, and on the basis of what may be understood either as intimate knowledge of and a genuine interest in his fellow men and women of Jefferson or his intimate knowledge of male gossip around the barber shop, he knows that she is around forty, has never been married. In accordance with a simple understanding of what this means, he observes, "I leave it to you fellows if them ladies that get old without getting married dont have notions that a man cant—" (CS, 170). This is not only prejudice and simplemindedness, however; other men in the shop know that this is "not the first man scare she ever had . . ." (CS, 171). There is thus reason, even if based only on hearsay, not to take Minnie's words for the truth. But facts are of little interest to the stranger, the youth, and most of the others. They do not listen to reason; simply to think of the possibility that a white woman could be lying, or to ask about facts, means that one is "a hell of a white man" (CS, 170) or simply a traitor.

At one point in the conversation it looks as if one of the men understands the role of the weather, the dryness, and the heat in what has allegedly happened. But ironically he brings up the weather only as a misogynistic explanation for why someone would be compelled to attack Minnie. We could not ask for a more direct indication of male bigotry in addition to racism, but it is important to notice that even if Minnie has become a laughingstock for these men, they are eager to "defend her," to the point of killing an innocent Negro. So whom do they defend? They do not take Minnie seriously: the whole town laughs at her behind her back, and they are not all capable of seeing her as an individual, a human being with her own problems.

As we read the realistic but almost unbelievable conversation in the barbershop we pause, because some of the characterizations of the speakers come as a surprise in the explicit, albeit indirect, judgment of the speakers. His face covered with shaving foam, the drummer from out of town looks "like a desert rat in the moving pictures" (CS, 170), and the youth, whose name is Butch, has "a strained, baffled gaze, as if he was trying to remember what it was he wanted to say or do" (CS, 171). McLendon is revealed to us in what we understand as probably a destructive masculinity, perhaps also modeled on the moving pictures to which we have already had reference in the story. His white shirt is open at the throat, he wears a felt hat, he is poised on the balls of his feet, his glance is bold and hot. He puts an end to all discussion about whether something happened or not in a memorable assertion which makes clear that arguments and reason, facts and truth, and even justice do not matter at all: "Happen? What the hell difference does it make? Are you going to let the black sons get away with it until one really does it?"

So the men in the barbershop join McLendon, some of them eagerly, others reluctantly and slowly, but one by one they get up and leave with him. Hawkshaw can do nothing and leaves right after the others. Two other barbers are left behind in the shop, and a brief exchange between them ends the first part of the story, adding to our impression of McLendon as a violent man: "I'd just as lief be Will Mayes as Hawk, if he gets McLendon riled" (CS, 173).

Behind the rumor that has set this all in motion is Minnie Cooper, who has experienced a spiritual and sexual drought for a long time now and who has reached her own dry September. Her situation has altered over the years; once she rode "upon the crest of the town's social life" (CS, 174). How empty her days have become can be seen from the following description:

> She was thirty-eight or thirty-nine. She lived in a small frame house with her invalid mother and a thin, sallow, unflagging aunt, where each morning between ten and eleven she would appear on the porch in a lace-trimmed boudoir cap, to sit swinging in the porch swing until noon. After dinner she lay down for a while, until the afternoon began to cool. Then, in one of the three or four new voile dresses which she had each summer, she would go downtown to spend the afternoon in the stores with the other ladies, where they would handle the goods and haggle over the prices in cold, immediate voices, without any intention of buying. (CS, 173)

Miss Minnie is the female character in Faulkner's short fiction that most resembles Miss Emily Grierson of "A Rose for Emily." They are both presented in retrospective capsule stories which emphasize family background, social life, sexual experience, and position in the town. The portraits are not identical but are similar enough to indicate the emptiness, waste, futility, and despair that unavoidably seem to be the lot of women not allowed to do anything because of their upbringing.

Minnie has had one love affair, with a bank cashier, and has consequently been reduced to the status of an adulteress in the eyes of the
town. No man cares to watch her on the streets anymore. She is filled
with unrest and despair so that to her, as to the men in the barbershop,
something must happen. When nothing happens to change her situation,
she is compelled to do something herself. Her fantasies, even the tragic
one about rape if indeed it begins with her, are created by her own
understanding of what people expect; that is, she tries to live up to the
expectations she believes the town has of her, even though she is not really a member of the community, not being allowed to contribute at all,
being forced to lead a meaningless life of boredom and idleness. Having
been born and reared to her position, she is also unable to get out of the
trap, because the town would not understand if she tried, and she would
not know how to live in a "real" world. Minnie is perhaps not really an
anachronism, but she should have been. The secluded, protected, but
ultimately worthless life she leads is not limited to her. The text shows
that other ladies in Jefferson, even married ones, have to fill their days
with meaningless activities. Minnie's situation is both a result of her
social position and of the rigid and stereotyped role a woman is supposed to fill and is prepared for through her upbringing. Minnie sees life
pass her without her participation, and she is not yet ready to accept the
role that her mother and aunt seem to find sufficient. She has turned to
drinking whisky, putting on a new dress each afternoon, and going out
to the moving pictures. Minnie's empty days "had a quality of furious
unreality" against the background of a mother who does not leave her
room and a gaunt aunt who runs the house. No wonder if Minnie in
desperation does something to prove that she is alive, to postpone the
descent of final darkness.

The first two sections of the story are told from a variety of perspectives. The narrator is in complete control of his narrative, even
though he is hardly noticeable. He shifts easily between the speakers in
the barbershop and his own descriptions of them and then moves on to
a capsule story of Minnie's life, his treatment of her varying from cold
objectivity, seeing her at a distance and from the perspectives of others,
to close-range observations that evoke pity and compassion. The narrator's sympathy for Minnie is obvious, and his criticism of a system which
makes life unbearable for women is as evident. Before returning to a
close reading of the text and following it to its conclusion, let us consider the narrator's function in "Dry September" a little further.

The third-person omniscient narrator changes point of view and
manner of narration freely.[7] Thus the reader is allowed to follow more
than one string of events as they unfold, always in chronological order.
By this narrative strategy, the author leaves one chain of events for more
urgent incidents elsewhere, to return at a later point in time. The tech-

nique allows him to avoid a direct description of the murder, because the story is at that point with Hawkshaw after he jumps out of the car. Allusions and metaphors leave no doubt about Will's fate, however, and the separate strings of events are closely related so that what happens on one level bears upon the events on other levels. More importantly, the tone and the setting of the story are powerfully symbolic of the ensuing action. The confident use of third-person narration to control the distance and distribute sympathy combines with the use of metaphors of dust and drought to create a stale, barren landscape. The metaphors suggest that the drought also applies to human beings and their interrelationships. There are even indications of a causal connection between climate, landscape, and social conditions and the terror and death that follow. It may thus be that terror and death, sensation at any cost, are not only given metaphorical emphasis by the nature imagery but are results of the complete drought in the lives of the characters involved. At any rate, Faulkner's narrative strategy in this story functions exceptionally well. Although close scrutiny may reveal how rigidly controlled the story is, the execution of its master plan is hardly noticeable. As Joseph Reed puts it, here the narrative control moves "beyond simple question of where to stand or empathetic attachment into a combination of almost Aeschylean artistry, involving distance, control, compulsion, dissective objectivity."[8]

The story picks up its line of action on a particular Saturday night in Jefferson, and we follow Hawkshaw as he hastens up the streets to find McLendon and company in a final attempt to stop them from going after Will. He walks through dimly lit streets, and images of drought, dust, and death dominate the text: "The day had died in a pall of dust; above the darkened square, shrouded by the spent dust, the sky was as clear as the inside of a brass bell. Below the east was a rumor of the twice-waxed moon" (CS, 175). A little later, just before the men find Will and drag him to the car, the moon is again described: "Below the east the wan hemorrhage of the moon increased" (CS, 177). The image of the moon may be interpreted in different ways, but in this context it seems to be used to cast a pallid light over the events of the story, making the dust into a silver shroud. Under the moon the men "seemed to breathe, live, in a bowl of molten lead" (CS, 177). The descriptions of the men out at the ice plant, calling the name of an innocent man of an inferior race so that they may kill him, while themselves only wanting to get out of there, away from the dust and heat and the moonlit night, are similar to those Faulkner employs in the war stories in which active combat is included, "Crevasse" and "Victory." The descriptions of the world as a wasteland are as powerful in "Dry September" as in the war stories, and it is significant that two ex-soldiers are active in the vigilante group. The drought has created a world of dust and despair; the imagery in the story not only describes nature but also the spiritual malaise and violence which seem to be the only things growing and thriving under such circumstances.

This section of the story is fast-moving and filled with action such as cars speeding along dark, dusty roads. Hawkshaw joins McLendon and company in the first car, and after Will is picked up, manacled and dragged into the car, he is placed in the backseat between Hawkshaw and the soldier, with Butch on the running board. No one listens to Will's prayers, and when in despair he strikes random blows and hits the barber on the mouth, even Hawkshaw strikes back. He probably knows that he cannot help Will; perhaps scared by his own reaction, he suddenly wants to get out. Since McLendon is not going to stop the car, Hawkshaw jumps out while traveling at high speed just after the car has turned into a road leading to an abandoned brick kiln with bottomless vats. He limps back toward town, and we do not see or hear the others until they pass him on their way back. Realism and rich imagery evoke a feeling of horror beyond repair, not in a handful of dust, but in a world filled with it:

> The moon was higher, riding high and clear of the dust at last, and after a while the town began to glare beneath the dust. He went on, limping. Presently he heard cars and the glow of them grew in the dust behind him and he left the road and crouched again in the weeds until they passed. McLendon's car came last now. There were four people in it and Butch was not on the running board.
>
> They went on; the dust swallowed them; the glare and the sound died away. The dust of them hung for a while, but soon the eternal dust absorbed it again. The barber climbed back onto the road and limped on toward home. (CS, 179–80)

Faulkner lets the most violent action take place away from the narrative, almost as in the tragedies of ancient times, but he does not do it for reasons of decorum. There is no doubt that Will Mayes is left behind, as the passing reference to the number of people in McLendon's car indicates. The precise information about the bottomless vats a little earlier is all we need to know what it means for Will to have "gone on a little trip." In this story Faulkner is much more interested in the creation of atmospheric detail to portray a landscape, a climate, and a community in a season of drought and a lifeless stasis that threaten to destroy life and all life-giving impulses. Direct description of mutilation and killing would not have served his purpose here as they do, however, in *Light in August*, a novel which shares much with "Dry September."

The only further reference to Will Mayes and the lynching party is in the whispered conversation of people in town as Minnie and her friends walk through the streets on their way to the picture show. We are told that there are no black people on the square, and we are given the dialogue of "coatless drummers in chairs along the curb" (CS, 180). The question "What did they do with the nigger? Did they—?" (CS, 180–81) gets an ambiguous answer: "Sure. He's all right"; "Sure. He went on a little trip" (CS, 181). If this is meant to be representative of the town's reaction and how much white people in general care, it is problematic to individualize guilt and responsibility. McLendon and a few of his like are responsible for the actual killing, but they have met no resistance and have in fact acted on behalf of the town, contributing to the upholding of the collective fantasy. The two chief hangmen, McLendon and Butch, are more than willing to take a white woman's word before a black man's. One should be careful not to charge only a few racists in the town with the slaying of Will, since nobody, with the exception of Hawkshaw, does anything to prevent the murder.[9]

The tragic action all begins with Minne and the rumor she has started. Why, then, does she tell her lie about the rape? The reference to the weather and to Minnie's own "dry September," meaning that her fertility and sexuality are coming to an end, is not a satisfactory explanation. Minnie may well feel that something must happen to make life bearable, but she is also prone to react rather arbitrarily. Idleness, boredom, and the long days with no meaningful activity except resting, dressing, walking, chatting, lie ahead. But there is more to Minnie's fantasies than the obvious and simple explanation indicated by Hawkshaw and others, that she is unmarried and getting old. Minnie's fantasies are also influenced by the dream factory in Hollywood. The life she seems to miss is not the life of marriage, children, duties, and responsibilities. Rather, it appears to be the glamorous and exciting life portrayed by Hollywood myth-makers. Late Saturday night, just after the town hears about the killing of Will, Minnie goes to a picture show:

> The lights flicked away; the screen glowed silver, and soon life began to unfold, beautiful and passionate and sad, while still the young men and girls entered, scented and sibilant in the half dark, their paired backs in silhouette delicate and sleek, their slim, quick bodies awkward, divinely young, while beyond them the silver dream accumulated, inevitably on and on. She began to laugh. In trying to suppress it, it made more noise than ever; heads began to turn. Still laughing, her friends raised her and led her out, and she stood at the curb, laughing on a high, sustained note, until the taxi came up and they helped her in. (CS, 181)

Minnie obviously experiences a fit of hysteria, and her friends speculate whether the rape had taken place at all. They do not understand Minnie's sexual pathology and are completely unaware of the possible causes behind it. Behind Minnie's desperate laughter and high screams is not only her failure to fit in to the social life of the small town, or her belief in Hollywood's impossible dreamworld, but most significantly her strong sense of failure because she is single. Minnie would not have despaired of being single if couples were not the accepted, institutionalized practice; she would not have despaired of growing old and losing her hold on men if being young, popular, and admired was not the social standard.

The focus in the section that ends with Minnie being taken care of by her friends, who administer ice and fan her, shifts from the observers on the street to the outside comments by the narrator but remains most of the time close to Minnie, almost intimately close as we see her put on her "sheerest underthings and stockings" (CS, 180) or follow her fight to suppress her laughter before entering the picture show. We know what she has done and still are drawn close to Minnie, feeling compassion and perhaps even anger on her behalf. This is indicative of Faulkner's mastery in handling narrative perspective and manipulating narrative distance.

The last section of "Dry September" has not received much comment, perhaps rightly so. It gives an additional view of McLendon, whose wife is sitting up waiting for him when he arrives home. McLendon, who has killed to defend the honor of a white woman who everybody thinks probably lied about being sexually attacked, brutally beats his wife for still being awake. Our impression of him is confirmed, if confirmation was indeed needed. Thus we are faced with an important question: Why did Faulkner choose to conclude the story with this glimpse of McLendon? The concluding paragraph, which depicts the sweating McLendon pressed against the dusty screen, panting in the heat, is perfect, a final return to the land of dust and drought summarizing everything that has happened in the course of the story: "There was no movement, no sound, not even an insect. The dark world seemed to lie stricken beneath the cold moon and the lidless stars" (CS, 183). Perhaps by concentrating on McLendon, the final section encapsulates the basic tensions of the story:[10] the violence of the men, the passivity and fear of the women, the wasted qualities of the world they live in. Yet Faulkner could have achieved the same effect, perhaps even enhanced it, if he had chosen a community point of view or returned to Hawkshaw while keeping the cosmic perspective. By choosing the ending he does Faulkner clearly signals the centrality of the role of women in this story and adds to his criticism of male brutality and stupidity. McLendon seems to be one of all the dead soldiers, accustomed to violence and action but now leading an inconsequential life in a small town where nothing happens. This does not, however, excuse him of anything: the text clearly condemns McLendon and the likes of him.

From the first to the last sentence of "Dry September," the reader is forced to react to the recurrent, almost insistent use of certain images. "Dust" is everywhere in the story, as a word, a part of the world it evokes, and a pervasive part of the dry, dark, and lifeless social space it creates. The dust is a leitmotif,[11] but its significance may change from situation to situation. The repetitions of the word, often in alliterative combinations, give the language an almost magical, compelling force, so that the reader establishes connections on the basis of sound and rhythm, as much as on the basis of syntagmatic structures.

But there are, as our reading has shown, many things beneath both the dust of "Dry September" and beneath the cold moon and the lidless stars. Because of, or perhaps even in spite of, the barrenness of the environment, people live, love, despair, and do foolish things in Jefferson; most importantly, they fight to keep some of their dreams alive, but they are deceived into believing in false dreams and subscribing to collective fantasies supported by the dreams on the silver screen. Of all the characters we meet in the story, only Hawkshaw seems considerate and interested in other people's lives in any real sense. A strong sympathy for Minnie is created in the text, but it is in part established because we as readers see that no one really cares about her at all, with the possible exception of her friends, who help her but also seem a little too eager to know what really happened.

Our reading of the story has emphasized the unfortunate lot of women. There are other important aspects of the story, both concrete and more abstract, yet they all seem to converge on the question of the role of women in society at a given time and place. One way of reading Minnie in "Dry September" is to emphasize elements she has in common with other female characters in Faulkner's stories, particularly Miss Emily Grierson.[12]

We sympathize with Minne, yet we remain critical of her behavior in general and of her role in the rumor in particular. Minnie clearly misuses her social position—which has taught her not to pay attention to other people or to show plain and ordinary respect for those "below" her status level—and exploits the violent racism she recognizes in the men in her community. The rumor itself is an example of how social position can be used with devastating effect. Minnie can expect the respect which any white woman of a certain quality deserves, and she can rely on the racial hatred alive in the community to achieve the effect she wants. She reveals no concern whatever about the consequences of her lies; to her it is only important to prove her value and for a final time have someone react to her femininity. This female power, which is assigned to most women in the better social layers of these traditional communities without any reservation, is misused time and again—often simply because it is misunderstood by the women themselves.

In the final analysis "Dry September" is a bleak, terrifying, and utterly convincing picture of a world out of joint, even if the cosmic perspective, despite the apparent indifference of both moon and stars, is a last indication that even this world will change, life will go on, rain will fall, bringing the season of dust and drought to an end, on the human level as well. One of Faulkner's most condensed and effective narratives, the story has a central position in his career as a short story writer. There are many significant relationships between "Dry September" and other texts within Faulkner's oeuvre, as one of the great stories from his major story-writing period and as a central text in *These 13* as well as in *Collected Stories*. It may profit from a reading in the context of these works but also in the context of the many short stories of deprived women, or as a story showing once more the outrage of a potential believer. Through Hawkshaw and the Jefferson setting, the story has important relations to "Hair," and through its picture of McLendon and also because of Minnie's rumor about a black man, it relates significantly to *Light in August*. More than anything else it is a powerful literary text and should be studied because of its literary qualities before considering its many possible and significant contexts, of which only a few have been hinted at above.

# Chapter 8

# The Hound

## TEXTUAL INFORMATION AND PUBLICATION HISTORY

"The Hound" is one of the stories in Faulkner's career that he revised and integrated so completely in a novel that he seems to have thought that it should not live on as a story in its own right. Despite the fact that it was included in *Doctor Martino and Other Stories* (1934), it was rewritten to become a Snopes story, part of "The Long Summer" in book 3 of *The Hamlet,* and was not included in *Collected Stories.* Since this last and inclusive volume came to represent Faulkner's short stories for a long period, the story version of "The Hound" was not available to most readers until it was published in *Uncollected Stories* in 1979. Faulkner's practice was by no means consistent in these matters: "Wash," for example, was included in *Doctor Martino* and then revised to become a part of *Absalom, Absalom!,* yet it was included in *Collected Stories.*

In the fall of 1930 Faulkner spent much time revising the galleys for *Sanctuary,* doing, as he said, "a fair job."[1] Accordingly, he had little time for short story writing, and consequently the number of new stories from this time is low compared to the enormous activity before and after. "The Hound" was submitted to magazines for the first time on November 17, first to the *Saturday Evening Post* as were so many of the stories of 1930. The story was rejected, then went to *Scribner's* and the *American Mercury* before Faulkner sent it to his agent, Ben Wasson, for him to sell it. Apparently Wasson was responsible for placing "The Hound" with *Harper's Magazine,* where it was published in August 1931 (Skei 1981, 68, 127). No prepublication versions are known. The text of "The Hound" in the collection is identical with the text in *Harper's.* Twelve of the fourteen stories in *Doctor Martino* had been published in magazines, of which the author revised only two: "Mountain Victory" and "Turn About."

The most central of all events in the story of Flem Snopes—because it finally leads to Flem's being killed—was presented in "The Hound," a story without any mention whatsoever of a Snopes character.[2] It is one of at least two stories that became Snopes stories only when Faulkner actually sat down and wrote *The Hamlet*. Faulkner's own statements indicate a conception of the Snopes story as a novel, which then produced certain stories, including ones not featuring the Snopeses that were later revised for *The Hamlet* (although he does not mention "Fool about a Horse"); yet I am more inclined to think that "Fool about a Horse" and "The Hound" were conceived and written without any conscious intention of their later inclusion in the Snopes legend. If Faulkner at the time of writing them knew that they were Snopes stories, there is no reason why he should not have made them that—even the market (the best-paying magazines) asked for more stories with the characters from "Spotted Horses."

There can thus be no doubt that Faulkner transformed "The Hound" into something completely different and in accordance with some of his main interests in the novel as a whole. Indeed, the expansion from story to novel (where the story elements broadly are retained despite the addition of different motivations and changes of detail) may prove which thematic interests Faulkner struggled to introduce or to strengthen in the novel and which he thereby weakened or overshadowed. The narrator's role changes, too, in the novel, because so much of the background stories of Houston and Mink must be told by an omniscient narrator—no storyteller within the story has this information, and neither of the two opponents associates much with the men around Varner's store. They may be marginal characters in their community and seem to be marginal also to the main story of Flem's ten years of usurpation of Frenchman's Bend and his rise to wealth, yet Faulkner has created a situation in which a Snopes is set up to undo another Snopes. Mink Snopes's reasons for wanting to do this seem simple enough, based on an ethos of family loyalty; but they also result from the human predicament, a struggle almost in cosmic terms against an indifferent and hostile world. The conflict with Houston begins (as does that with Cotton in the short story) within sharply etched class distinctions, but Mink's self-understanding is also based upon prejudiced preconceptions of human value. His hope for help from Flem is based on an understanding of kin or clan, which Flem, as a representative of a new society, has set aside. Mink is hopelessly trapped in a rapidly changing world, and his situation, defined by a special time and place and culture, transcends these limitations to become a description of *conditio humana*.

## READING "THE HOUND"

"The Hound" is in many respects a superb story, central in Faulkner's short story career as well as in one of his major works in the novel genre, the Snopes trilogy.[3] "The Hound" is a penetrating and perceptive psychological study of how a man under enormous pressure behaves and reacts, and it is also a study in envy, revenge, and guilt. Ernest Cotton is typical of the country people we meet in the world of Frenchman's Bend, the world of *The Hamlet*. He is one of those who seem to have been deprived of all but the most basic of cultivating or civilizing forces. What little they have shall be taken from them, what they achieve shall be usurped and destroyed. In the backwoods world of Frenchman's Bend, people usurp and swindle and trade and deal, trying to get the best of those closest to them in a society where there is little to be taken and little to be shared. Character after character is divested of everything but life and some sort of pride, and they are thus pitched against enormous odds. "The Hound" is one of the darkest of the tales about such people, because there is little room for the comic or humorous in such a barren world.

Some characters seem to be more perseverant and patient than others, either because of what may seem to be an inborn or inherited trait or because they have been conditioned by their upbringing and environment to react in such ways. They simply do not know of any other way to live, but they protect themselves and their own against all intruders because change is always a threat and because they know how little it takes to disturb the balance that at least keeps them alive—the balance between their account in Varner's store and the cotton or corn they produce and deliver at harvest time. In addition to the general economic and social system, their particular and individual situation may further account for the almost incredible stamina they show. When they are threatened by outside forces, they react, often violently and viciously, but in accordance with an age-old understanding of right and wrong. Cases are taken to court time and again in this world, but people like Cotton feel that they have been taken advantage of and unjustly treated also by the justice of the peace, and so they have to take over when the law does not give them their due. This creates a human drama—at times tragic in its dimensions—that seems to suit the short story very well—or vice versa.[4] "The Hound" is in some ways such a drama, in which stubborn endurance through hardships, toil, and poverty suddenly yields to an inhuman pressure, and a man is compelled to act contrary to his nature and, by implications given in the story, contrary to nature.[5]

The protagonist of "The Hound," Ernest Cotton,[6] is one of the lowest among the low, poorest among the poor; a loner who can barely make ends meet, a man who has so far been successful in nothing except survival. Cotton is a bachelor,[7] and he lives in a log cabin floored with clay. He is underfed, and his only clothes appear to be the overalls he wears daily. He endures his barren, lonely life of hard work, little food, and no pleasure because he knows of nothing else: he has an unconscious understanding of his place in the great chain of being, he accepts creaturehood and fights nature without much hope of ever eking out more from it than what he needs to keep himself alive. If Cotton had been left alone he would probably have led this same monotonous life of hard labor; he would have endured, as thousands of his fellow men have endured, the same kind of life in deep poverty without complaints and without being aware of a different, better life. If they by chance should happen to become aware of it, which they were likely to do living in deep poverty in a land of plenty, they would still, more or less stoically, accept their social position, their poverty, their ignorance, and in some cases their exploitation by the rich landowners, as inevitable. They would not be the ones to question the ordering of nature nor the ordering of the society of men. Cotton would never have done this either if he had not been treated inhumanly by his well-to-do neighbor, Houston. Cotton cannot help hating Houston, and through the conflict with Houston he comes to understand the injustice of the world, man's great capacity for injustice to other men—especially those below him who are already down on their knees. Cotton even seems to think that this poverty is undeserved, since he knows that he works hard, asks for nothing, and endures. Naturally and inevitably he comes to hate Houston's dog, which gives the story its title: "A dog that et better than me. I work, and eat worse than his dog" (*Uncollected Stories*, 157).[8]

Cotton kills Houston, and the story opens on the very sound of the shot that kills. It is important that it opens on the sound, that the killing has already happened, has become a thing of the past, of *was*. There is no turning back, nothing that can come undone; everything is irreparable, inevitable. Cotton listens to the outrageous and unbelievable sound of his own gun, and we know that for the rest of the story this sound will be in his ears and that running away from it will be of no help.

The opening paragraph describes the effects of the shot on Cotton: the sound, the noise, which was "the loudest thing he had ever heard in his life" (*US*, 152) and which continues to build long after the smoke of the black powder is gone, long after he felt the shock of the shotgun into his shoulder, long after the horse galloped away. This is how information is given to us, indirectly, a little at a time: we hear about the empty stirrups and the empty saddle of the horse, but only in a panoramic overview of the scene closing the first section of the story do we see the body "lying on his face in the road" (*US*, 153). The narrator has a very narrow perspective, concentrating on Cotton and the act just finished and then on the immediate reactions, for which Cotton has prepared himself. Only the sound, "too loud to be heard all at once" (*US*, 152), has surprised him. Everything else is as expected, leaving no doubt about the premeditation of the killing. He knows that, having committed the murder, he should want to run, so he sits down and counts slowly until sound and echo are gone and only silence can be heard.

This very dramatic and effective opening reveals nothing except the killing and the killer's immediate reactions. He has done what he had planned to do, but one small thing went wrong. The first shot made so much noise that he was too late to take a second shot, and so "the hound too was gone" (*US*, 152). We know from title as well as from this failure that the hound will function significantly in the text, which has created obvious expectations in the reader for background information. Who is Cotton? Why did he shoot the man on the horse? What drives a man to this point? And, in spite of the premeditated and well-planned murder, will he get away with it? The story's introduction has prepared us to expect a text split between action and reaction, between what Cotton must do after the killing and the emotional strain this puts upon him.

When the story continues it promises to give this kind of background information, in a different kind of narrative looking retrospectively back on Cotton's life. It begins by telling us that Cotton was a bachelor and that he lived in a chinked log cabin four miles away from the scene where we left the corpse in the road. But this is told only in preparation of Cotton's coming home after the killing, and the outside narrator chooses to stay very close to Cotton and to tell the story from his perspective. Since we are allowed to listen to direct and quoted or reported speech and thought—even when Cotton is alone and thinks to himself—a rather strong irony is at work and becomes decisive in our final understanding of Cotton. The narrative perspective dramatizes Cotton's solipsism (Ferguson 1991, 98), indicating his inability to understand other people's lives. The narrator seems to have imposed certain limitations on himself, almost as if he wants the story to tell itself and to avoid explicit commentary save for those found in descriptive passages of Cotton's habits and thoughts. The narrator chooses to report what Cotton feels, thinks, and plans, and he leaves it at that. After the killing, having washed his shoes and cleaned the shotgun, Cotton goes to bed and lies down, even though he does not expect to sleep:

> It was dark after the fire burned out; he lay in the darkness. He thought about nothing at all save that he did not expect to sleep. He felt no triumph, vindication, nothing. He just lay there, thinking about nothing at all, even when he began to hear the dog. . . .

He knew this dog's voice. It and the galloping horse with the flapping stirrups and the owner of the horse had been inseparable: where he saw one of them, the other two would not be far away— a lean, rangy brute that charged savagely at anyone who approached its master's house, with something of the master's certitude and overbearance. . . . (*US*, 153)

The perspective from which we as readers follow the story is thus clearly Cotton's. He is prepared for the psychological effects (he would not have known nor understood the term) of the killing, and he seems to be calm, thinking of nothing, not even reacting with anger, fear, or self-reproach when he hears the hound that he should have shot with its master. Cotton seems to know intuitively that death, or having shot someone, is something you cannot forget about quickly. It would take time to "move that irrevocable distance" (*US*, 153–54), and Cotton becomes aware of his second mistake: he had forgotten about the body. Listening to the dog in the bottom, he is reminded of the dead body lying in the road, and thinking of "nigger talk" about how a dog would howl at the grave of its master, he suddenly finds himself "bolt upright on the pallet" (*US*, 154). He knows he has to act, get up in the middle of the night, stumble into the darkness of the woods, and crawl his way through the briars and brambles of the undergrowth to bury the body of a man he himself has shot, probably while being attacked by the dead man's vicious hound. No wonder then that the text tries to establish some sympathy for Cotton before he is sent out on his terrifying mission: "So he lay with his gaunt, underfed body empty with waiting, thinking of nothing, listening to the dog" (*US*, 154).

When Cotton enters the woods, it is as if nature itself resists what he is doing. Creepers and bramble seem to "spring out of the darkness and clutch him with spiky tentacles," but he forces his way through the "musing impenetrability" toward the sound (*US*, 154). In scenes of unmitigated horror, terrifying in the simplicity of their cold narrative directness, Cotton drags the body by the shoulders to the rotten shell of a cypress and, using the plowline he has brought with him, manages to get the body inside the trunk. The body catches on something inside the stump, and Cotton has to jump up and down on it until it suddenly falls, leaving him dangling by the rope that he has been smart enough to tie to a limb. He fights furiously not to be buried with the corpse and makes it to the top of the edge of the hollow trunk.

The scene is grotesque, nightmarish, terrifying. Cotton acts calmly in accordance with a plan he has made, as if he has expected trials of this sort after the killing. But the calm is only apparent, and beneath it is the despair and terror that we as readers feel:

"I ain't never been so tired," he said, leaning against the house, the wall which he had built log by log. "Like ever thing had got outen hands. Climbing that stump, and the noise the shot made. Like I had got to be somebody else without knowing it, in a place where noise was louder, climbing harder to climb, without knowing it." (*US*, 155)

Cotton seems on the verge of understanding that what he has done is so terrifying that it has changed him and that what he has done seems to have grown too big for him to handle. And still the hound, absent during the burial of the corpse, is alive, howling again from the river bottom when Cotton goes back to bed. Little by little the hound seems to become something more and other than just the faithful and savage dog of the dead man; it cries and howls as from inside Cotton's head, as if to remind him of what he has done, as if to be his sense of guilt haunting him. Cotton had not prepared for this eventuality.

So far we have been close to Cotton, followed his movements and thoughts, analyzed his feelings, wondering what went on in his mind. The narrator has kept this perspective, but in the third part of the story this changes. We meet other people outside Varner's store: five men in overalls—with Cotton as the sixth—sitting on the top step and the county sheriff as the seventh in a chair. The men talk about Houston, who is missing from the area. So we finally get a name for the dead man, and we get some of the information we need in order to understand how and why Cotton felt compelled (apparently) to kill his neighbor.

Houston is described as "that prosperous and overbearing man," and the men who discuss his disappearance seem to agree that "overbearing" is an accurate description of his behavior (*US*, 157). He is also said to be secretive and as "well-fixed as ere a man in the county" (*US*, 156). He had taken advantage of Cotton by letting a hog of his winter on Cotton's corn; then, when the case was taken to court, Houston was awarded the hog but had to pay for the wintering of it. Moreover, he had to pay one dollar as pound-fee for a stray.[9] More than this measurable injustice, Cotton feels that Houston has done this on purpose, and he hates seeing the rich neighbor leisurely riding on horseback with his well-fed dog running alongside while he struggles day in and day out to make ends meet. Cotton may indeed have felt that Houston encroached upon him and upon his self-respect.[10] Up to that point in time Cotton has accepted his lot and gone about his work without any fuss: he is in the eyes of the local people and the narrator a mild man in worn overalls, but there is a limit even to his patience and endurance. One might argue that Cotton in anger and hatred lost his perspective and moral judgment, but in his undefined and limited set of clear-cut values he senses that there is no other solution to the problem with Houston than to kill him. All the injustice Cotton has ever experienced becomes embodied in Houston, and killing him is the only way that the poor, illiterate man can maintain his dignity and even restore some of his pride. Houston has disrupted and in a sense destroyed Cotton's world, and it would not be possible for him to go on doing what he had done without some kind of reaction. His patience and his endurance had come to an end, and he had to act. The killing does not solve any problems but still seems inevitable. Cotton will have to endure more hardships because of his murderous reaction,[11] and when detected he does little to hide his crime. Before detection, however, he does everything conceivable in a traumatic fight with nature to conceal what he has done.

"The Hound" centers more and more on Cotton's behavior as the story progresses. His vain attempts to calm down after the murder, his symbolic washing of his shoes and shotgun, his relentless and terrifying struggle with the decaying corpse, his own frailty, his guilt, and his human dignity are important and central elements in the story. Interwoven in the probing and penetrating psychological description and analysis of the mind of a common, hardworking man forced to become a murderer through circumstance is a background story which seems to indicate that to any unprejudiced observer Cotton is a sympathetic character. This does not mean that murder is condoned or accepted in the story—the course of events is in itself proof of this as Cotton lives in hell from the very moment when he hears his shot. Nor does the text leave any doubt about the premeditation of the act. Yet there are mitigating or extenuating circumstances in Cotton's background, and still the simple facts of the story are such that we may agree with Carothers (1985) that "Cotton murders Houston because of the latter's overbearing manner" or even that, in a comparison with Mink's killing of Houston in *The Hamlet,* "Cotton's murder is . . . more horrible than Mink's, being less susceptible to rational explanation" (127). Perhaps one of Cotton's remarks about Houston and his dog—that Houston was "Setting that ere dog on folks' stock" (*US,* 157)—is more of a reasonable accusation than all the others, even if it gives no reason for killing the owner of the dog. One can understand a farmer's reaction to this, but if this could not be tolerated, even to kill the dog would seem a drastic solution. The dog is still alive, still howling, and is of course instrumental in betraying Cotton's guilt.

After the talk outside Varner's store, Cotton is the last one to leave, and in the dark he loads his shotgun, enters the bottom, and fires at the leaping body of the hound. He keeps telling himself that the dog is dead and flings the shotgun away in a slough. Cotton still cannot sleep, so he spends his nights in a chair in the doorway, watching, listening.

If "The Hound" had been a story of detection, it would have been told from a different perspective, and the hunt would have become central. Also, the fact that a black man hunting for squirrels finds Cotton's shotgun and hands it in at Varner's store would have been decisive (as it probably is to the sheriff in this story, even if nothing is made of it). Cotton denies ownership and returns home to watch the first buzzards circling down and disappearing among the trees. Cotton does not react much: they will devour the dead dog, he thinks, which should not take long, but still more birds arrive, and so he knows he has heavy work to do ahead of him. Then he hears the dog again. Cotton remains calm on the outside. He cooks his supper and eats, but then time is up. Armed with an axe only this time, he "descended through his meager corn patch" (*US*, 160), and we read in mounting horror and even disgust as Cotton cuts an opening in the trunk and drags the body out of it, with the whimpering dog at his feet:

> "Git away," he said, still without being conscious that it was the dog. He dragged at the body, feeling it slough upon its own bones, as though it were too large for itself; he turned his face away, his teeth glared, his breath furious and outraged and restrained. He could feel the dog surge against his legs, its head in the orifice, howling. (*US*, 161)

Even Cotton has to turn away, because of the rotten body, to which he could find his way simply by letting his nose guide him. As readers, we most certainly do not wait for more gruesome or morbid images, not because we sympathize with Cotton, who once again is more tired than ever before, resting before he takes hold of the legs of the corpse and starts pulling away in the approaching daylight. But the screw of horror is turned once more: when Cotton throws the body into the channel, he sees only three limbs instead of four; he runs back toward the stump only to meet the fighting dog again—and the sheriff: "We got him. You can come out, Ernest" (*US*, 162).

Ernest Cotton is seen from the outside and described by the narrator during the conversation at Varner's store as "a mild man in worn overalls, with a gaunt face and lack-luster eyes like a sick man, whittling a stick with a thin hand, thinking about killing them" (*US*, 157). It seems as if Cotton, having made up his mind to take revenge and kill Houston, is willing to face any and all consequences of this action, even if it means living through nightmares of many sorts. When arrested he seems to make no resistance and accepts his lot. But sitting in the car, handcuffed to the sheriff, he plans suicide and makes an attempt, which fails. In prison, with lots of black prisoners in jail for minor offenses, Cotton, a murderer, is still thinking that he is better than the blacks, simply because he is white. He tries to explain to them that what he had done was all right, or would have been fine if the body had not started coming to pieces. Almost without voice after the suicide attempt, he still tries to tell himself and others that bad luck has brought him to jail, and he has to be silenced by a black prisoner who wants to hear "no truck like that" (*US*, 164). The feverish attempts to explain how competent a killer Cotton really is seem to indicate mental imbalance, which is only to be expected. Yet it is also a final attempt to keep his self-respect. Little is left of the dignity he so desperately upholds and for which he may be said to have murdered his neighbor. We do not know if he has to take this final blow, this final offense, and watch the black prisoners get food before he does. It should thus be fair to say that Cotton acts within character at all times and that there is little in the story to surprise the reader once he or she has come to understand Cotton's pattern of behavior. Yet we need to take a closer look at Ernest Cotton in order to explain his actions and interpret the story as a whole.

His patient and unrewarding work as a farmer had taught Cotton both to expect little and to endure. In his struggle to bury Houston's body Cotton finds himself in what appears to be an inescapable trauma, a nightmare in which even nature resists what he is doing. Despite his final failure, the lasting struggle, combined with a strong feeling of guilt, is another example of perseverance and single-mindedness.[12] The problem of evil and guilt and the question of what it takes to make a man kill under a given environmental pressure are both at stake in this story. "The Hound" also demonstrates that normality is highly relative and that a mild man who is talking quietly with his neighbors not only may be thinking about killing one of them but potentially is a killer. Cotton may well be feeling guilt, and the hound itself takes on a symbolic quality to represent this guilt, but he nevertheless sticks to his personal understanding of right and wrong, justice and injustice, and even when imprisoned he still thinks that Houston deserved what he got. So Cotton makes no attempt to escape his evil deed, and through the last scenes in the story, a kind of stubborn persistence and patience are felt.

Cotton's endurance must be seen in relation to his ignorance: he knows no better life, and he defends it violently when he feels that it is threatened. He is a man trapped by nature, lost in nature, and terrified by nature, mostly because he has committed murder and has thus acted contrary to nature. Ernest is completely alone, or so he thinks, and he needs to be left alone. Nature's resistance to what he is trying to do—bury the corpse, kill the dog—reflects a struggle within Cotton himself, and the vicious and undying dog may represent Cotton's own conscience and guilt, elements of his own nature against which he also fights.

Despite these psychological and symbolic interpretations of the story, there is also a realistic level at which Ernest Cotton fights nature almost directly and finally has to give in to it. Cotton stumbles for many a night in the impenetrable undergrowth and darkness of the woods where he has hidden the body of his neighbor, but nature will neither hide the body nor let Cotton remove it easily from where he first hid it. He is just as trapped in the darkness and mist of the woods as he is in a dark and inescapable trauma. When he finally is taken prisoner and tries to commit suicide, nature (his own body) again resists, and it seems to Cotton that he must be the eternal loser, beaten by an invincible enemy: the nature of the world and in himself.

Gripping, intense, and self-contained, the extraordinary strength of "The Hound" is a result of the third-person "limited" narration, in which we as readers are invited to share Cotton's agony from the moment he hears the sound of the shot that kills Houston until he runs in terror back to the trunk for the missing limb of the dead body. Only seldom do we get the relief of an outside view. Most of the time the anguish and terror through which the protagonist goes is so intense that we cannot even be pleased when the inevitable happens and Cotton is apprehended. As James Ferguson (1991) phrases it, "our reactions at the end of the story are not those of relief or triumph but of exhaustion—and of compassion for Cotton" (76). These are ambiguous reactions: relief and triumph because the madness comes to an end and the killer is caught, but compassion for the killer? How is this—which I think is a correct description of the final response to the short story—possible?

The sympathy which readers may have for Cotton, without in any sense condoning murder, seems to be based not only on the text's description of him. He is not at all presented as a victim of social forces, but he clearly has had little opportunity to improve his situation. He is a loner but apparently accepted and treated with respect by his neighbors, as we can witness in the conversation outside Varner's store. Even the sheriff's polite arrest of him, calling him Ernest (and not Cotton, which seems to be a nickname), testifies to a respect by his fellows, which we must take into consideration when trying to understand his behavior. Sympathy may also arise from the simple and human tendency to insist on the rights, at least the right to retain human dignity, of the low and unfortunate. There is no doubt in the text that Cotton economically and socially belongs to the lowest of the low: "Cotton was driven to an extreme in what was originally an admirable endeavor, the preservation of his self-respect against the encroachment of Houston, who is time and again described as 'overbearing'" (Jones 1957, 37). Yet the enormous impact of the story is a result of the way Faulkner succeeds in letting us as readers share the unbelievable and horrifying agony of a murderer, both through the chain of terrifying events which follows the murder and through watching the effects of this evil act, despite all subtle causes for it, on the mind of the murderer. The ease with which the story is told and the complete familiarity with people and places that it exhibits come from its being placed in the heart of Yoknapatawpha County. It even draws on some of the major thematic interests of the Snopes trilogy, if only by letting us visit Varner's store and meet the clerk who is a Snopes or by being a first version of what became a central episode in *The Hamlet*.

# Chapter 9

# Mountain Victory

## TEXTUAL INFORMATION AND PUBLICATION HISTORY

"A Mountain Victory" (the title of this story in all versions before *Doctor Martino and Other Stories*) was sent to the *Saturday Evening Post* in September or early October 1930, most likely on September 24, and the *Post* bought the story, after it had apparently been returned to Faulkner, who in a letter on October 4 (?) wrote, "Here is 'A Mountain Victory' with the surgery which you suggested performed and included."[1] Five days later an associate editor replied that the clearer motivation in the short story "fixes everything up nicely," yet another letter from Faulkner indicates that he had been asked to make further cuts (in the proofs), and he stated that he had removed "one unnecessary chapter."[2] This "chapter" is easily identifiable as part 4 of the twelve-part story (see below). The correspondence shows that the revisions and cuts were handled very quickly, although it does not explain why the story was not published by the *Post* until December 3, 1932, which is both surprising and noteworthy.[3]

Very few of Faulkner's short stories were sold at the first attempt. Faulkner usually sent his stories (unless he felt that a story suited another magazine better) to the *Post* first, and in 1930 the *Post* bought three stories (including the virtually forgotten "Thrift" and "Red Leaves," both also published in 1930). The reasons why Faulkner submitted most of his stories to the *Post* first may be many and complex, but one of them is certainly that it paid better than any other magazine and also that it paid upon acceptance—not when the story was printed. "Mountain Victory" was thus a success story from a commercial point of view; like "Red Leaves," it is a success story from whatever angle it is considered.

Yet Faulkner had to put in a lot of work with this story before its magazine publication, and he revised it considerably more, although insignificantly before it was included as the penultimate story in *Doctor Martino and Other Stories*. He only revised one more of the previously published stories for this collection—"Turn About," which, incidentally, also had been sold to the *Post* on the first attempt.

Two prepublication versions of this story are extant, plus one version which may well be later than the *Post* printing and related rather to the preparation of *Doctor Martino*. The earliest version is a manuscript of eighteen pages, and a forty-two-page-long typescript appears to be based on this manuscript. Both typescript and manuscript are divided into twelve parts, given roman numerals. There are a number of differences between manuscript and typescript, but Faulkner had the habit of expanding and clarifying during the typing process. The most important expansion is probably that descriptions of the Negro's inability to stand much cold and Weddel's even greater concern for him because of this are added in the typescript.

In a few cases paragraphs in the manuscript have been reduced or left out in the typescript version. The last paragraph of part 5, in which the girl's inscrutability and profound patience are stressed and said to be typically female, is, for instance, left out. In the later versions concrete observations and descriptions of her impoverished life replace general statements about "that implacable and hidden world in which women live."[4]

The most significant changes are not between manuscript and typescript but between the typescript and the printed versions. The removal of part 4 of the typescript in the *Post* printing has already been noted.[5] It presents a closeup of Hule and his sister as they watch Weddel getting ready to take his bath. Vatch interrupts and beats up both his sister and brother. The girl is at the center of this scene, and Hule mistakenly accuses her of being just as eager to kill Weddel as Vatch is. The two youths seem to join forces again because of the threats from Vatch. Another closeup, this time of Weddel as he lies in the loft thinking of home, is left out, probably because the text dwells on this side of his character in a number of other instances.

Faulkner's great concern for this particular short story is not only shown by the fact that he revised it before using it in a collection; the revision seems to have been done thoroughly, even to the extent that a new typescript was made. This forty-six-page typescript has the handwritten editorial comment "Thirteenth story" on the first page, and there are also marginal references in the typescript to what must be galley numbers. This version does not include section 4 of the first typescript and was used as the setting copy for the story in the collection.

## READING "MOUNTAIN VICTORY"

"Mountain Victory" has until recently been given only cursory treatment by scholars and critics, but even those who claim that it has been ignored seem to do little to improve our understanding of this magnificent story.[6] It was early recognized as one of Faulkner's best, for example, in a review of *Doctor Martino and Other Stories*, and Malcolm Cowley certainly thought highly of it (Jones 1994, 527), as did Irving Howe (1975), who regarded it as Faulkner's best writing about the Civil War (264). Most often the story is mentioned and given brief treatment in studies of wider interest than one single story: in studies of Faulkner's Indian characters, for example, or his black or women characters. Being more of an autonomous story than most of Faulkner's short stories—that is, having fewer links to other texts—the story most certainly deserves extended treatment as a work of literary art in its own right. The text is a slow, at times almost static, narrative, and despite the dramatic conflicts that develop and reach a climax, the story has an absolute unity of time (from evening to morning), of place (a log cabin in the Tennessee mountains), and of action (few characters, all contributing to the final tragedy). Add to this the stark poverty of the resident family and the defeat and loss of the war veterans, and we have all the ingredients of a tragic encounter in which elementary and basic forces are set up against one another.

The story's plot is superbly handled, even if readers may find it overworked and unnecessarily complicated at times. Some of the characters may approach caricatures or types, but they are sufficiently individualized to become believable as living people. The black servant seems to come straight out of conventional comic writing, and one could wish for a more realistic portrait. The story is also a very literary short story in the sense that it makes use of conventions but also parodies them. The strange couple of Major Weddel and his servant Jubal is but one example of this; the white-trash family is another. Faulkner gives conventional descriptions, and then the text quickly moves beyond these stereotypes. People become "real," and their problems take on a significance which transcends the narrow circumscription of their lives to tell something about being alive in the world and even something about literary representation.

Readers may find too much Faulknerian language in this story; some of his idiosyncrasies in descriptions of character and behavior tend to repeat themselves a little too often. Words like *quizzical, motionless,* and *sardonic* seem rather pointless in most instances.[7] In memorable scenes of the whipped and wounded war veteran (he has lost an arm) lying on the hard floor in the empty hayloft and thinking of home, Faulkner's language is at its most poetic, conveying strong emotions, a generosity of understanding, and a closeness to character which shows his range as a short story writer. If his best short stories, analytical and dramatic, violent and desperate—as so many of them are—ever created empathy in the reader, this is one of the texts in which it happens.

Most of Faulkner's characters carry with them the burden and the blessing of a living past, be it the Civil War, family matters, lost pride, guilt, or remorse. They have to adjust this past and their own present in order to have some degree of freedom in the future, or to have a future life at all. The wounded war veteran on his way home in "Mountain Victory" is an example of this. The slowly unfolding but carefully structured story in which important ethical values are tested ends violently and conclusively, yet the problematic motivation behind the protagonist's decision not to negotiate for his life lingers on in the reader's mind as if the story were an open one.

All through "Mountain Victory" there is a sense of irrevocable tragedy, of unappeasable destiny, and we watch a conflict unfold from what should have been a normal encounter between strangers. Although the text gives external motivation for the conflict, this chance encounter seems to become a force stronger than the individuals and their part in it, and their very existence is threatened with a ruthlessness that seems inevitable.

The skeleton of this story in eleven parts is very simple, almost anecdotical in its brevity. Major Saucier Weddel, on his way home to his plantation in Mississippi after four years of fighting in Virginia, halts at a cabin in the Tennessee mountains and asks for shelter for himself, his servant, and their horses. In the poor white family of five, the elder son, Vatch, has also been to the war. He hates his enemies with uncontrolled violence, and no one can stop him when he smells rebel blood again, although the others do not want any more killing. He is a Tenneseean and has fought for the Union, which may further explain his hatred of the major and his class in the South. His younger brother, Hule, tries to persuade Weddel to take him and his sister away with him the next morning, but never seems to have really made up his mind whether to help the major to escape or to help his father and brother in preparing the ambush. He and Weddel are shot and killed, and Jubal must then die because he has seen it all.

But this is the skeleton or fabula of the story, and even if it is arranged chronologically and narrated from the outside in the third person, the discourse is something else and more than the story we can extract from it. The story is among the best Faulkner ever wrote, and we shall follow its slow development with its shifting perspectives before attempting to respond to the text as a whole and discuss its possible interpretations.

Faulkner seems to have divided his story into sections as the need arose for complete shifts of perspective. Some of the parts are told from the servant's point of view, although the narrator only allows the characters of the story to tell who they are in relatively limited stories within the larger framework of the story proper. Yet he seems more willing than most Faulkner narrators to share the responsibility of the narration with his characters, even to the extent that they tell stories in their own words. "Mountain Victory" becomes almost dialogic, and it certainly deserves the designation *polyphonic,* since so many and so disparate perspectives are chosen for the main narration.

In the opening part of the story we watch the strangers, or intruders, described as a "cavalcade," toil up the trail in the Tennessee mountains from the window of the cabin they are approaching. Five people watch, unaccustomed to visitors, and we can almost feel the tension rising as the strangers come closer and one of the three men goes to fetch his rifle. He has recognized the rebel cloak worn by the man on the thoroughbred horse, and even though the war is over, as his father tells him, he appears not to be through with it.

From the window we watch with the poor family of five, Unionists in a state within the former Confederacy, and we get an almost scenic view of the mountains in relief against the valley and other mountain ranges. But most of all we get a detailed description of the two persons coming up the slope on their horses. One of them is described as a "shapeless something larger than a child" (*CS,* 744), and until we get closer to him he is only referred to as a "creature" since he is seen at a distance and difficult to make out. This "creature" comes onto the porch and knocks at the door, and the father of the family sends his wife to "go and see" (*CS,* 746). Tensions seem to be strong among the family members, but the older man, the father, is clearly the head of the family, even though the oldest son, Vatch, is in strong opposition to him. It is likewise obvious from the wife's behavior when she meets first the servant and then the other man, Major Saucier Weddel, that the husband makes all decisions in this family: "I'll ask him" and "I'll have to see" (*CS,* 747) are both telling replies. When the husband comes into the hall where she is, things are settled at once; the visitors are allowed to stay the night, and Jubal takes the horses to the stable.

The opening of "Mountain Victory" is both scenic and dramatic. The narrator keeps his limited perspective so that the reader gets his information about the strange intruders at the same time as the family in the cabin on the mountaintop does. They do not know that the tired and friendly visitors will disrupt their lives, even if they have a violent and apparently uncontrolled male member of the family, Vatch. The text gives away information about the strangers slowly, and some of the characteristics of the persons as well as some of the reactions we notice can only be understood later on. The rider on the thoroughbred keeps the reins in his left hand; only later do we learn that he has but one arm. Vatch's reaction also becomes clear and perhaps even excusable later on. We know that the strangers come from fighting "them Yankees" (CS, 746) in the Civil War and that they are on their way back home but need to rest. The scene is set—in "the chill, wet light of the dying April afternoon"—for a confrontation between opposite classes, traditions, and lifestyles, and the opening section makes clear that this is not going to be a chance encounter among strangers. We know who lost the war, and that two of the losers now visit at least one of the victors, but we do not know what kind of "mountain victory" the title refers to. A one-armed beaten war veteran from Mississippi, with his black servant; a white-trash, redneck family on a mountaintop, poor, probably illiterate, living in a log cabin with a plank lean-to. A young man who still hates everything that reminds him of the rebel soldiers; a small, barefooted woman with an expressionless face, the mother of three; the father, a big man with pale eyes; and a young boy of seventeen and his twenty-year-old sister, both shoeless, she dressed in a garment made from flour sacks, beaten and mistreated by her father and brother. On the one side we have the losers in a war, probably with nothing to come home to; on the other side we have the victors in a war who are also the eternal losers in the poor hill country of Tennessee, with their dilapidated cabin and their lack of everything but the barest necessities. They are worlds apart, and their chance encounter could have been a friendly and peaceful one; yet we know from the very beginning that tragic events will unfold, and when we finish part 1 we know that whoever ends up victorious in this story will also have lost something.

As we read on in the story we discover that Faulkner has chosen a surprising and very effective perspective by following the scene in the kitchen through the eyes of the young girl. She is watching through a crack in the clay chinking between the logs, and accordingly she cannot see everything but can comment on what she sees and hears. The narrator lets us see her from the outside, but we also get close enough to follow her emotional reactions and hear her breathing the major's name into the crumbled wall. What she sees in the room is described as if by her, but there is little doubt that the voice and wording come from the narrator, even though he returns to the girl time and again to maintain his perspective on the scene.

Having chosen to present the arrival of the visitors from the cabin window, with the whole family as viewers, it is perhaps not very surprising that Faulkner uses a similar method in the second section of the story. Yet it is significant that the girl's point of view is chosen. She is in fact the only character within the story who for natural reasons could be used to spy on the scene in the kitchen. Her father and older brother do not want her to see or be seen by the stranger, Major Weddel. The role assigned to the girl in the narration of the story also indicates that she will play an important part in the plot, since she is hardly chosen as focal point for technical reasons alone. What Faulkner achieves by using the girl in this central position in part 2 is, on the one hand, simply to get a part of his story told from a revealing point of view, outside the action but still close to it. On the other hand, the girl's reactions when she sees Weddel add a tone of calm despair, of deprivation and poverty, and of impossible hopes and dreams. If we read for the plot and watch for all the elements that contribute to drive the story toward its end, the girl's position becomes extremely important. The narrative desire is almost based on the girl's desire—a desire for a man, for Weddel, for a different world, for getting away at all costs. When, with her eye to the crack, she first hears the major state his name, this is how the text presents her reaction, which includes a first closeup of the major:

> "Soshay Weddel," the girl breathed into the dry chinking, the crumbled and powdery wall. She could see him at full length, in his stained and patched and brushed cloak, with his head lifted a little and his face worn, almost gaunt, stamped with a kind of indomitable weariness and yet arrogant too, like a creature from another world with other air to breathe and another kind of blood to warm the veins. "Soshay Weddel," she breathed. (CS, 749)

By using the girl's point of view the text in a very concrete sense "stages" the conflict between the two ex-soldiers from the Civil War in a limited space with the few props that the kitchen offers. The confrontation between the sitting Union soldier and the standing, one-armed rebel officer is lifted to a new level of significance because of the girl's understanding of them or, rather, because of the narrator's diction and imagery in his description of her thoughts and reactions. On the story level it becomes very clear that Vatch hates the intruders, largely because of his wartime experience. He threatens Weddel by showing him cartridges from the war, asking if Weddel would know them better if one exploded in his face. He tries to make Weddel drink whiskey, but Weddel refuses because of his stomach. Later, when he tries to bring the drink to Jubal, he is stopped and forced to go out the front door. We know this is because he is not supposed to meet the girl, but we also know that she has seen him. Five times we hear her breathe or say "Soshay Weddel" to herself, "into the crumbled dust beyond which the voices came, not yet raised yet forever irreconcilable and already doomed, the one blind victim, the other blind executioner" (*CS,* 750). The text leaves little doubt about the direction events will eventually take. But so far the dramatic tension has just started, and the plotting of the story which will bring the final tragedy about has also just begun. Much of the motivation is found in Vatch's hatred of many things he either does not understand or that he fears, but motivation of a different sort is found in the girl's repetitive invocation of Weddel's name: "It's like a music. It's like a singing" (*CS,* 751). The motivating forces behind the further development are wonderfully complex, and the dream of living in a place where women wear shoes may be as important as the nightmares filled with running and yelling rebel soldiers.

The next section of the story is simpler, more straightforward in its narrative method. We watch Weddel take the whiskey tumbler to his servant, and we listen to them talk in the barn, in addition to getting detailed descriptions of Jubal's work on "a pair of thin dancing slippers" (*CS,* 752), followed by mild comedy when Jubal drinks the Tennessee corn whiskey. In the midst of all the tension, poverty, and almost claustrophobic imprisonment the story conveys, it is a relief to listen to Jubal's incessant and meaningless talk, although he is so much a caricature from the "old massuh" school that many readers have been critical of Faulkner's portrait of Jubal in this story. It is easy to agree with such criticism, because Jubal's simplicity, fidelity, and stubborn consistency are exaggerated and heavy-handed. And yet he is also portrayed as very role- and class-conscious and is in many ways the master of the major, perhaps even being the one who has made it possible to survive the hardships of war. Weddel's relationship to Jubal may well be based on the old code, and there is no doubt who owns whom, even after the war; yet Weddel's concern for his servant is exemplified time and again in the text, so there can be little doubt of the emotional ties between the two. The way Weddel has tried to take care of his servant, who always seems to be cold, is perhaps the single most important fact in the girl's total infatuation with Weddel and what he stands for.

In the development of the plot, the whisky Jubal drinks is more important than Weddel's fetching his heavy revolver before he decides to bathe in the well house. As noted about the prepublication versions, a brief part 4 followed at this point, with the girl and her younger brother watching Weddel take his bath. Having seen how the girl's perspective was employed very successfully in part 2, it is easy to understand that Faulkner chose to delete this section. It did not bring the story forward at all, and it emphasized elements that had already been made clear and that the narrative returns to later on.

Of all the characters in the bleak and barren log cabin on the mountaintop in Tennessee, the twenty-year-old girl and Jubal have been more in the foreground in the text and in our reading of it than the basic conflict, which seems to have more to do with "that dark and smoldering and violent and childlike vanity of men" (CS, 750). When we read on, Jubal and the girl dominate the scene, together at the same time in the lean-to kitchen. Jubal complains about the weather, and the girl discovers that his feet are wrapped in fur. Her reaction, not surprisingly, is "Hit's fur. He taken and cut up a fur coat to wrap his feet in" (CS, 755). Later on she disobeys her father and brother and enters the room where Weddel is to get confirmation of what she has suspected: that Weddel had cut the fur from the sable lining of his cloak. But this is later on, in a development to construct a fascination for Weddel parallel to the text's deliberate rhetorical strategies that establish the major's humanity as a result of a long and difficult lesson he has been through. Right now the girl asks Jubal where they live, and he is more than happy to give his version of "Countymaison" and "de Domain"—the plantation in Mississippi that he left with his master four years before. He also tells a vivid but brief tale about the trip that Francis Weddel made to Washington to see the president, a story Faulkner readers know well from "Lo!"

As Jubal talks on and the girl listens, it is as if he were back home, while the girl, "her big, smooth, young body cupped soft and richly mammalian to the rough garment" (CS, 756), seems to take everything in, as if she is looking into a world she did not know existed. The family members seem to have discussed the visitors, because suddenly the girl confronts Jubal with Vatch's suspicion that Weddel is a Negro himself. Jubal is horrified but knows why such a blatant misunderstanding is possible: "It's caze yawl aint never been nowhere. Ain't never seed nothing. Living up here on a nekkid hill whar you cant even see smoke" (CS, 756). Other questions are easier to handle, as whether girls wear shoes all the time at Countymaison. The girl repeats the question, she asks if the major is married, and then combines the two thoughts into a statement almost painful when the reader reaches it: "'I dont reckon he'd have any time for a girl that didn't have any shoes" (CS, 757). In the meantime she has found another jug of "dat ere Tennessee spring water," and Jubal has another drink. The drinking is another minor yet important part of the plot development of the story.

What the text has pointed forward to and returned to whenever it seemed to go in another direction—the confrontation between enemies in a war already decided—assumes central position in the next section of the story. Four men are seated about the supper table, and the father confronts Weddel directly, asking him if he is "a nigra" (CS, 758). Weddel's answer shows his arrogance but also a deeper understanding of a conflict he probably did not expect but has felt rising from the first moment: "'So that explains it,' he said. 'I was thinking that he was just congenitally illtempered. And having to be a victor, too'" (CS, 758). Weddel's answer, that he is not a Negro, is followed up by a question from the father: "Who are you?"—perhaps the most central question in the text if we think of Saucier Weddel as its protagonist or "hero," and since so much of the text from this point on centers on Weddel and his understanding of identity, self, being alive.

The father asks the questions, but Vatch is the real antagonist, with his face lowered and hard, and Weddel addresses him: "'I think I know how you feel,' he said. 'I expect I felt that way once. But it's hard to keep on feeling any way for four years. Even feeling at all'" (CS, 758). Weddel and Vatch have both been to the war: Weddel is tired of war, and he is defeated. Vatch is one of the victors and has lost all decency and respect for people. Weddel feels nothing, whereas Vatch feels a mad hatred. Weddel, having fought and lost, has learned a lesson in humility; Vatch has learned nothing. Weddel's comment is on a different level than Vatch's reactions, swearing and splashing whisky across the table. Weddel also shows an arrogance and cynicism which appear to be typical of him but which later on seem to yield to more life-giving forces, consideration and compassion, which ironically prove to be fatal.

But he tells his story, which shows that the question "Who am I?" can only be answered by describing one's background, heritage, history—all the forces that shaped and molded him, including those from later years of deprivation and fear. His heritage is proud, but he describes elements of it with an irony so strong that it seems as if he has discovered some of the injustices and wrongs of the old system. He ends his brief biographical sketch by saying that he was "a major of Mississippi infantry in the corps of a man named Longstreet, of whom you may have heard" (CS, 760). When Vatch comments on his having been a major, Weddel answers: "That appears to have been my indictment; yes" (CS, 760), an answer and an attitude probably much different from the one he went to war with.

When Weddel has told his story, Vatch tells his, a tale of how he gave a rebel major an extra eye after having had to crawl a long way to get to the right distance with his musket. The gist of this bloody tale is that he would not mind doing the same thing to another rebel major, but Weddel assures the father that he does not mind Vatch and his violent ways. Weddel is carrying his revolver and seems prepared to use it if necessary, but direct confrontation is averted since the girl suddenly stands in the room where she is not allowed to be. The father has to wrestle with Vatch to keep him back from doing whatever he is planning, and he sends the girl out of the room. Twice we are told that Weddel does not catch the name used by her father. His mind is set on other things, his hand hidden inside his coat pocket, and in a final face-to-face confrontation with the father, Weddel is told to take his horses and go. A description of Weddel's eyes, "like those of the dead, in which only vision had ceased and not sight"(CS, 762), strongly and scarily reminds the reader of the eyes of the rebel major that Vatch told about a little earlier in the text.

A very brief scene, flickering yet distinct, gives a glimpse into a family structure and a way of life both painful and revealing, and not only because the girl, who is again in the center, has discovered kindness and consideration in what Weddel had done for his servant. The scene shows a meaningless misuse of power when the father enters the room where the girl is and beats her with a leather strap in punishment of her behavior. If we as readers did not quite understand the urge and despair in the girl's behavior—her interest in Weddel, her dream about wearing shoes, even later her scheming to escape—we do now, not because she is beaten by her father but because she appears to consider herself fortunate since it is not Vatch who comes after her: "I was afeared it would be Vatch" (CS, 763).

The two following sections of this fairly long short story are insignificant in the sense that they only drive the story closer to its fatal resolution without adding to it. They contribute to the building of the plot, which includes Jubal's getting totally drunk and falling headlong to the floor, followed by the major's refusal to leave without him. The father commands his youngest son, Hule, to fetch the horses, but Weddel cannot leave Jubal behind—not after four years. Whereupon the father says, "I have warned you" (CS, 765). Hule helps Weddel getting Jubal up into the hayloft, and the stage is set for what we fear will be a final and deadly confrontation at dawn. The plotting creates this situation, but there are two actors—the girl and her younger brother—who have their own plans and therefore add to the complexities and intricacies of the concluding parts of the story. But the basic plot is clear: Weddel is warned, he has been given his chance to get away, but his servant is dead drunk, and he cannot leave him behind. The outcome should be clear, but the text has prepared us for some sort of intervention or interference from the girl.

Weddel lies on his back, side by side with the snoring Jubal, and he contemplates his situation—having lost a war and being trapped on his way home to what must be ruins—and inadvertently he sums up some of the things that make life so important and so difficult:

He lay rigid on his back in the cold darkness, thinking of home. "Contalmaison. Our lives are summed up in sounds and made significant. Victory. Defeat. Peace. Home. That's why we must do so much to invent meanings for the sounds, so damned much. Especially if you are unfortunate to be victorious: so damned much. It's nice to be whipped. Quiet to be whipped. To be whipped and to lie under a broken roof, thinking of home." (CS, 766)

This is a key passage in "Mountain Victory," a linguistic moment of sorts in which the story indirectly comments upon itself, pointing to names and sounds that sum up and make our lives signify. He lies thinking of home, which is perhaps the next best thing to being there, except home may not be there any longer and will most certainly be different now. Only the name, Contalmaison, the sound of it and the thoughts of it, seem real. Weddel seems to have found a peace he has sought after for a long time, and he still feels alive, because he has not "lost the privilege of being afraid" (CS, 766).

His thoughts come to an abrupt end because of a sound he hears, and Hule appears with a message from his sister involving a ladder he may climb to get into her room. The boy seems unable to understand that Weddel refuses to meet his sister and threatens to kill Weddel, but he more or less gives in and tells Weddel to shoot him. Weddel tries to explain why he is not interested in the boy or the girl: all he wants is to go home. But so much of the boy's hopes, including his sister's dreams that perhaps have been transferred to him from her, depends on Weddel's willingness to let the two of them escape with him, and he does not quit easily. "I'll work. We'll both work. You can get married in Mayesfield. It's not far" (CS, 769). Weddel still refuses, even though he must understand that his chances to get away alive are very small and that he is in dire need of help. Perhaps this is the very reason: he knows he has reached a point of no return, and his thoughts of being afraid and hence alive and happy come back to him: "I'm just afraid. I think my luck has given out. I know that it has lasted too long; I am afraid that I shall find that I have forgot how to be afraid" (CS, 769). He repeats his refusal to leave in the darkness of the night when the father also appears and tells him to "Take what is yours, and ride on" (CS, 770). The father gave a warning earlier; now it is repeated and specified: "You have till daylight" (CS, 770). The boy also offers to show Weddel a shortcut down to the valley, but Weddel answers in a much more concrete fashion this time: "I cant. He wants to go home. I must get him home too" (CS, 771). And so we follow the story to its last section, into the "thick cold dawn" of the following morning.

Everything that has been prepared in the story now converges, intertwines, and reaches its closure in intense, dramatic, and finally tragic fashion. The outcome seems unavoidable, not so much because we have witnessed how different family members take an active interest in

Weddel and the possibilities he represents either for retaliation, final revenge for the nightmares, or for escape and a new life. The story moves toward its resolution also because of generic expectations and conventions. The deliberate and detailed concentration on certain characters, on complex and rather particular motivation behind characters' behavior, combined with the hero's peculiar understanding of what it means to be alive, has set limits for possible conclusions and irrevocably taken us to a final rendezvous. As readers we have no reason to expect a quiet and peaceful departure from the mountain, nor do we expect any changes in Weddel. We fear that the young boy and his sister may make a last desperate attempt, and we are afraid of the consequences. The only thing that may be surprising in the final section of the story is the elaborate planning and scheming by Hule, the young boy, which finally seem to put him in an awkward and untenable position where he does not really know what he is doing or what he wants to do. We know that he has given Weddel advice about a hidden path he should follow, and then he emerges from a copse and makes a final attempt at persuading Weddel to take him and his sister with him. He tells Weddel that his father and brother know the path, too, but still appears to think that it is possible to slip away. What he intends to do when he understands that Weddel will not take them is not entirely clear. He says, "Come on, then. We got to hurry" (CS, 774), which must mean that he still offers to help, but this time most likely by fooling his father and brother who are lying in ambush to kill Jubal, who is riding the thoroughbred. Hule tries to keep Jubal back all the time, and Weddel gets suspicious; later, too late, the boy reveals that he has told his father and brother that Weddel would be riding the good horse, and he tries to get Weddel and Jubal off the path he had advised them to take. Hule seems to have made a last attempt to trade with life and death in order to get Weddel to take him and his sister away from the mountain cabin. When that fails he seems to be willing to let Weddel and Jubal ride into the ambush; since he is unable to keep Jubal and the thoroughbred behind, however, he knows that the confusion about the horse Weddel rides will not help him. When he finally cries out for them to get off the path, he may be motivated by guilt and therefore makes a last, desperate attempt to save Weddel's life.[8]

Perhaps our attempts to understand the boy's motives are not very important after all, since the text has set its course and small deviations do not matter much. Weddel could not leave earlier because of his servant, and he could not possibly trade with his own life, even if ambush and death might be the outcome. Thinking and talking to himself, he has given expression to a worn-out peace and quiet which only death can bring, and when he leaves the gaunt and bleak cabin in the Tennessee mountains he feels that he is still alive because he is afraid. Weddel's experience during the war has changed him, but he still acts within character and consistently. He is afraid that he has forgotten to be afraid, but he comes to realize that he is still alive in a deeper sense of the word:

> "And so I am running away," Weddel said. "When I get home I shall not be very proud of this. Yes I will. It means that I am still alive. Still alive, since I still know fear and desire. Since life is an affirmation of the past and a promise to the future. So I am still alive—Ah." (CS, 772–73)

Weddel is then killed because he could not possibly trade with his newly won insights, with the humility and humanity that seem to be internalized in his character and which the brief encounter on the Tennessee hilltop puts into relief. The actual shot that kills Weddel is not heard, not described, until after the fact. The thin grimace on his face when he "rowelled the sorrel" was "still on his dead face when he struck the earth, his foot still fast in the stirrup." In the path lies the body also of the boy, "the face wrenched sideways against a stone, the arms backsprawled, openpalmed" (CS, 776). But Jubal is alive and on his hands and knees when the two men arrive. The father discovers his youngest son and looks down at him "like he was waking from a dream" (CS, 777), while Vatch does exactly as in his story about the other rebel major: he backs away to get at the right distance for a rifle shot. The story ends before the sound of the shot, with Jubal watching the gun "become a round spot against the white shape of Vatch's face like a period on a page" (CS, 777), and the story ends after one more sentence.

"Mountain Victory" shows the irony involved in the use of "victory." Victory appears to be an illusion: it may well be better to have been beaten if it means having been taught a lesson in humility and humanity. Vatch is one of the victors in the Civil War, but he has lost himself and all chances of a peaceful and happy life afterwards. Vatch is the victor in the mountain, too, killing the two "intruders," but he is also a loser, not only because of the ambush and his execution of the two strangers but because a young boy with a vain dream of a better future, his brother, lies dead in the path. Mr. Compson's remark to Quentin in *The Sound and the Fury*—"Victory is an illusion of philosophers and fools"—comes to mind here, but it is necessary to discuss the underlying motivation behind Weddel's actions and also to look more closely at his thinking about victory and defeat now that we have followed this slowly developing text to a conclusion that seems to have been a part of its beginning.

The most important elements in the story clearly transcend the interpretive level, at which the Civil War and its effects on people is empha-

sized, and the reading and analysis above have accordingly only emphasized those aspects when explicating passages referring directly to the
wartime experience. On a superficial level the conflict in the story is that
between a Confederate officer and a Union soldier, and the action is in
a sense the aftermath of the great conflict. Moreover, racial attitudes are
at stake, and the racism is also fueled by a strong class hatred. But the
local, private, timebound conflicts are transferred to a different level, so
that more basic and universal problems pervade the text, and we experience a struggle with personal and existential problems on the part of
more characters than the protagonist himself. The existential conflict
may not be central enough in the story to show how all textual elements
derive from this key conflict and contribute to it, yet in an interpretive
move relating to the text as a totality, I think this aspect deserves notice.

Major Saucier Weddel, a company commander in Jackson's Army of
the Valley, is completely alone, lost, and defeated, but he has something
which sets him apart from numerous other estranged and alienated figures in Faulkner's short fiction: He has a set of ethical norms to guide
him, and having had them put to a final test, he knows that they are still
valid. Other characters go through experiences where their very existence is threatened in order to reach an uncertain set of values, which
they may later try out and have confirmed. This is true for a number of
stories describing uncertain experiences or memories of them in a child
narrator's voice, such as "Uncle Willy" and "A Justice."

Let me end with a note on "the dream," to which I have so often
referred in the reading above and which is central in so many of
Faulkner's short stories. The dream in "Mountain Victory" is stronger,
more pathetic, more moving because it is so modest, so naked, and so
completely out of reach. It has nothing to do with what is commonly
known as the American dream, even though numerous Faulkner characters live and suffer because of their firm belief in the myths of opportunity and social mobility. The dream may indeed be very modest, and in
its simplicity and limitation it demonstrates better than any narrative
how naked and cruel life can be for some people. The young girl in
"Mountain Victory" is one of the most moving examples of this. She is
not the principal character of this story, but we get very close to her and
can see how she suffers badly from a harsh and loveless family situation.
She does not know much about a different life, but she senses it in the
person of Saucier Weddel. Her situation is by far worse than those experienced by Miss Minnie or Miss Emily, in materialistic terms as well as
in psychological ones. She is, together with her mother, who is beyond
all hopes and all dreams, the weakest character in the white-trash family in the dilapidated log cabin in the Tennessee mountains, which is an
unusual place for Faulkner to use as setting.

The dream in itself adds a touch of human frailty, helplessness, and desire to the story. In the girl's situation it comes as no surprise that the dream also has sexual overtones; but this does not by any means reduce the urgency and need for a more meaningful life because her present situation is unbearable. Her older brother is the one who treats her most mercilessly, but there is not much help or comfort to find in the other members of the family. She has nothing to look forward to; poverty and ignorance have made her imprisonment inescapable. The girl is warm, mistreated, dreaming, inscrutable, and profoundly patient,[9] but since she is the weaker person in a family who needs her (or her work, rather), there is little hope that she will ever be wearing shoes or even see the different world which she has sensed in the name of Saucier Weddel.

In the ruthless and sublime inevitability of "Mountain Victory" Faulkner creates a drama in which conflicts far beyond those immediately related to the encounter and the action are described. In my opinion there is thus every reason to compare this story with "Barn Burning" or "Red Leaves," for example, because of obvious intertextual relationships and because of the treatment of a particular existential experience which transcends the limits of the story elements in the text. It tells a dramatic and tragic story, and it does so with a great storyteller's mastery over technique and theme, character and conflict, sound and symbol. It tells a story but signifies a lot more than the story it tells.

# Chapter 10

# Pantaloon in Black

## TEXTUAL INFORMATION AND PUBLICATION HISTORY

The textual information about "Pantaloon in Black" is simple. The story was written and sent out at a time when Faulkner used Harold Ober in New York as his agent, and it is also written so late in his career that the reworking of old drafts into new, completely different stories no longer was Faulkner's habit or practice. The story was sent to Ober in a letter that he records as having received on March 18, 1940. The file card in Ober's records for this story also reveals that the story was received on this date. Ober wrote a brief (and misleading) synopsis of the story on his file card and noted that it should go to "*Harper's* last"; after four unsuccessful attempts with other magazines, the story went to *Harper's,* which received the story on July 9, 1940. It was sold exactly a month later for four hundred dollars. Ober's files record a twenty-four-page typescript, and a carbon of a typescript of this length is in the University of Virginia Library (Meriwether 1971, 306). The magazine version of "Pantaloon in Black" was used virtually unchanged in *Go Down, Moses,* and Faulkner accordingly seems to have seen no need to integrate this story more fully into the text of what he always considered to be a novel. The story was printed as a short story again in *Uncollected Stories* (1979).

If one insists that *Go Down, Moses* is about Ike McCaslin and his repudiation, one is bound to be troubled by the apparent inconsistencies in narrative tone and by the fact that Ike is missing from large parts of the book. If, on the other hand, one holds that a central theme of the book concerns relations between blacks and whites,[1] one may be seriously troubled by the hunting stories with their wilderness theme. Furthermore, if the book is viewed as the story of the tainted McCaslin family, "Pantaloon in Black" does not necessarily belong in it. Yet the fact remains that Faulkner included the short story in the book, even in a very important position, after "The Fire and the Hearth" and before the first of the wilderness stories. This choice may become understandable if we emphasize both the theme of racial injustice and the aspect of the book which has been referred to as the world or society of a Southeren plantation. Go Down, Moses centers significantly on and around the McCaslin place: all the characters of any significance in the book relate to this place in some way or other, and even in the book's present time (early 1940s) this place seems to form the stable and unchanging center of a society in miniature.[2]

The apparent singularity of "Pantaloon in Black" has led critics to argue that it is not integrated in Go Down, Moses and hence does not belong there, and that it reduces the coherency of the volume as a whole. For our purpose in the reading and interpretation of "Pantaloon in Black" as a short story, this critical debate need not concern us directly. Yet I do think that the alleged marginality of the story in Go Down, Moses comes as a result of the problematic status of "Pantaloon in Black" as a double-voiced text with a black character as a dominant central consciousness. The text is in itself difficult—some would say impenetrable or unintelligble[3]—and so the structural problems it seems to be responsible for in the longer work may in part stem from inherent conflicts of race as well as of reading in the short story itself. The place of the story within the larger framework of Go Down, Moses will be addressed again at the end of this analysis. When we follow the story in its poetic and violent development, we do so by using the text from Uncollected Stories, reprinted from its periodical publication in Harper's (even though this story, contrary to many others reused in the novel, appeared virtually unchanged in Go Down, Moses),[4] and leave all questions about integration and function in Go Down, Moses aside.

## READING "PANTALOON IN BLACK"

A "Pantaloon" is a character from Italian commedia dell'arte with a function similar to that of a clown. According to Mikhail Bakhtin such a stock character has the function of criticizing social structures and laying bare any sort of conventionality. He has "the unique right to rip off masks, the right to rage at others with a primeval (almost cultic) rage" (Bakhtin 1981, 163).[5] This is very close to a description of the otherwise problematic rage that Rider expresses when his wife has died and is buried. He does not at all know how to continue on his own, nor why he should go on alone in a world no longer graced by her living presence. The marginality of the character, developed and individualized from its stock characteristics, gives "Pantaloon in Black" a strange subjectivity, a haunting closeness. The third-person narrative is both limited in its intimate focus on the black protagonist and the use of a language which clearly belongs to the narrator, who is at a distance from the events but who employs his language to create everything from deeply felt sympathy to raging intensity and pitiful compassion on the part of the reader. "Pantaloon in Black" shows a narrator—and ultimately an author—in complete command and control of his material and perspective; yet at times the emotional impact is so strong that it threatens to break the boundaries of storytelling, until everything is contained and confined by the peremptory ending offered us by the white deputy and his wife. Susan Donaldson (1992) finds "contending narratives" in *Go Down, Moses* (128), and nowhere do they seem more in opposition and conflict than in "Pantaloon in Black." We must be aware of the conflict and tension in the main narrative of the story between the perspective of the black character, Rider, and the narrative voice through which the protagonist's consciousness is filtered. James Ferguson maintains that Faulkner in this short story is able to get "the best of two worlds: the kind of controlled intensity that derives from limiting the perspective to a single consciousness and the suggestion of a rich range of experience clearly beyond that of the protagonist" (99). Even more characteristic of the language in "Pantaloon in Black" is Faulkner's superb translation of strong feelings into images of what Rider sees, hears, and touches. Richard Gray observes that the text turns emotion into sensory experience and by implication becomes an interrogation of systems of speech.[6] The contending narratives of the black man in his agonizing struggle to be allowed to join his dead wife and the white deputy's rambling stereotype of racist attitudes in his master narrative of prejudice and stupidity almost force us to consider what storytelling finally is about and to reflect on the cultural, racial, and ideological motives behind the different narratives found in this story.

"Pantaloon in Black" opens *in medias res*: We are present with Rider at the side of the grave where the pine box containing his dead wife, Mannie, now rests. The opening sentence strikes a note of calmness and controlled despair and indicates how sudden and unexpected Mannie's death has been. (We are never informed about the causes of her death.) We are reminded of her presence, not only in the coffin but in the character of Rider and in the very language of the narrator: "He stood in the worn, faded, clean overalls which Mannie herself had washed only a week ago, and heard the first clod strike the pine box" (*US*, 238). "Mannie herself" stands out, gains foreground effect, and the intolerable loss is thus made clear from the very beginning of the story; even if the outside description of Rider gives no direct indication of his grief, it prepares the reader for his immediate reaction at the graveside, which is to take one of the shovels and bury the coffin in dirt as quickly as possible. Soon the grave is filled so that it resembles any other,

> marked off without order about the barren plot by shards of pottery and broken bottles and old brick and other objects insignificant to sight but actually of a profound meaning and fatal to touch, *which no white man could have read.* (*US,* 238; my emphasis)

The word "read" seems of the utmost importance here. It refers specifically to the inability of white people to understand the signs and symbols of a black cemetery, but it also seems to imply the impenetrability for the master race, the white man, of the traditions, culture, and rituals of the black race. It also signals to white readers that they should expect a text—literary and cultural—which they may find problematic and of which they may only have touched the surface, even when they think they have understood it. If readers pay heed to this warning in the text, they may be less prone to marginalize the text and its chief character, because the text has already marginalized most readers, so that part of the challenge in reading "Pantaloon in Black" will be precisely to work from both these marginal positions and see how it comes to signify. It should also serve to remind us that race is a key issue in the text, even when it concentrates on Rider's unappeasable grief and few white characters are involved. In the world of the plantation system, whiteness is ubiquitous anyhow.

The text gives small bits of information about Rider directly and indirectly, in the midst of the descriptions from the burial. We know that he is enormously big and strong, that he works at a sawmill, and that his aunt has raised him, all this from small remarks completely integrated in the text about the burial. Rider leaves the cemetery, but he does not want to leave together with his aunt. A person from his sawmill gang tells him that he should not go home because Mannie will be "wawking yit" (*US,* 239), yet Rider hurries toward his own home. Entering the lane that leads to the house he rents on this late Sunday evening, he is alone and not alone in a country lane with footprints and marks of hoof and wheel, with unbearable memories even in the air of the August evening. Nowhere in the text are Rider's emotions more powerfully rendered than in the poetic and emotional description of a deserted, dusty country lane in August on the night of his wife's burial:

> It was empty at this hour of Sunday evening—no family in wagon, no rider, no walkers churchward to speak to him and carefully

refrain from looking after him when he had passed—the pale, pow-
der-light, powder-dry dust of August from which the long week's
marks of hoof and wheel had been blotted by the strolling and
unhurried Sunday shoes, with somewhere beneath them, vanished
but not gone, fixed and held in the annealing dust, the narrow,
splay-toed prints of his wife's bare feet where on Saturday afternoons she would walk to the commissary to buy their next week's
supplies while he took his bath; himself, his own prints, setting the
period now as he strode on, moving almost as fast as a smaller man
could have trotted, his body breasting the air her body had vacated, his eyes touching the objects—post and tree and field and house
and hill—her eyes had lost. (*US*, 239)

The dead wife is not only a loss, a deprivation, but a void even in the
world of the senses. Her body has vacated the air he is now passing
through, and nothing will ever be the same. This is made abundantly
clear in the almost pitiful beauty of the narrative (very much the narrator's even if he still keeps within Rider's perspective) about Rider and
Mannie's brief, undemanding, uneventful but perfectly happy married
life. Rider is twenty-four and has always made good money at the
sawmill. Six months ago he saw Mannie and said goodbye to "all purposes nameless" (*US*, 240). He had known Mannie all his life, but he
suddenly saw her for the first time and was "thu wid all dat" (*US*, 240).[7]
Renting the last house in the lane from Carothers Edmonds, he had built
a hearth in it and started a fire there on the night he married, intending
to keep it burning like Lucas Beauchamp had done for forty-five years.
The image of "the fire on the hearth" is significant also in this story, not
because of what it shows of endurance and durability but because of the
expectations attached to it. The general renovation Rider has done to the
cabin is important but carries none of the symbolic value the building of
the hearth does. Mannie even baked a cake every Saturday "now that she
has a stove to bake in" (*US*, 241). Rider and Mannie may well have had
little, but to them it was all, and the text leaves us in no doubt about the
sincerity and value of this life. We are thus almost forced to ask why
those who have so little must lose it all, and Rider obviously struggles
with this question, which, since it is caused by Mannie's death, should
be a question addressed to his maker. Yet some of his reactions clearly
indicate that he wants to set other things right, too, in this unjust and
unequal society, having lost all that matters to him. His actions should
not only be understood as his means of escape—killing so that the law
or the white people will put an end to his life and reunite him with
Mannie. Rider knows the Southern code well enough to manipulate it to
serve his purposes, and the text shows indirectly and ambiguously but

convincingly that Rider places himself in a situation in which his oppressors can get to him, thus giving him the freedom from "breathing" that he so much wants.

Let us return to the narrative itself as it unfolds and develops after the drive forward has been halted to allow the narrator to tell about Rider's married life, the complete change this meant to him, and the dreams for the future he in a very concrete way had built into it. The fire on the hearth should have burned on into a bright and happy future, but it was not to be. Rider returns home, but putting his hand on the gate, he realizes "that there was nothing beyond it" (*US,* 241).[8] Everything reminds him of his wife, and he suddenly wonders what he is doing there, although he knows that he needs to eat. He has completely forgotten his dog, but it now joins him, and they both enter the house:

> They mounted the steps and crossed the porch and entered the house—the dusk-filled single room where all those six months were now crammed and crowded into one instant of time until there was no space left for air to breathe. . . . (*US,* 241)

The dog leaves him to stand outside the door, howling because Mannie's ghost appears. Rider talks to her, calling upon her to wait, but she fades away and disappears. "Den lemme go wid you, honey" (*US,* 242) is Rider's final prayer, but he knows and feels that his will to live is stronger than ever knew. The "strong and indomitable beating of his heart and the deep and steady collapse of his chest" (*US,* 242) is an example of the repetitive and frequent insistence in the text on "the will of that bone and flesh to remain alive" (*US,* 242), even when his conscious wish and deliberate actions indicate that he does not want to stay alive—he wants to join Mannie. The reader may overlook the importance of the recurrent descriptions of Rider's breathing, but it is vitally important to notice how Rider's natural and inevitable will to stay alive without Mannie, with painful memories of her and an intolerable grief that threatens to suffocate him, is juxtaposed with his deliberate attempts to hold grief at bay until he can find a way to successfully join her. Rider actually struggles with his own breathing—"his chest arching and collapsing until he stopped it presently and held himself motionless for perhaps a half minute" (*US,* 243)—and he fights to keep himself from screaming out loud. Grief is portrayed very strongly in these portions of the text, and it is definitely a grief related to what Faulkner later would call the "old verities of the human heart." Rider, in the same Faulknerian metaphor, definitely "grieves on human bones."[9] Rider's actions—the forces behind them and the codes regulating them—may be difficult for a white man to interpret, yet his grief is human and universal, not black and local.

Unable to find peace, unable to stay at home, Rider makes his way to the sawmill, accompanied by the dog beneath the August moon. He works like a wild man, and during noon break his aunt's husband comes with food and words from his aunt that only the Lord can help Rider. Rider does not even want to listen: "Whut Mannie ever done ter Him? Whut He wanter come messin' wid me and—" (US, 245). In the next moment he is working again, trying to make physical strain stop his breathing, stop his thinking and remembering. He accomplishes the incredible feat of lifting an enormous log, and one of the onlookers is certain that it will kill him. The daring and wild physical test is not meaningless within the text of the short story, which is of course what matters here. Rider survives his suicidal log-lifting test and quickly leaves the sawmill, so that at sundown we watch him in the river swamp, buying a jug of illegal whisky from a white man. The white man notices Rider's eyes, "which had been strained and urgent this morning and which now seemed to be without vision too" (US, 246–47), and tries to take the gallon jug back, offering Rider a pint for nothing instead. Rider does not accept the offer; he has paid, the jug is his: "Look out, white folks," (US, 247) is his response to the white distiller before he turns his back upon him, and as readers we should remember this warning, which seems to be directed against *white people* as a group, because it is of no consequence in the conversation with the liquor dealer.

Accompanied by his dog, Rider moves on through the cane-stalks in the twilight, feeling still that there is no air, no room to breathe in, talking to the jug he carries and drinks from, daring it to fight him and his strength. This may easily be interpreted as the talk of a madman who is losing his hold on reality, but within the "project" we have established on the basis of the text's insistence on the conflict between the will to live and the wish to die, it makes sense: "Come on now. You always claims you's a better man den me. Come on now. Prove hit" (US, 247). The liquor is of no use, has no effect, does not abate his anguish or despair. The liquor does not even go down his throat but "sprang columnar and intact and still retaining the shape of his gullet, outward glinting in the moonlight." Rider decides he has "misread de sign wrong" (US, 248) and knows that the whisky will be of no more help. Again we are reminded of the semiotics of this short story, of the importance of reading and interpreting signs correctly.

Extreme physical feats and strong liquor have been put to a test and have failed. The next remedy in the text, not at all sought by Rider but offered to him by his aunt and uncle, is religious faith. He admits to his aunt that drinking has been of no help, but he refuses to get down on his knees and pray. Even if his aunt calls him by the name of his childhood, "Spoot," he cannot see why God, who knows everything, needs to be told of his fate. "Awright. Hyar Ah is. Leff Him come down hyar and do me some good" (*US*, 249), Rider responds, and just after midnight he is at the mill again. The dog, having followed him on his various missions, is gone now, which should prepare us for a new development, an escalation of the dramatic action, a denouement. Rider is, in his extreme situation, finally and completely alone. He chooses strange words to express this, but they leave little doubt about the premeditation of the path he has chosen. He knocks loudly at the barred door of a shed where gambling is going on, calling out, "Open hit. Hit's me. Ah'm snakebit and bound to die." Inside he repeats that he is "snakebit and de pizen can't havm me" (*US*, 250), and even if the watchman tries to have him thrown out, his six dollars allow him to enter the game of dice. Again, casting the dice, he tells that he is snakebit, and also that he perhaps accordingly "kin pass wid miss-outs. But dese hyar yuther boys—" (*US*, 251). In other words, Rider knows exactly what he is doing, planning his own death by violence, and even if he therefore can accept the crooked game, he thinks of the other black men who have been deceived out of most of their wages for years by the white dice player, Birdsong. Rider grabs Birdsong's arm, and a second pair of dice falls out. The white man reaches for his gun, but in one continuous movement, almost in slow motion, in one of Faulkner's unparalleled 101-word sentences, Birdsong gets his throat slashed. This sentence, says Susan Donaldson, "suggests nothing so much as angry, rebellious energy spilling over the boundaries designed to contain it—in this case, the hierarchical relations of race and even the narrative confines of the story" (Donaldson 1992, 143). Read in the context of Rider's project, it is suggestive of even more, and it is still within the confines of the story as Faulkner masterfully controls it.

The concept of the "diceman" is important here. It functions not only in the clever plotting and patterning of the action in the story but carries strong symbolic significance. Rider has already numerous times contested God's planning and the wisdom of divine acts, and the diceman indicates a sort of fatality or randomness which makes it futile to even think of humans as having a free will. Rider's vision, now that he seems to have lost all vision in his eyes, is even more bleak than this, because the white people invariably seem to have an extra pair of loaded dice to use against the blacks. So it is not only in a more general, philosophical sense that the dice are loaded against human beings; in the case of the black people of the South they have another pair of dice thrown against them whenever the master race decides to do so. In this story Faulkner's penetrating study of race relations takes him far beyond the vision he entrusted to Mr. Compson in *The Sound and the Fury*, of "man who is conceived by accident and whose every breath is a fresh cast with dice loaded against him" (108).[10] The killing of Birdsong—the diceman himself—may be read as an act of symbolic violence, bringing death in its wake and hence "new life" to Rider.

Rider has thus committed the act that will free him from his prison, from the anguish of breathing, from the unappeasable grief he experiences. Rider's development began within the short story as the mourning of a dead and cherished loved one but has moved deliberately and carefully through a dust-filled and moonlit August landscape to the point of violent killing, which becomes at the same time "a gesture of farewell and a refusal."[11] He has acted in solidarity with his fellow workers at the sawmill, and he has carried his plan to its horrific conclusion without being stained by the blood of his victim.

And so Rider's story ends here, with the killing of Birdsong, whose name may warrant interpretation, although it is too simplistic to use it to indicate how much against and contrary to nature Rider's act is. We get to know a little more about the whole clan of Birdsong people, and we are also told by the deputy that the victim "has been running crooked dice on them mill niggers for fifteen years" (US, 253). Rider's story comes to a conclusion by the killing, in the sense that the narrative from his perspective ends, along with the narrator's carefully selected and forceful, rhythmical prose. The rest of the short story is then told from the deputy's perspective, still in the third person, but the deputy is allowed to tell his version of what happened after the killing in his own words, relating the "facts" to his wife who is busily getting ready to go the picture show. The strong emotional force of the narrative up to this point is replaced by the rambling, prejudiced, racist narration given by the deputy. The function of this second narrative must be seen in relation to the primary narrative. It works to confine, contain, and, unsuccessfully, negate the impact and the implications of the narrative about Rider's grief. In one sense the terrible suffering and the violent action of the first narrative are brought under control through the deputy's storytelling. We are given the white perspective on Rider's grief, and we see how completely misunderstood everything is from this angle. Yet Rider's rebellion could only be temporarily successful—the first information we get in the second narrative is that it is all over. The lynching of Rider and the coroner's verdict of his death are mentioned parenthetically as the narrative prepares to switch to the deputy's point of view and let his voice take over the actual narration, so that the narrator of the story only provides stage directions and indirect comments by allowing us to see the lack of interest on the part of the deputy's wife.

The deputy has had a rough night and is a "little hysterical" (US, 252), and his opening remarks, general and broad and extremely racist, should be read in the context of his physical and mental condition, even if the text seems to undercut some of the hardships of his nightly work:

"Them damn niggers," he said. "I swear to Godfrey, it's a wonder we have as little trouble with them as we do. Because why? Because they ain't human. They look like a man and they walk on their hind legs like a man, and they can talk and you can understand them and you think they understand you, at least now and then. But when it comes to the normal human feelings and sentiments of human beings, they might just as well be a damn herd of wild buffaloes. Now you take this one to-day—." (US, 252)

The deputy's wife thinks it no wonder that two or three men can walk into the prison and get away with a prisoner, because the sheriff's men in her opinion do little but sit on their backsides and talk. The deputy does not respond to her but goes on with his story. From the general remarks about the lack of human feelings in black people, he tells about Rider and his grief, understanding nothing. The irony is almost too obvious, since the first narrative has shown a human being in deep emotional trouble. The deputy's story is fond of hyperbolic statements and rich imagery, which in another context (for example, among his friends around the courthouse) might have evoked laughter. The deputy's version of Rider's grief has his general racism at its basis, and since this version by necessity is contrasted with the previous narrative, it is revealed as superficial, wrongheaded, and stupid. This does not help much, however, on the story level, since the deputy's story is told "after it was over" (US, 252).

There are elements in the deputy's narrative that are realistic and significant in their own right, however. The murdered diceman, Birdsong, is only one of forty-two votes which may be decisive even in an election to the sheriff's office. Also, the sheer manpower of the Birdsongs indicates that the law enforcers are reluctant to protect their prisoner when they have arrested him. They know that the Birdsong people will come and claim their kind of justice, and the sheriff and his deputy are not likely to make much resistance.

Rider makes no attempt to escape, but he asks not to be locked up. The sheriff tells him—and his aunt, who suddenly shows up—that "them Birdsong kin" most certainly will come to get him, even if he also says that "interference with the law can't be condoned" (US, 254). So they lock him up, with his aunt in a corner of his cell, and he breaks out by ripping the steel door out of the wall, yet only because he cannot stand being locked up: "Ah ain't tryin' to git away." Unable to stop Rider, the sheriff's people do not shoot him down, since "if it wasn't going to be the law, then the Birdsong boys ought to have first lick at him" (*US*, 255). The prison guard forces a group of chain-gang blacks to grab Rider. The deputy's description of the fight before Rider was finally brought down is finally a relief because its humor, despite the cruelty and violence, breaks through and gives comic relief to an incredibly evil, painful, and grotesquely inhuman narrative: "now and then a nigger would come flying out and go sailing through the air across the room, spraddled like a flying squirrel and his eyes sticking out in front of him like the headlights of a car." Laughing, with tears "big as glass marbles popping out of his eyes," Rider's last words to us are "Hit look lack Ah just can't quit thinking. Look lack Ah just can't quit" (*US*, 255), which the deputy does not understand at all and asks his wife about. But she, as we know, is going to the picture show and has expressed a wish that her husband "take him out of my kitchen, anyway" (*US*, 252). What I have called Rider's project is thus confirmed by him in the very last of his words in the text, and Rider obviously knows perfectly well what lies in store for him: the Birdsong boys and his death.

The deputy gives the final glimpse of Rider, weeping and fighting in the prison. For once in his narrative he relates something that he does not think he knows everything about and understands better than anybody else. Inadvertently, he thus opens space for a real and tragic view of a suffering human being, deprived of everything and now even misrepresented to the full in a racist master narrative. Susan Donaldson is clearly right when she claims that "Nowhere else in the stories in *Go Down, Moses,* I would argue, is the confining power of narrative more chillingly demonstrated than in the peremptory ending offered by the deputy" (145).

The primary effect of "Pantaloon in Black" is to demonstrate how a simple and primitive man is capable of grief and sorrow which none of the other characters in the story seem to understand and which no one has experience enough to handle.[12] The hard, tough, apparently untouched Rider, who has lost his wife, displays an intense and desperate grief which tears him apart, although he is not able to articulate his loss—at least not so that the white people can grasp it.

In the development of *Go Down, Moses* one may understand the role and function of "Pantaloon in Black" as an intervention in order to slow down the pace of the narrative and to add drama and tragedy in a very concrete way where tragedy has only been remembered and hinted at before. This story, in which grief and loss and murder come in close succession and cause a man to go mad, greatly underscores and emphasizes the incredible stamina, endurance, and other admirable human qualities that must have been necessary for many black people simply in order to survive. "Pantaloon in Black" adds to the world of the plantation, but with its looser connection to the McCaslin world it also prepares us for sojourns into a somewhat larger world, one not limited by the boundaries of the plantation and where people's lives are not bound to it forever by the frail but everlasting threads of kinship, blood relations, work, and debts. "Pantaloon in Black" thus prepares us to enter a world where "The Bear" can take place, but the question of race still looms central and large all through the novel. Despite the greater design, the long and lasting conflicts, the many and futile attempts at setting things right and reaching a deeper and broader understanding of racial questions, it is very much possible that "Pantaloon in Black" is the strongest and most convincing of the individual stories that combine and interconnect to form *Go Down, Moses*.

# Chapter 11

# Red Leaves

## TEXTUAL INFORMATION AND PUBLICATION HISTORY

Faulkner sent "Red Leaves" to the *Saturday Evening Post* on July 24, 1930. It was accepted at once and published on October 25 of the same year. This unusual and easy success accounts for the lack of any textual problems regarding this story. There are two prepublication texts of "Red Leaves": one untitled, twelve-page manuscript and one carbon typescript of thirty-six pages. The story was revised for *These 13*, and that version was used in *Collected Stories* (Skei 1981, 64). Parts of the story were used in revised form in *Big Woods* (1955) as a prelude for "The Old People." "Red Leaves" is also one of the most anthologized of Faulkner's stories.

Even if the publication history and the sequence of the prepublication versions do not present any serious problems, we do not know with any kind of certainty when the story was originally composed. I see little reason to speculate that it was written much earlier than the date when it went to the *Post*. We have no indications that Faulkner struggled with this material through one or more revisions and complete recastings. If he had done so, available manuscript material from the period indicates strongly that the composition story of "Red Leaves" would also have been possible to trace. It is on the other hand reasonable to think that it took some time from the conception of this complex story, built on historical and anthropological material and myths, to its completion. But I doubt that it took years, and we cannot date a short story as "written" or "composed" at the time of the first idea for it or link it to another work because of minor similarities (an image, a name, a phrase). The same procedure could be used to prove a story to be linked to a work ten or fifteen years in the future. Diane Jones's discussion is an

example of an unwarranted need to find an earlier date for the composition of "Red Leaves," using a possible earlier composition of "A
Justice" because of Quentin Compson's role in that story and the use of
a "twilight" passage, as well as because of Lewis Dabney's speculation
about the development of the name Yoknapatawpha (Dabney 1974, 24),
which in the manuscript of "Red Leaves" is used in an early experimental form (Yo-ko-no-pa-taw-fa). Jones finds it possible to date "Red
Leaves" between *Flags in the Dust* (September 1927) and *As I Lay Dying*
(winter 1929), which may be as good a guess as any but certainly not a
better guess than relying on factual information and accepting that while
an accomplished work of literary art grows and develops over some
time, it is written, becomes a literary text, when it is realized in its final
form as understood by the author, not the world of publication (Jones
1994, 320–21).

The story in "Red Leaves" does not change substantially from manuscript to typescript, which, of course, would have been both unusual
and surprising. The typescript is typical of Faulkner's practice of expanding by adding details, filling in background stories, rethinking names of
characters and places; but the only significant addition in the typescript
is a more elaborate and informative description of Issetibbeha and his
wife (Blotner 1974, n. 95). The *Post* text includes a number of changes
from the extant carbon typescript.[1] Only in the *Post* text are central
events in the story placed in historical time. The hunt and burial of the
Man in the present of the short story is dated to 1840, while Doom's
New Orleans trip took place at the end of the eighteenth century.[2]
Faulkner seems to have been thinking a lot about time, both in the sense
of historical events or periods and as the time needed to do things, when
he went back to "Red Leaves" and revised it for *These 13*. The time it
takes to move the steamboat becomes five months instead of five weeks,
which seems much more realistic and reasonable if we consider the distance and the means by which it was done. Other, less important time
markers are also changed.

For our reading and interpretation of the story the different ways in
which Faulkner divided it into sections may be given some significance,
although one should not assume that this automatically adds to the
story's meaning. But it clearly changes the reading experience and con-
nects scenes, events, and actions in particular patterns, setting them off
from other patterns. Changes in perspective and the shifting between
narrative units normally generated Faulkner's need for divisions and sections in his long short stories. In stories such as "A Rose for Emily,"
"Dry September," and "Mountain Victory," the divisions occur where
the narration changes, and even if we have textual evidence that sections
could be moved about or even deleted, the divisions appear to be well

warranted and almost natural. Not so, perhaps, in "Red Leaves." In the *Post* printing with its four parts, the first part is taken up by the discussion between the sixty-year-old Indian called Three Basket and another Indian whose name we do not get until much later, Louis Berry. This part corresponds to the opening part in *These 13* and subsequent printings. The second part in the *Post* printing is clearly two separate narratives. The first one is an outside and very sweeping historical narrative about Doom and Issetibbeha, the corruption of power, and the introduction of slaves in the Indian community. The second narrative picks up the conversation between Three Basket and Louis Berry, more or less where the narration broke off at the end of part 1. Accordingly, the division of part 2 in the *Post* into parts 2 and 3 in subsequent printings follows the pattern we know from other Faulkner stories and is a natural place to divide the text if it is to be divided at all. In other words, the three sections seem a much better solution than the two sections in the *Post*, but it would not have made much of a difference—except perhaps for the narrative pace and the reader's experience of the speed and flow of the text—if it were printed without section divisions at all.

Part 3 in the *Post* corresponds to part 4 in subsequent printings. Accordingly, part 4 in the *Post* is divided into parts 5 and 6 in *These 13*. The division is natural and reasonable but not inevitable. There is no change in the narrative pattern, no shift of perspective, and so the narrative just glides on from the new part 5 to the concluding part 6. But the new division is sensible, since it marks the successful end of the hunt ("You ran well. Do not be ashamed" [*CS*, 338]) and the beginning of the preparations for the burial of the Negro. What is achieved by this last section division is that the sixth part comes to stand as the conclusion of this remarkable story, a strong and very moving conclusion, which in part is achieved because it has been allowed to be a separate unit of the longer narrative.

We should always be cautious when we attach significance to technicalities of this sort; the almost lyrical language and the deeply serious thematic concerns of the story cannot be reduced or enhanced significantly by a division into fewer or more sections, and the concluding paragraphs and lines of a short story will always have a particular impact simply by being the end of the narrative, the summing up of the reading experience. But to the extent that the structural device of sections has an effect at all, it is in the creation of a shorter, separate concluding section. All other divisions come naturally from changes in the perspective of the narration, changes that would have been recognizable and significant even without sections and roman numerals.[3]

Most readers and critics have responded to the story in six parts, as printed in collections and anthologies, and "Red Leaves" has always been considered one of Faulkner's best short stories. Critics who have felt the need to single out one story as his very best have often mentioned "Red Leaves." James Ferguson (1991) writes about "the incomparable 'Red Leaves,' probably his greatest achievement in the genre" (35–36). One may be more tempted to rate this story very highly as a Faulkner critic or scholar than as an "ordinary reader" because of its central place in Faulkner's work and world, with so many different perspectives and interests that can be related to much of his best work. We shall not pursue this line of argument and instead concentrate on a reading of the text of the short story, referring to the most pertinent of the criticism and scholarship devoted to this text, and relating it to other texts only when and if this is necessary for our reading.

"Red Leaves" appears to be independent of genre conventions and free to include all sorts of material that drive it relentlessly toward ends implied by the very narrative or which stem from a mythical structure underlying the narrative and concretized in it. The myth may as well be Faulkner's own; the point is that it functions and gives the story additional significance, because the concrete and realistic elements of the tale become general, universal, and anthropological, independent of time, place, and characters. A stage is set, and the characters enact a human drama of cosmic and eternal significance. But it is vitally important to remember that the story is a concrete and very detailed narrative, with a historical background, of an event with its basis in a tradition which creates problems in the lives of the Indians of Yoknapatawpha County. The story is a fictional narrative from a fictional country, and I shall not even attempt to compare fiction to fact here, nor shall I speculate on the artist's right to distort, make up, and lie about a historical past. Fiction does not claim truth in the ways many critics apparently have thought it does when they comment on "Red Leaves." This kind of investigation is interesting in itself but it is of little or no interest when we read and analyze the story. Its narrative power, its literary techniques, its success as a literary text are much more important from my point of view.

## READING "RED LEAVES"

"Red Leaves" is structured around a burial ritual that builds a basis for the rest of the story to rely upon. The ritual sets forth that the body servant of the Chief, a black slave, must die simply because tradition requires it. This pronouncement is followed, quite logically, by the servant's running away, by a hunt for him before the Chief's corpse starts smelling too bad, and eventually and inevitably by the capture of the slave. The ritual is a human institution insofar as the Indian tradition is concerned, but it may also be seen as more or less a law of nature that the slave must follow his master to the grave.[4] The Indians have had a very close relationship with nature, and their laws and traditions seem to have been made in order to enhance their possibilities for survival in the wilderness by adhering to the laws of nature. Behind the tradition which requires the slave to follow his master to the grave lies the assumption that man is part of nature and that all living things must die. The time one dies is nonetheless of some importance. It is more important to human beings than to any other among nature's creations, and most important to the civiliized, cultured human beings for whom death appears to be one of those reprehensible things which cannot be controlled. Whether man lives in close contact with nature or has lost all such contact, he alone is capable of thought, of consciousness, and this may account for the human tragedy (the existential dilemma) played out in "Red Leaves." In a study of this story Edmond L. Volpe (1975) remarks that "the human being is the only living organism that has the power to contemplate its own extinction" (122).

It is more problematic to follow the text of "Red Leaves" than for most other Faulkner stories, since the reader must feel bewildered and disoriented for a long time. Much in the text becomes understandable and meaningful only in the light of what follows later on in the narrative. The reader has to suspend understanding and explication or has to revise his response and perhaps even return to earlier descriptions to confirm his own reading. This is particularly true for the part of the text before the background story (in section 2). After the panoramic and retrospective narrative of the recent history of the tribe and its leaders, the narrative returns to the present situation, and through shifting perspectives, dramatic manipulation of distance, and gradual changes in the pace of the narration the story is brought to its inevitable end—that it is problematic to follow the text does not give us an excuse to discuss it only on the basis of a final response. It may be even more important to follow the text when it demands to be reread, but "Red Leaves" also deserves to be discussed in a number of different contexts.

The opening section of "Red Leaves" introduces us to the world of the Indian plantation through an outside description of two Indians on their way toward the slave quarters. Their dialogue is not easy to follow or understand, and even if this opening in the middle of serious events—the death of the Indian chief, referred to as the Man—leads us straight into the central elements of the short story, we really need the incredible historical background offered by the second section to be sure that our guesses as we read the first section are correct. The dialogue is about serious matters, but it is kept in a light tone, and the tendency of one speaker to correct the other creates further uncertainty. The easy talk between the two Indians also provides much information, since it centers on the institution of slavery on the Indian plantation. The whole exchange becomes a nostalgic lamentation of the old ways, before the slaves and all the work they meant, but returns after a while to the serious and urgent problem at hand: the dead Issatibbeha and his black body servant who has run away.

The two Indians on their way to the slave quarters know that they will not find what they are looking for, because the same thing has happened before. We do not yet know what, but the two Indians talk about the slaves all the time and compare the present situation with the lot of slaves belonging to the clan in "the old days." They are very negative in their evaluation of the black slaves, because having slaves means a lot of work and a lot of trouble, but also because they cannot understand people who prefer to sweat. The blacks are accused of being like horses and dogs and even of being worse than the white people. Worse than that, their flesh "has a bitter taste, too" (CS, 314). But the old days cannot be restored by eating black people. They have become too valuable for that.

In the slave quarters they have acted out their rituals for the dead chief and for his servant who must follow him. Three Basket knows that the one they look for is not there; he has run away, as has happened before. The two Indians seem to find it strange that the slaves do not like to die: "'They cling. It makes trouble for us, always. A people without honor and without decorum. Always a trouble" (CS, 316). So the two Indians, having completed an almost ritualistic errand, decide to visit the new chief, Moketubbe, who is now the Man and "can wear the shoes with the red heels all the time now" (CS, 316). We learn that Moketubbe has been wearing these red-heeled slippers behind his father's back, and it is even insinuated that this may lie behind the untimely death of Issetibbeha: "He used to wear the shoes behind Issetibbeha's back, and it was not known if Issetibbeha knew this or not. And then Issetibbeha became dead, who was not old, and the shoes are Moketubbe's, since he is the Man now. What do you think of that?" (CS, 317).

There is much in this first part of the story which indicates conflicts, rituals, objects, and attitudes that will become clear or understandable only later in the text. What is most important so far is perhaps that we have been introduced to the burial ritual, and because of references to what has happened before, we come to expect a hunt for the runaway slave. We have also speculations about an unnatural death because of a pair of red-heeled shoes, and we have a strong impression that slavery is a burden on the Indians but also that they seem to keep slaves for profit (and thus they are too valuable to eat).

The narrative of the events surrounding the death of Issetibbeha breaks off, and in the second part of "Red Leaves" we get the historical background for the present situation; but it does not go further back than to the father of Issetibbeha and the time when he, having learned his devious ways among criminals in New Orleans, came to power in the Indian clan. Briefly we hear how the first Man—Doom, from du Homme, as his French friend in New Orleans called him—had a stranded steamboat moved twelve miles on cypress logs and how a girl from a good family came to him six months later and soon gave birth to Issetibbeha. Later on, having sold forty slaves and not knowing what to do with the money, Issetibbeha travels to New Orleans and then to Paris, from which he brings those items of "European finery" that really serve to describe an Indian culture which has lost its roots and its close contact with nature, has become an anachronism, and is on its slow but steady way toward extinction. We also learn how the institution of slavery was established and developed into a regular slave trade of breeding blacks and selling them to the white people, and we learn how much of the European finery in the chief's house was brought there. We get some of this in sweeping and broad summaries, but when the question of slavery is brought up the narrator allows us to listen to the discussion and the final decision which took place some fifty years before the present of the narrative. The conflict, beginning very early in Moketubbe's life, between him and his father over the red-heeled shoes is dramatized and in part rendered as dialogue. We even follow the thoughts and fears of Issetibbeha when he wonders if his son's lust for the slippers may be a threat to his life, but the narrator is careful to limit his omniscience so that at times the text is allowed only to guess (indicated by the use of the word *perhaps*) what the Man may have been thinking.

The background story is fantastic, almost legendary or mythical, but this is the kind of narrative, despite its fantastic elements, that Faulkner referred to as the best of gossip—the old tales and talking. We are allowed to be present at the creation of myths that become history and are used to explain and defend the present situation because they are given narrative form, told, passed on, to become the accepted truth. And since history repeats itself, with rituals being performed as in the old days and with unexpected and mysterious deaths, even the most unlikely story of the past is believable. Something has nevertheless changed, despite all repetition and despite all the traditional customs and rituals, and it has changed for the worse. The disruption of the old ways, of the traditional lifestyles, seems to have come with slavery, but we should keep in mind that the narrative perspective is kept close to the Indians (except for the section when we follow the fugitive slave). We see a world "going to the dogs" (CS, 323), but we see it from the perspective of a couple of Indians whose understanding of the ways of the world, of the black race, and of life in general are transmitted to us by a narrator who refrains from explicit commentary and evaluation yet whose narrative voice leaves little doubt about the absurdity and inhumanity of Indian traditions and institutions. Much of the corruption may be said to result from white influence on the lives of the Indians, but we should also note that parallel to a description which shows Indian decay and corruption a picture emerges of a strong and vital black counterculture. If there is life and energy and vitality anywhere in the world of "Red Leaves," it is in the slave quarters, in the slaves' rituals, their sense of community, their ways of taking care of their young, and in the traditions which they only vaguely remember from the old world.

This part of "Red Leaves"—a "capsule story" about the corruption of a natural life and world[5] testifies more than anything else in the story to the slow but steady decline of traditional and natural life among the Indians, which they, not always too unwillingly, have been subject to. The red-heeled slippers, a symbol established as a kind of leitmotif in the story, carry the symbolic value of power, since they belong to the Man, but they are also deadly as a result of the envy they create. These slippers are totally useless, as are most objects from the civilized world which are now in the steamboat-house. The storyteller in "Red Leaves" takes his time to present these objects and their uselessness, and we would misunderstand the seriousness of the story if we think that this is done just for fun or mockery or if we experience it as a kind of comic interlude before the story turns to the existential conflicts of the hunt and matters of life and death command all our attention and interest. Money, especially if one does not have any use for it, corrupts, and the money with which the slippers and bed and mirror and everything are bought is earned by selling slaves.

We meet Three Basket and Louis Berry where we left them at the end of the first section, and from the slave quarters they are now on their way to Moketubbe, the new Man, who will have to lead the hunt. The problem is that Moketubbe is a "supine obese shape just barely alive," who forces his "big, tender, dropsical feet" into the red slippers (CS, 335). He is a small man but weighs two hundred and fifty pounds. To him even talking is travail, but since tradition requires that he lead the hunt for his father's runaway slave, he has to be carried in a litter. He cannot breathe when he has the red-heeled shoes on, and he does not move or react at all when Three Basket indirectly tells him that he has to lead the hunt by telling how it was when Issetibbeha hunted for three days for the body servant of his father, Doom.

Save for a brief anecdote about Issetibbeha's bed, including a description of how his newest wife, the young one, was unable to sleep in it and preferred a pallet on the floor, this part of the text prepares the hunt, which must begin immediately since the dead chief cannot be buried until his slave is there with him and the waiting dog and horse. In the meantime hundreds of people eat and drink and dance. Waiting for the burial rites, they even have to leave the plantation to fetch more food, which is also as it should be. But the narrative leaves the dead chief and the celebration behind and turns to the hunt, and "Red Leaves" changes from dark and wry comedy seen with an ironic detachment on the part of the reader to a story of pursuit and capture, carried out in accordance with tradition and giving the impression of a ritual that must be allowed to run its course. The ritual's resolution is inevitable and preordained because it follows a basic pattern from which there is no deviation, neither within the hunt nor within narrative representations of it. But a hunt can be seen from different points of view, and "Red Leaves" becomes the great story it is through the ingenuity of its handling of perspective and distance. Still told by an outside narrator in the third person, the narrative nevertheless succeeds completely in keeping the slave's point of view, so that we as readers experience the horror of his situation with him, through him, even from the inside of his mind as he runs for his life, hides from the pursuers, visits his people even though he cannot as a dead person be among the living, and returns to the woods to escape his pursuers, who seem to be relaxed, simply waiting him out, waiting for him to despair, wear himself out, turn himself in. We suffer with the slave in existential anguish and pain, and we understand fully why he does not want to die and even, as he himself comes to realize, why his desire to live is so strong, so deep, so intense. At the end of the section, on the fourth day of the pursuit, the unnamed slave is bitten by a cottonmouth moccasin, and he knows that it will only be a matter of time before he is caught, days before his death. The scene is among the most famous in all of Faulkner's writing, with good reason:

> At sunset, creeping along the creek bank toward where he had spotted a frog, a cottonmouth moccasin slashed him suddenly across the forearm with a thick, sluggish blow. It struck clumsily, leaving two long slashes across his arm like two razor slashes, and half sprawled with his own momentum and rage, it appeared for the moment utterly helpless with its own awkwardness and choleric anger. "Olé, grandfather," the Negro said. He touched its head and watched it slash him again across his arm, and again, with thick, raking, awkward blows. "It's that I do not wish to die," he said. Then he said it again—"It's that I do not wish to die"—in a quiet tone, of slow and low amaze, as though it were something that, until the words had said themselves, he found that he had not known, or had not known the depth and extent of his desire. (CS, 334–35)

The fear of dying seems to be replaced by a desire to live, and the slave's understanding stands in direct opposition to the one expressed by the Indians Berry and Three Basket. And even if the slave knows that he is about to die, he must also know that his race is so strong and vital that it will outlive and outlast all his pursuers. Just before he is bitten by the snake he comes face to face with one of his pursuers, and the confrontation carries symbolic importance. Within the short time span of the hunt the slave is bound to lose; in the longer perspective, however, things look different: "the Negro, gaunt, lean, hard, tireless and desperate; the Indian thick, soft-looking, the apparent embodiment of the ultimate and the supreme reluctance and inertia" (*CS*, 334).

It may be tempting to ask why the slave, given his superior strength and vitality, does not manage to escape. He cannot possibly escape, because he is in a sense already dead. Even his own people consider him dead, and the demands of ritual as well as of myth and genre cannot let him get away. Even if we think in realistic terms, the slave is under a terrible strain and in fact allows the moccasin to strike him. At the time he is bitten he also knows that he has accomplished something, that he has escaped his pursuers for many days, and that he deserves the praise from his captors: "You ran well. Do not be ashamed" (*CS*, 338).

From the point when the moccasin strikes the narration shifts again, and the perspective is now that of the pursuers. Consequently, we see everything at a greater distance. Even if we get close to the slave in the concluding section, the distance of the dramatic perspective is kept until the story reaches its conclusion. In the final section the slave is brought back to the plantation, and even if he wants to eat, and then to drink, he is incapable of both. He does not say much, and although there is nobody to hear him he has something to say, a message, a statement, a final farewell to his people:

> He looked back at the house, then down to the quarters, where today no fire burned, no face showed in any door, no pickaninny in the dust, panting. "It struck me here, raking me across this arm; once, twice, three times. I said, 'Olé, Grandfather.'" (*CS*, 340)

The slave seems to insist that his death is finally not given by the Indians but can be understood and explained "within the confines of his own cultural references, by his own totemic grandfather," as Gene M. Moore puts it.[6] The Indians fail to understand any of his reactions, and they just urge him on so that the decomposing and smelling body of Issetibbeha may finally be buried with horse, dog, and body servant.

Having read the story and reflected on it, we most certainly find that our attitude has changed a number of times and that we have been surprised not so much by descriptions and surface details as by the almost unnoticeable and minute changes that little by little undermine one understanding and substitute another for it. As we read on our understanding must be revised again, or perhaps we carry with us different attitudes and different explanations and understand that we shall perhaps not be able to "decide" or make up our mind about this marvelously complex story. James Ferguson, who thinks "Red Leaves" is probably Faulkner's finest short story, explains its complexity and richness by saying that it is "at the same time detached and engaged, tragic and comic, grim and funny, remotely sardonic and intensely moving" (93). This is a fair evaluation, but there is still a lot more to be said about the text, not least because it so often says one thing and means another.

The significance of the burial ritual to the meaning of the story is obvious. The whole story is centered around it, and it is the most important structural device in the narrative. Its importance is also evidenced by the title of the short story. "Red Leaves" is clearly intended to mean the autumn leaves, *les feuilles mortes,* which as a natural part of the cycle of the seasons must wither and fall. Faulkner himself explained the title thus:

> Well, that was probably symbolism. The red leaves referred to the Indian. It was the deciduation of Nature which no one could stop that had suffocated, smothered, destroyed the Negro. That the red leaves had nothing against him when they suffocated and destroyed him. They had nothing against him, they probably liked him, but it was normal deciduation which the red leaves, whether they regretted it or not, had nothing more to say in.[7]

We have seen that the narrative of the pursuit—the central narrative unit in this long story—is handled so that the focus is divided between the slave's desperate hiding and running and the Indians' pursuit and eventual capture of him. Throughout the story we are offered very different perspectives on what is going on, and we can simplify the narrative complexity thus: One perspective shows us by way of satire, dialogue, and a capsule story what the Indian culture has been and has become through white influence and interference; the other gives an existential discussion of a human being's struggle with his fate and the inevitability of death. Even if it may sound complex, it is a gross oversimplification. The Indians are not only satirized and the slave is not simply a nonconformist to a natural ritual. Furthermore, the question of corruption is not explained only by the introduction of slaves in the Indian society; slavery is only the major symbol of the corruption and degeneracy to which the Indians fall victim. The background story of Doom[8] is in fact proof that the Indians are corrupted in other ways than by the institution of slavery. The bimonthly whisky delivery is another piece of evidence to the same effect.

"Red Leaves" is probably the best example among Faulkner's short stories around 1930 of culture's influence on nature; the story is also about the "vanishing American,"[9] about the declining wilderness, and the emerging of a modern civilization. The story is also "a terrifying existential confrontation with the reality of death,"[10] but this does not reduce the significance of the nature-culture conflict which is at the base of "Red Leaves." The influence of the greedy white man upon the primitive and natural Indian is also shown, but most important is perhaps that three cultures are juxtaposed in this story.

It is tempting to suggest that the institution of slavery with its basis in actual history was another tool Faulkner used to get his story told, and that the story first and foremost is a "compact and inevitable . . . fable of life,"[11] an existential study. In such an argument slavery and the abuses of it would only form a macabre humor and a vicarious comment upon an originally white institution. It may be more to the point, and also a more valid interpretation of the story, to see in it the effects of the white culture on the natural life of the Indians. It is possible, perhaps even probable, that Faulkner in the Indians saw an opportunity to find a "middle" race in his treatment of racial problems in his South; likewise that he in the natural wilderness where the Indians had a stable society saw primitive qualities of more lasting value than the more ephemeral and elusive qualities found in the white village culture. Moreover, Faulkner's Indians are often representative of a race treated unjustly, thus giving him ample opportunity for social criticism.[12] Yet this works in strange ways in "Red Leaves." The corruption of the Indians seems to come from the inside: we see a steady degeneration among its leaders, and we see the upholding of institutions that have become obsolete and meaningless. We see Indians complain about having slaves and still keeping in bondage a people who within the limits of "Red Leaves" are much more vital and carry within them promises of survival and a better life, perhaps in a better organized and more equal and just future society. When critics comment on Faulkner's fictional treatment of the different races they often seem to forget that the Indians are hardly treated more unjustly by white men than black men or other white men are in his fiction. In addition, there is plenty of evidence in Faulkner's Indian stories of the Indians' mistreatment of their own race.[13]

To see the clash of different worlds in "Red Leaves" as a clash between nature and culture, one must draw attention to the fact that the story is rich with symbols, most of which show what the white man has brought to the Indians and how useless and out of place these things are—at least until the Indians adjust to a new and different way of life, to a world where a natural life cannot be led.[14] In the Indians' repetitive and nostalgic remarks about the old days when no blacks forced them to organize work for the slaves, there is little more than a general misunderstanding of what the old days were like and a lazy attitude toward life. The old-time Indian territory is of course pictured as a precapitalistic Eden, but we should not fail to remember that rituals requiring sacrifice were part of that Eden:[15]

> A year later Issetibbeha returned home with a gilt bed, a pair of girandoles by whose light it was said that Pompadour arranged her hair while Louis smirked at his mirrored face across her powdered shoulder, and a pair of slippers with red heels. They were too small for him, since he had not worn shoes until he reached New Orleans on his way abroad. (CS, 320)

Another symbol of Indian degeneracy and corruption is Moketubbe himself, who is "already diseased with flesh, with a pale broad, inert face and dropsical hands and feet" (CS, 321). Moreover, in his inertness and almost mystical behavior Moketubbe's degeneracy is also shown on a moral plane. He has a strange kind of shoe fetish, limited to the red-heeled slippers, and thus implying his yearning for power. The envy, suspicion, and struggle for power within the leading family of the Indian tribe change and become more refined as a result of the chief's knowledge of the world of culture and civilization. The struggle itself and the very desire for power are not products of the modern world—even if power becomes more significant, procuring manufactured goods, whisky, and the luxuries of the white man's world.

How things change over the years in the Indian camp is demonstrated in the emotional speech rendered by an old Indian. The plight and burden of the black slaves on the Indians are central elements in the otherwise rather nostalgic outburst, which also serves to underline the estrangement from nature to which more recent development led:

> "This world is going to the dogs," he said. "It is being ruined by white men. We got along fine for years and years, before the white men foisted their Negroes upon us. In the old days the old men sat in the shade and ate stewed deer's fine flesh and corn and smoked tobacco and talked of honor and grave affairs; now what do we do? Even the old wear themselves into the grave taking care of them that like sweating." (CS, 323)

This description of ancient days in the Indian territories of Yoknapatawpha country, compared to the life they are forced to live now, almost ridicules ancient days and ways of the Indians. It is nonetheless obvious that as the white men have closed in on the Indians, cleared the forests, tilled the soil, and killed the animals that they hunted and depended on for a living, new ways of life have had to take over, and these are not necessarily better ways of living. A life in close contact with nature has been replaced with a life in which the Indians exploit and use other people to make a living, and the great profit they make enables them to buy useless things which further threaten to disrupt and destroy natural life. The "benefits" of civilization have come too quickly; the Indians have not been given time to adjust their own culture to the demands of a new situation, and they have not been adaptable enough to change with the incessant changes of the world around them. Faulkner does not directly portray man in nature and the advantages of natural life, nor does he imply that civilization is an improvement. "Red Leaves" is nevertheless a story about natural life corrupted, and there is little doubt that some of the values and qualities inherent in the old lifestyle of the Indians would have been beneficial to a modern world.

"Red Leaves" effectively demonstrates various oppositions between nature and culture found in many of Faulkner's short stories around 1930, although this opposition is not the author's principal concern. The story gives vivid images of man in nature and of natural man, and in the old Indian's reminiscences of how it once was we get an impression of an easy, leisurely life in accord with nature. In the slave's attempt to escape from his pursuers we see a human being who has never lived close to nature and who is terrified by nature itself and eventually caught by it, almost directly.[16] Numerous black characters in Faulkner's fiction share an irrational fear of nature, believing that some hidden force in nature may strike and hurt. In some ways nature seems to embody all the oppression and fear that they suffer in their daily lives and for which they cannot give the actual explanation or reason, since that would lead to more suffering. But "Red Leaves" also gives strong textual evidence that the black race will endure.

To destroy nature is also to overcome nature, to suppress the unsound and destructive forces in oneself to become more considerate and moderate. This duality of the term "nature" is exploited very carefully and cleverly by Faulkner in a good many stories, and in "Red Leaves" he has excellent material for an investigation of man's nature, morals, and culture since he has presented three different races at various stages in their development, although the white race is marginal to the story proper.

"Red Leaves" indicates that the life and culture of the Indians are associated with natural or cyclic processes of death, decay, and new growth, "the deciduation of Nature," in Faulkner's words. The Indians we meet give the impression that they are not afraid of dying and that death stands in some sort of relation to the life one has led on earth. Yet from Doom's first visit to New Orleans and his—and later, Issetibbeha's—corruption to a degeneration that has definitely continued in Moketubbe, a life in close contact with nature and with the changing seasons has become more and more of a false memory. It is not true for the time of the main narrative in "Red Leaves." The slaves, in their quarters made from brick, bury their drums and keep watch over them, burn their sticks and rely on their fetishes, and seem to form one unified group, even if they are constantly sold away from the plantation. The roots of the black slaves are deep and strong, and Three Basket and Berry, visiting the quarters, feel that the slaves not only "are thinking something" but also "knowing something" (CS, 315): "They were like a single octopus. They were like the roots of a huge tree uncovered, the earth broken momentarily upon the writhen, thick, fetid tangle of its lightless and outraged life" (CS, 315).

When the song and the sorrow become one and the same, when loss and deprivation and pain become text, when the narrative must resort to poetical language to strengthen the emotional forces underlying its desire toward the end, when the poetic and narrative impulses are fused (Ferguson 1991, 36), we have the best possible text by the young and searching writer. Faulkner's outrage, compassion, and profound understanding of what it takes to create a story which is story and poem at the same time makes "Red Leaves" possible. Poetical in its symbolic richness and terrifying in its realistic descriptions, "Red Leaves" will haunt the reader long after he has finished reading it.

# Chapter 12

# A Rose for Emily

## TEXTUAL INFORMATION AND PUBLICATION HISTORY

"A Rose for Emily" is William Faulkner's most famous short story. It appears for the first time on the short story sending schedule for October 7, 1929, and was Faulkner's first story to be accepted and published by a national magazine (*Forum*, April 1930).[1] Slightly revised, the story was included in *These 13* and later in *Collected Stories*. It is Faulkner's most anthologized short story, and it has received far more critical attention than any of the others. Most critics do not rank it among his very best. Yet it is definitely a very cleverly executed story with superb descriptive passages and a surprise ending, and it is easy to see why other critics consider it a masterpiece of short fiction and find it to be among Faulkner's greatest work in the genre.[2] It is possible that the story was conceived and written prior to 1929. In a letter to Horace Liveright in 1927, Faulkner tells his publisher that he is "working now on two things at once: a novel, and a collection of short stories of my townspeople."[3] We do not know that this collection is the same as the one which was called *A Rose for Emily and Other Stories* in the contract for what became *These 13*, yet Joseph Blotner (Blotner 1974, I:692) takes it for granted that it was this collection to which Faulkner referred in February 1927.[4] It is of course entirely possible that Faulkner wrote a number of early drafts for stories and then revised them considerably later on, but I doubt very much that he was working on a collection of stories at this early time, and I am even more doubtful about his having enough stories about his townspeople to make up even a slight volume. We know, however, that he was working on lots of miscellaneous story material on and off between novels, so it is perhaps most probable that the letter really expresses an intention and represents an attempt to inquire as to the publisher's reaction. It is likely that Faulkner tried to figure out if he had enough short story material for a book as early as 1927, since there are early versions of "As I Lay Dying," "'Once aboard the Lugger—,'" and "Idyll in the Desert" with page numbers (after repagination) indicating that they were part of a longer typescript. Yet the three stories mentioned above do not deal with Faulkner's towns-people at all, and we can only speculate that he had other stories for the planned volume, one of which may have been "A Rose for Emily." If Faulkner had any stories about his townspeople, an early version of the story about Emily Grierson would certainly have been one of them, but the story as it was published in 1930 is in all respects a much stronger story than the one told in the earliest versions to which we have access, whether they originate in 1927 or 1929.

"A Rose for Emily" is the first story about Faulkner's townspeople in any real sense, and it is the first story in which a community point-of-view—through a first-person plural narrator, a "we"—is used with easy mastery and without any of the limitations that a first-person, outside narration may entail. The story sold relatively quickly and easily, so Faulkner did not have to rewrite or revise it substantially in 1930, although he may have rewritten it several times before the final version. There are numerous important changes from the extant six-page manu-script fragment to the extant carbon typescript, a complete, seventeen-page version, and the *Forum* text is a further and substantial reworking of the story, basically by deleting too explicit descriptions and too abstract formulations. It is very difficult to know when Faulkner made the changes of the typescript version, most likely by typing the new version. The story went first to *Scribner's* and was rejected and then to *Forum*, which bought it on January 20, 1930, if we are to trust a handwritten note on the carbon typescript. This may be taken as an indication that the typescript was the one he sent to *Forum* and that revisions took place later. Yet the note on the carbon typescript may simply be a record of a sale, not necessarily of the story in the exact form it has in the typescript. Without any evidence, it still seems most likely that Faulkner took out material and condensed the story after it had been rejected and before he sent it out again (see also Skei 1981, 14, and Jones 1994, 88).

Michael Millgate (1966) deals very competently with the changes from manuscript to typescript to published text, and he uses them to show Faulkner's growth as an artist (262–64).[5] In manuscript as well as typescript there is a long conversation between Emily and her servant Tobe, who is the beneficiary of her will but who has arranged to go to the "poorhouse." Faulkner expanded this conversation, which takes place shortly before Emily's death, in the typescript, and the dialogue makes it absolutely certain that Tobe knows what is in the upstairs room and has known for a long time. They also discuss how the town will react when Emily's secret is revealed.

It is worth noting that Faulkner expanded this scene from manuscript to typescript, even if this was a practice he usually followed, only to remove it completely at a later stage. The changes from extant typescript to published text (obviously based on a new typescript, now lost) are extensive and substantial. The simple fact that sectional divisions are included in the published text but not in the typescript is indicative of a final stage of composition, not only revision in the ordinary sense.[6] It is an obvious guess that Faulkner deleted so much material in order to keep the story's secret until the very end, since to reveal Tobe's knowledge would have "diluted the final episodes" (Millgate 1966, 264). This must be the main reason why Faulkner left out a central scene in the typescript version of the story, but one may also guess that such a scene represented another and perhaps more serious violation of the first-person narration than other such episodes in the story, involving an omniscience that does not normally fit in with the limitations of this perspective.

There is no doubt that the revisions of "A Rose for Emily," like those in "Dry September" with the transposition of its opening sections, are evidence of Faulkner's growing craftsmanship and sophistication as a writer of short stories.[7] The withholding of crucial information in "A Rose for Emily" is done almost inadvertently, and the text seems to be filled with detailed description of the new times and the destruction of the old ways, as if to put off the gruesome facts for as long as possible. The narrator seems to share so many of Emily's attitudinal responses to the modern world that we accept that the narrator is not always forthcoming. As the final text came to stand, "showing" prevailed over "telling" in the key episodes of the long time span covered in the story, and the story makes its points and reaches its conclusion through a direct narrative with numerous ambiguities and ironies implied in its very telling. It is vitally important for a character like Emily to retain her enigmatic status as long as possible in a text purporting to tell the innermost secrets of a wasted life, and if critical response to Emily's character is proof of anything, she certainly became an enigmatic, elusive character, as well as a symbol of many things.

## READING "A ROSE FOR EMILY"

"A Rose for Emily"[8] is a gothic tale in the sense that it creates a doom-laden atmosphere in which an old spinster who is totally shut out from the teeming outside world lives in a decaying mansion with one of the floors closed. Emily apparently refuses to accept the passing of time or change in any sense. But, unlike in most gothic fiction, the chief protagonist and her house are very much in and of this world, although she has felt compelled to end all association with her fellow townspeople. Faulkner has been said to write about events that were expected to happen but never actually took place, and it has been maintained that he based his story on an actual couple.[9] In answer to a question whether the story came from his imagination, Faulkner said that it did but maintained that "the fact that young girls dream of someone to love" exists a priori.[10]

Because there are a number of situations over a period of years described in "A Rose for Emily," and because Emily reacts to these in different ways, we shall have to follow the story fairly closely to watch events unfold, not only because of Emily's refusal to adjust and change but because of the incredible changes in the world around her which simply leave her behind as an anachronism. Most crucial confrontations in the story have their basis in Emily's feeling of being different and better than the ordinary men and women of Jefferson, but her actual reactions must be described in terms of the motivation in individual and social psychology that the text implies. Also, Emily easily becomes a symbol, emblematic of a lost cause, of good old days, of a time when women knew their place and had few if any outlets for their frustration and anger.

We shall return to the many possible interpretations of "A Rose for Emily" after having followed the text of the story, but there is little reason to enter into long discussions of Emily as character or as a result of a certain rhetorical and narrative strategy (in which case she comes to signify much more than an old spinster in a decaying mansion). Trying to stay close to the text and explain this narrative of Emily's life will have to do. More specialized approaches, concentrating on one aspect of the text or one character trait in Emily, from many and different theoretical bases, abound in Faulkner criticism, although it is probably fair to say that we do not need more—general or specialized—interpretations of this story unless they build on what has already been written.[11] In this volume I find it sufficient to give an introduction to the story before reading it by paying close attention to the text of "A Rose for Emily" more than to the many possible contexts in which each and every turn of the story may be placed. Having read the story, my textual comments and contextualization are restricted to: 1. the narration of the story and the very special use of a first-person plural narrator and perspective on the events; 2. the oppression and deprivation seen in Emily's situation (and shared by many female characters in Faulkner's short fiction); and 3. Emily's resistance to change and the importance of time and change in the story. All these elements will obviously also be integrated parts of the reading of the text, since there is no such thing as an "objective" or "innocent" reading of any text and certainly not of "A Rose for Emily" and since the formal aspects of the story, including the handling of the narrative, cannot be overlooked as the reader follows the text from beginning to end.

"A Rose for Emily" is located in Jefferson and is thus one of many Faulkner stories from "The Village." The story is told by an anonymous, first-person narrator in the plural ("we") who seems also to be a marginal character in the story and who seems to be very cautious, willing to postpone judgment and wait for new events to happen, although now and then using language which discloses his attitudes and value system. The narrator's position undergoes subtle changes from section to section, and even though Faulkner may have felt the need to have him present at the climactic opening of the upstairs room near the story's ending, he also lets him have access to information which does not come from having watched, eavesdropped and listened to secrets and which simply do not fit in with the implied restrictions of the first-person perspective. The corporate narrator is clearly an individual and a male, but he identifies with a group or with the townspeople in general. Anyhow, it is vitally important to remember that in "A Rose for Emily" the distinction between the narrator's role as narrator and as character is important and that it likewise is useful to distinguish between narrative perspective and narrative voice and not use the less precise and less productive concept of point of view. We shall return to these and related questions later on.

"A Rose for Emily" is clearly told from a community point of view, so that the narrative voice in the story is the voice of "our town" and "we," a group which is contrasted with "they" in some of the story's parts. The narrator seems to adopt the thoughts and attitudes of his townspeople regarding the old lady in the decaying mansion, and we get a sympathetic portrait, so that we as readers feel sorry for Emily. Yet there are many ironies in this position, since time changes, and what the town "thinks" changes too, more so than the views and opinions of the narrator and the group to which he belongs, or so it seems. This inevitably implies some of the limitations of the first-person narrative, and this again makes it extremely difficult to account for the intimate knowledge and the inside information which the "we" narrator has.

When Miss Emily Grierson died, "our whole town" went to her funeral. During the long years of isolation and what one might think would be oblivion, the town has remembered Miss Emily. She has become a "tradition, a duty and a care" (CS, 119). These types of responsibility may indicate the attitudes to Miss Emily of three consecutive generations in Jefferson.[12] The reason for telling the story is the fact that Miss Emily has died; this is the first information that is given in the story, and it is the starting point for a story to which episodes and incidents are added as they, by way of association, implication, or closeness to the narrator, come to his mind.[13] All this is of course an illusion, but it is an extremely carefully and skillfully arranged illusion. The seeming casualness with which the story is told should not be allowed to deceive us into believing that this is a straightforward reminiscence about a lady who has just passed away.

On the contrary, after the initial paragraph announcing her death we get a panoramic description of the area in which Miss Emily's house stands, "lifting its stubborn and coquettish decay above the cotton wagons and the gasoline pumps" (CS, 119), and the rich and extended scenic description reflects the position Emily herself has in the modernized town. She has also become "a sort of hereditary obligation upon the town" (CS, 119), a reminder of a past that for other reasons also lives on in Jefferson and of which the reader is reminded by a reference to the cemetery and the soldiers who fell at the battle of Jefferson. As we read on the story turns from the present of Emily's death to the time when her taxes were remitted "into perpetuity" (CS, 120), and then moves forward chronologically to the new mayors and aldermen in modern times who try to collect taxes even from Miss Emily and thus overthrow another of Colonel Sartoris's ideas from what to them must appear to be ancient days. Emily refuses to pay, but the narrator cleverly sets up a dramatic situation which makes it natural to invite the reader into Emily's house with the deputation from the board of aldermen. The interior of the house may well be modeled on gothic tales, but it seems most of all to be dark, worn, unchanged, decaying, and shut off from the sun and from life outside. No visitors have been there since Emily stopped giving china-painting lessons ten years before, and we get the impression that it is unlikely that anyone else will be admitted. The worn furniture and the "close dank smell" (CS, 120) protect her from a world of change, apparently a threatening world to her, but she has of course also walled herself off from other people and from being alive in a real sense by closing her front door for good.

The description of Emily herself, the first one from close up and the most memorable passage in the whole text, is more ghoulish than anything else. The narrator, who seems to have expressed a kind of sympathetic understanding of the stubborn resistance to modern ideas and a positive attitude to the old value system Emily represents, seems to wipe out all such notions in the portrait of "the small, fat woman in black" (CS, 121):

> Her skeleton was small and spare; perhaps that was why what would have been merely plumpness in another was obesity in her. She looked bloated, like a body long submerged in motionless water, and of that pallid hue. Her eyes, lost in the fatty ridges of

her face, looked like two small pieces of coal pressed into a lump of dough. . . . (CS, 121)

The reader cannot but react to this passage with wonder and unease: Why the comparison to "a body submerged in motionless water"? Is this simply another way of describing her long and lonely years in the decaying house? And why has she shut herself off from the rest of the town? Why has she become a tradition and a care? We expect to get more of the background story, and when the narrator has told about the tax deputation, he moves straight on in the second section to describe how another deputation had been "vanquished" thirty years earlier. And we read on, in this most familiar of all Faulkner texts, about the smell, which had started two years after her father's death and shortly after her sweetheart—the one and only—had left. Men of a different and older generation did not accuse Miss Emily of the smell, but simply crept across her lawn and sprinkled the house and the cellar, which they broke open, and so the smell went away. From this episode the narrative moves backwards two years to her father's death, when she finally released her father's body just before they had to "resort to law and force" (CS, 124). The story events are important as scenes from a life deprived of so much as to be finally, totally, and completely alone save for her servant, but the town's reactions, as narrated by the plural narrator, are as significant in our reading of the text. We only hear a few words about a sweetheart and may even be a little surprised by the choice of designation for the young man who deserted her, and then we are told that he probably left because her father had driven all suitors away, because they were not good enough for "Miss Emily and such" (CS, 123). We also learn that people start feeling sorry for her because of her father's behavior but also because of "insanity in the family" (CS, 123). The reader is thus prepared and should not be surprised whatever happens next. We already know that Emily's loss of her father almost drove her crazy, and we may wonder what happened when the "sweetheart" deserted her later on, when she did not have a father or anyone else to cling to. The narrator is generous in his understanding and sympathy on behalf of the town, accepting that Emily's behavior is inevitable and excusable.

In the third and fourth sections the story of Miss Emily and her boyfriend, Homer Barron (a Yankee, a day laborer, the foreman of a construction company paving the sidewalks), is told, mostly as gossip, in small glimpses of what people said and thought, how they spied on them when they drove in a yellow-wheeled buggy on Sunday afternoons, how they whispered, felt sorry for her, and then decided to give notice to her relatives because a Grierson could not, after all, fall as low as this. In between all the gossip some real and serious information is given: the narrator re-creates the scene in the druggist's shop when Emily buys rat poison, at a time when two female cousins were visiting her. The narrator and the rest of the town "sat back to watch developments" (CS, 127), a detachment that is really hard to believe given the active interest in every detail of Emily's affair with Homer Barron. But waiting apparently pays off: "we" learn that she buys a man's toilet set in silver, with the monogram H.B., and think that they will be married. The townspeople have become Miss Emily's allies against her cousins, and they think that Homer will return or simply has left to wait for Miss Emily when he disappears. He returns at dusk one evening after the cousins have left: "And that was the last we saw of Homer Barron" (CS, 127). The narrator has already established a connection between Homer's disappearance and the smell and repeats this by referring to the sprinkling of lime. And then the text recapitulates what it has told so far in a more-or-less chronological narrative about Emily's life from the moment Homer disappeared until her death at the age of seventy-four.

So we are back where the story started, and in the fifth and last section we see Tobe admit ladies at the front door and disappear. We hear about the funeral on the second day, with the town coming to look at Miss Emily, and the narrator gives extensive attention to the very old men of Miss Emily's generation who come to her funeral:

—some in their brushed Confederate uniforms—on the porch and the lawn, talking of Miss Emily as if she had been a contemporary of theirs, believing that they had danced with her and courted her perhaps, confusing time with its mathematical progression, as the old do, to whom all the past is not a diminishing road but, instead, a huge meadow which no winter ever quite touches, divided from them now by the narrow bottle-neck of the most recent decade of years. (CS, 129)

This may seem unimportant compared to the discovery of the fleshless grin of Homer Barron in the bed in the closed-off, tomblike room upstairs, and the even more macabre discovery of "a long strand of iron-gray hair" (CS, 130) on the second pillow in the bed. But only in a certain way of responding to the text. The ending is of the surprise type, yet it does not at all come as a surprise with the exception perhaps of the extra turn of the screw of horror—the implication that Emily has slept beside her dead lover for some forty years. The text has prepared its reader for the discovery by numerous repetitive suggestions and hints and by creating a character and conditions for it to develop its worst sides. And so we have no more questions on the story level of the narrative; we know what has happened, and the narrator, despite his propensity for gossip and his curiosity and voyeuristic tendencies, seems to have given us sufficient material to analyze and perhaps even understand why Emily acted the way she did. But this leaves the question of what the story signifies beyond the not-so-simple but still intelligible events of the story as such. And here another question becomes important as well—the question of time—a huge meadow which no winter ever quite touches because Emily apparently also has refused to accept time and change, loss and deprivation, by creating her own temporal and spatial enclosure, by arresting time and making it stand still within her decaying house, unwilling to take notice of change.

A rose for Miss Emily? A tribute to her, who kills not to be deserted, who clings to those who rob her of that which she has not, who shuts herself off from the world with a dead lover and lets the mad, mad world go by outside? Why not? Emily is a victim because she belongs to another time and a different world than that which emerges in her lifetime, and she flatly refuses to give up her internalized ideals and ideas because she has been given nothing in exchange for them. The reader cannot and will not condone Emily's behavior, but at the same as she is depicted as a product of a certain era and place she is also a victim of that era and place, of ideas and attitudes and behavior of a bygone age which should have been buried with the veterans in the cemetery in Jefferson but which still is a part of the present, although a dead part of a changing world.

Having followed the text of "A Rose for Emily," asking some interpretive questions, let us return to the narrator's role in the story. There are too many changes in personal pronouns throughout the story to accept "the town," "our whole town," or a representative spokesman for the town as the narrator of the story. There is reason to believe that the question of narration—or even of narrative distance or point of view—is too complicated to be explained fully without a lengthy discussion of the limits of narratology, but it is necessary to stress that the voice of the community in "A Rose for Emily" only applies to portions of the story. Since our total understanding and appreciation of the story largely depend upon the thematic subtleties which a close study of the narrator's role may yield, the structure of the narrative must be discussed at some length. Apparently much of Emily's character lies in the eye of the beholders, and it is accordingly worthwhile to see who they are within the short story itself.

"A Rose for Emily" is, as we have seen, divided into five parts: the first four of which differ little in length, while the fifth part is shorter. The basic elements of the story are told in fragments, a little at a time, with a confusing sequence of elements typical of much of Faulkner's writing of this period. The chronology is, after all, not too confusing, if we do not insist on pinning every event down to an exact date, as some critics have done with extraordinary results.[14]

The intriguing shifting of pronouns in "A Rose for Emily" raises many questions, and there is some reason to venture the guess that Faulkner did not care too much about accuracy or exactitude here. This assumption offers no solutions to the narrative problems, and the very fact that Faulkner carefully revised the story, omitting some material from the final parts of it, indicates a great degree of control of the narrative. Nevertheless, there seem to be clear distinctions between the "we" of parts 2, 3, and 5 and the "they" (various ones in part 2) of the story, while the "we" in part 5 is the introductory "we" implied in the term "our whole town." What "they" do in part 3 is later done by "we" in part 4 (that is, saying "Poor Emily" behind the curtains, spying on her). If for a moment we test the validity of the first-person ("we") narrator, he has much of his information from general gossip around the town and some firsthand observation. But he must be exceptionally well-informed to know what a special meeting of the board of aldermen discusses or to describe the paper and handwriting of Miss Emily's letter to the mayor. Furthermore, we are allowed to see Miss Emily open the bottle of poison at her home and read the label on it. This may of course only be dramatic presentation, but the question remains: How does the "we" know this? The point of view is rather limited, and the narrator must have access to what appears to be relatively secret information. Does he (the single mind behind the "we") know this through the druggist who sold the poison and speculate on what it was like when Emily arrived home? Are we forced to resort to the explanation that an omniscient narrator is at work in certain specific cases, while the verisimilitude or factuality is maintained when, for example, the Baptist minister's experience with Miss Emily is never divulged? Or should we assume that the spokesman behind the "we" is a close friend of the druggist? This may sound far-fetched, but is not altogether impossible. Then the same spokesman would have to be closely related to the presumably young man on the board of aldermen, and he must be one of the smaller group of "we" in parts 2, 3, and 5, with an intimate knowledge of Miss Emily (having been suitor?); and he must belong to her generation and share many of the then dominant attitudes about the protection of ladies and aristocratic codes of behavior. This explanation may find some support in the fact that the same "we" presents Emily and her father, and it is this "we" who best understands Emily's refusal to let her father be buried:

> We had long thought of them as a tableau, Miss Emily a slender figure in white in the background, her father a spraddled silhouette in

the foreground, his back to her and clutching a horsewhip, the two of them framed by the back-flung front door. So when she got to be thirty and was still single, we were not pleased, exactly, but vindicated; even with insanity in the family she wouldn't have turned down all of her chances if they had really materialized. (*CS*, 123)

And further:

We did not say she was crazy then. We believed she had to do that. We remembered all the young men her father had driven away, and we knew that with nothing left, she would have to cling to that which had robbed her, as people will. (*CS*, 124)

Here it looks as if the "we" is at a distance to the young men Emily's father had driven away, but this knowledge and understanding of Emily and her father is so intimate that it may just be a narrative stance. The paragraph does not leave much doubt about his being a representative of the average opinion of the townspeople, yet the "we" figure knows more than "they" do:

Already *we* knew that there was one room in that region above stairs which no one had seen in forty years, and which would have to be forced. *They* waited until Miss Emily was decently in the ground before they opened it. (*CS*, 129; my emphasis)

The many ambiguities and the added mystery resulting from this bewildering use of personal pronouns in "A Rose for Emily" are in the text we study, and accordingly we have to come as close to an understanding of their effects as possible. But far as we may stretch an interpretation based on a limited "we" sharing Miss Emily's gruesome secrets, the main impression of the story lies in its central character itself, as our interpretation has attempted to show.

If we bring in the "anonymous voice" which so many critics have found in Faulkner's fiction, this voice is heard clearly in many of the village stories. This voice may, indeed, be "the author seeing himself distanced as one more perspective on the scene, one more legitimate but not conclusive point of view," to use Olga Vickery's apt description of this narrative device (Vickery 1964, 299). In Faulkner, Vickery says, "authorial exclusion is replaced by authorial transcendence." Faulkner had plans for a book about his "townspeople" as early as 1927, and in "A Rose for Emily" and many other village stories he appears to be watching these people in some crucial moments of their lives, arresting their motion for a moment to create a tableau and show them in all their struggle and despair, without comments but with a pervasive voice which ultimately distributes sympathy and antipathy and conspires with the reader in creating the artifice which he chooses to construct.

Miss Emily shares a number of characteristics with other female characters in Faulkner's short fiction. Elly in the short story bearing her name is protected and refuses to be so. She is deprived of what she feels are her obvious rights and revenges herself on her parental authorities by becoming sexually active and choosing her own partners. Her older sister in Faulkner's short fiction, Miss Emily Grierson, is also overprotected and strongly controlled. As is the case with Zilphia Gant and Miss Minnie Cooper, Emily's suitors are kept away, and all three women miss what ordinary girls have. Emily's father's hold on her (or, rather, her father-binding) is so strong that this may account for her problems with men after his death.[15]

Emily belongs to a generation whose beliefs and codes of conduct she lives by. Living in an old and once fashionable house on what had been the most select street in the town, Emily is brought up to believe in the dominant attitudes about chivalry, protection of ladies, and "aristocratic" codes of behavior. Her father leaves no doubt about her place in relation to him, nor about the obedience he expects from her, and he also seems to have induced in her a feeling of responsibility to her position and status. Emily feels she is better than most other people and can hence explain and justify her own strange acts by reference to her exclusiveness. Emily has always been an aristocrat and has been overprotected by her father with the horsewhip; moreover, by being a Southern lady to whom at least the first couple of generations respond with reverence and awe, she has become used to being different. Emily thus simply acts out her alleged position, and her sexual and social roles make it easy for her to find defense mechanisms to explain and justify her deeds.

In "Elly" Faulkner presents a young girl in an ordinary white family in Jefferson who feels suffocated because of the limitations of her social position and the fact that she is a woman. She reacts violently while she is still young, and, since the result is fatal, her story is much simpler than Emily's. Emily reacts to a series of crises throughout her life, and we shall have to look at her reactions in more general terms than we have to do in Elly's case. Miss Emily is characterized by different generations' reactions to her as well as by her own reactions to a series of crises: the death of her father, the tax exemption, and the affair with Homer Barron and his disappearance.

When her father dies Emily denies that he is dead, and the "we" of the story explains this as normal, or at least, expected behavior. Emily only does "as people will," but she has become compulsively possessive and is clearly a case of abnormal psychology. Her father ran her suitors off; now that he is dead he is still the only one she has to cling to. The loss she suffers when she finally has to give in to social pressure and let her father be buried is therefore important. It is, in point of fact, the only time she gives in to public opinion, the only time she acts out of character. When she later fears that Homer Barron, her Northern "beau," is about to leave her, she poisons him, hides the corpse in a sealed room in her house, and thus gains possession of her lover forever. With the exception of her father's death, Emily carries her head high in all situations. She treats everybody with overbearing, does not yield an inch to any modern demands about taxation or the like, and keeps her pride and strong will as a kind of bulwark against an unbearable, hostile outer world where, little by little, new generations with modern ideas take over the leadership. Emily may be a monument in the small town, but she is a fallen monument, and in the daily life of the community she is nothing but a living dead person—even though the narrator may have some strange reason for perpetuating the memory of her long after general interest has shifted from her and the lifestyle to which she adheres to the building of a better world outside and around the anachronistic and aristocratic lady in her decaying mansion.[16]

The contrast between the town and Miss Emily is an important one. Emily has always insisted on doing things her own way; she never accepts or concedes to behavior considered normal by the townspeople. Perhaps the town grudgingly accepts and even admires Emily because of her ability to be herself—they do not learn of her horrible murder until after she is dead. The monumental old lady passes respectfully and respected into the town's history. She

> had gone to join the representative of those august names where they lay in the cedar-bemused cemetery among the ranked and anonymous graves of Union and Confederate soldiers who fell at the battle of Jefferson. (CS, 119)

The inference that Emily has been brought back to the age she always lived in—some fifty or sixty years back—can be made. Emily is an anachronism, as she is the only survivor of an old order, or at least the only one of those with a clear memory of past glory who has refused to adjust to the changing world around her.

Emily does "what people will"—she clings to the few certain things there are in her life, and she refuses to accept change or to change herself. With madness in the family, her murder by poison and concealment of the corpse are explicable acts, despite their horror. Her tragedy is not motivated only in her protected and sheltered upbringing or in an oedipal bonding to her strong father. Her solution is to destroy in order not to be betrayed, to conceal not to be discovered, to withdraw to be let alone with her memories and problems.[17] Her "solution" is not a workable one; isolation and withdrawal may help her survive, but she is nevertheless among the living dead.

Emily's solutions to the problems of adjustment and change can be described in sociological and psychological terms: she is able to keep her untenable position only by seclusion from the ordinary world, and she has to resort to introversion and a number of defense mechanisms to survive when social pressure threatens to destroy her position. Emily is capable of doing so because she has a reality of her own.[18] Emily's feeling of loss and deprivation and her fear of change—change that may take away what little she has left—account for some of her reactions. In her case psychology and madness may be needed to explain her reactions, and she is thus different from the other female characters we have discussed above. To a certain extent, however, Emily is also acting out what she has reason to believe is her alleged role as a woman, no matter how misunderstood it is.[19]

The gothic tale about Miss Emily is also a tribute to the old and stubborn lady in her decaying mansion. It presents an isolated individual against the community, delineating some of the possible explanations for the isolation, and this story may also be seen as, in the author's words, another instance of "man in conflict with his heart, or with his fellows, or with his environment."[20]

# Chapter 13

# Spotted Horses

## TEXTUAL INFORMATION AND PUBLICATION HISTORY

"Spotted Horses" was published in *Scribner's Magazine* in June 1931. Revised and expanded and in many ways completely changed to serve new functions, the story was incorporated in *The Hamlet* (book 4, "The Peasants"). Malcolm Cowley created a new, long short story version of this material for *The Viking Portable Faulkner*, a version which has often been anthologized. "Spotted Horses" was not included in *Collected Stories*, which is in keeping with Faulkner's not quite consistent practice, and was accordingly not available in its short story form until the publication of *Uncollected Stories* in 1979. In its superb blend of comic and tragic elements, "Spotted Horses" is one of the funniest short stories Faulkner ever wrote, but it still includes elements of basic human misery and reckless inhumanity. The short story version of the narrative about the Texas ponies sold in Frenchman's Bend is inferior to the part of *The Hamlet* using the same material, but I still find the short story to be worthy of being included among Faulkner's twelve best short stories. I find no valid critical reason for using the Cowley text in my study.

The textual problems related to the prepublication versions of "Spotted Horses" are among the most complex in all of Faulkner's short story career, even if we keep the manuscript and typescript for *The Hamlet* out of our discussion, which will be kept at a minimum, anyhow.[1] The earliest extant version of the "Spotted Horses" material after *Father Abraham* (and related versions of this) is likely to be the typescript entitled "As I Lay Dying" and paginated 204–221.[2] This version has no outside narrator and is simply rendered as dialogue, without quotation marks and without identifying the speakers. This dramatic method allows for the use of numerous country voices but also requires that the story of the horse auction be told in retrospect. "As I Lay Dying" thus deals with the aftermath of the auction, with special emphasis on the confrontation between Mrs. Armstid and Flem Snopes but leaving the Vernon Tull incidents out.[3]

The next version of "As I Lay Dying" is a complete, twenty-two-page typescript paginated 1–14, 14B, 15–21, which introduces "I" and "my uncle," who is a Jefferson judge, on their way to the store to enquire into what Tull wants to sue Flem for. The narrator is this young nephew of the judge, and he is a character very much like Charles Mallison, who would play a significant role in later novels and in the Snopes saga. The story of the sale of the spotted horses is again told in retrospect, and undue emphasis is placed on the outcome of the auction, at least if compared with the intensity, color, excitement, and humor of the published short story and of this episode in book 4 of the novel.

Faulkner sent a story entitled "The Peasants" to *Scribner's* on August 25, 1930, more than a year after "As I Lay Dying" had been rejected. In a December 30 letter to the editor of the magazine, Kyle Chrichton, we learn that Chrichton has thought back on this piece but wants it cut down considerably. If we rely on the short story sending schedule, then "Aria Con Amore" should be the revised version of "The Peasants," although the one extant version of "Aria Con Amore" that we know is very far from the published story. Telling the story of the horse auction and its aftermath, the fifty-nine-page carbon typescript of "The Peasants" (numbered 1–16, 16–58) really has more of the material in the final version than "Aria Con Amore" has, although the narrative handling of the latter is closer to the one chosen for the final and published story, since "The Peasants" is told in the third person by an outside narrator. For "The Peasants" we also have an eight-page manuscript fragment and an additional page 16 of a different typescript.

In "Aria Con Amore" Suratt (later Ratliff, of course) has become the narrator, and we also know that this was the title under which Faulkner submitted the story to *Scribner's Magazine,* which makes it more than likely that this is the latest prepublication version. The published version is indeed very different from this one, and since the magazine accepted the story but wanted a new title, there must have been a completely different version with this title, used as setting copy for the magazine printing. No such version has appeared, however.

"Aria Con Amore," narrated by Suratt in the first person, is his version of the spotted horses sale, told in retrospect but basically consisting of what he told to the men sitting on the porch of the store—Mitchell and Bundren and Eck and I.O.—including questions and comments from the listeners, most of them from I.O. Mrs. Armstid's tragic situation is central in this version, even to the point where her attempt to get her money back from Flem makes up the first paragraph of the text. Because of the differences between this typescript and the published magazine story, one must presume that the extant typescript is an early version of the one that went to the *Post* and to *Scribner's* (Skei 1981, 47).

The final solution to the problems of narrative form, and to the question of which story elements to include in "Spotted Horses," should no doubt be seen as an important step in Faulkner's development toward *The Hamlet*. We are still in the early months of 1931, and Faulkner's final success with this central episode in his first attempt at writing about the Snopeses most certainly is part of the reason why he tried to turn so much of the early Snopes ideas into short stories, apparently without attempting to make a more sustained effort at the novel. But he knew, or would soon learn, that short story material rooted in the same idea, theme, narrative strategy, or even time and place alone could later be revised and help structure longer works, novels, from which short story writing kept him away, a fact he often complained about. In a very productive period which produced numerous short stories and a series of great novels, Faulkner also returned repeatedly to this single episode from the Snopes material, writing so many pages of manuscript and typescript that the total page count is equivalent to that of a complete, fairly long novel.[4]

## READING "SPOTTED HORSES"

In "Spotted Horses" Faulkner finally returned to the structure applied in *Father Abraham,* but reduced the introductory material to the minimum necessary to introduce Frenchman's Bend and the Snopeses to an outside audience, presumably a town audience in Jefferson. This background material may be said to delay the story proper, perhaps even to the extent that the drama of the immediate situation, which is the reason for the narrative, is diluted. The need to give such background information about the rise of Flem Snopes in Frenchman's Bend is obvious, yet it functions much more convincingly and adds power to the story about the horse auction in the broader context of *The Hamlet*. Nevertheless, the oral storytelling situation also allows for these introductory or digressive elements; they are accepted as parts of the rhetorical setup of a good yarn, and intimate familiarity with people and customs is a prerequisite for the good storyteller. The story is recounted to people who cannot be assumed to know anything about Flem's arrival in Frenchman's Bend nor the later development there. But we should also notice that Faulkner was very much aware of the problems with the background story and that he deliberately changed some of the mythology he had used in *Father Abraham* and would reinstate in *The Hamlet*.[5]

The narrative situation with the storyteller and his audience allows Faulkner to tell an oral tale and to use all the tricks of a natural-born storyteller in order to keep his audience's attention, create suspense, and evoke laughter. Suratt's storytelling is performance on a very high level, and he knows very well that he only has a story to tell as long as he has listeners who urge him to go on. The narrative situation is in a sense doubled in this tale: Suratt tells the story to a captive audience, and the story he tells is basically how and what he told (including responses from central characters on the porch of Varner's store) at an earlier point in Frenchman's Bend. In "Spotted Horses" Faulkner thus finally succeeds in creating distance to his story, yet also keeping the familiar and intimate relation of the story to those involved in it, that is, those suffering from the events recounted in the story. This also explains how hilariously comic elements can blend with the account of misery and human tragedy so perfectly that the one never dominates the other.

There seem to be two serious problems involved in the narration of this hyperbolic tale. The one already noted is the need to incorporate a fairly detailed background story, and Faulkner does this with moderate success in the magazine version, at least if compared with the novel. The other problem is that our attention seems to be very deliberately directed toward the narration of the story, the narrative process itself, so as to detract from the story and its thematic implications. Suratt's reason for telling this story, in which he is both narrator and character, may not be existential in any profound sense, but there is little doubt that the story is skillfully arranged in order to give structure to the experience, add narrative form to an episode involving many people. But by giving narrative form to his experience, by memorizing and telling about the horse auction episode, Suratt almost inadvertently repeats a former event and a former story by telling it again for the first time. There are numerous indications in the text that Suratt understands more of his story now than before but keeps wondering about its implications, so that the text implicitly invites the reader to fill its gaps and lacunae and to help in the creation of a textual meaning that goes beyond the surface meaning of a text about "puerile folly" and the lure of the gaudy horses. It is possible that "what is told is virtually submerged in the telling" (Ferguson 1991, 116), but the significance of the telling, with its ordering of events in a recognizable pattern to make it understandable, should not be underestimated. When we are invited at the very moment when legends or myths are created to witness, so to speak, the creation of the record of Yoknapatawpha County, we should listen to the tale as it unfolds, because it is only in the telling of the events that they make sense, gain importance, signify.

"Spotted Horses" is straightforward oral storytelling by a first-person narrator who addresses his audience now and then, invites them into his tale, suggests that they know people he mentions, and quickly establishes the immediate reason for telling the story of the spotted horses: One of them "flew right over my team, big as a billboard and flying through the air like a hawk" (*US,* 165), the very morning of the day he is telling the story, on his way to where he has sat down to spin his yarn. And even though the story is told after the events, in retrospect, it is told very shortly after the auction, while the runaway Texas ponies are still being chased all over the countryside.[6]

The anonymous storyteller is easily identifiable as Suratt, the sewing-machine agent, and in this text everything comes from his mouth, from his perspective, in his voice, even when he quotes direct speech by other characters. The first paragraph makes clear that the narrator is also a character in his own story, not the central one, but he has been present and participated in the events he is about to recount. Moreover, the background story that he uses to frame the story of the horse auction is proof enough to listeners and readers alike that he knows the area, its people, its secrets. When, in the course of his storytelling, he refers to a trip he made up to Bundren's and back, he gives added motivation for his seemingly unlimited knowledge about everyone and everything in the region.

The opening words of the story set the tone of the narrative which is to follow; it defines the speech act to be used and establishes as truth something which the story as a whole will confirm but for which there is never any proof: "Yes, sir. Flem Snopes filled that whole country full of spotted horses." As readers we have no reason to doubt this opening statement, and the narrator brings in evidence by referring to "folks running them all day and all night" (*US,* 165) and, then, of course, also by his own experience with one of them on his way to where he now is.

Flem Snopes is responsible for bringing the horses into the county, and so it is only reasonable that we get to know this person. The narrator appears to shake his head when he says, "That Flem Snopes. I be dog if he ain't a case, now" (*US,* 165), which is in preparation for a detailed, condensed, informative, and ironic tale about the Snopes clan and how Flem one day came from behind the desk in Varner's store as if he had always been there:

And he wasn't there but a year or two before folks knowed that, if him and Jody was both still in that store in ten years more, it would be Jody clerking for Flem Snopes. Why, that fellow could make a nickel where it wasn't but four cents to begin with. He skun me in two trades, myself, and the fellow that can do that, I just hope he'll get rich before I do; that's all. (*US,* 166)

Trade and barter, money and profit are thus clearly central themes in the tale to which we are listening. The reader is in no doubt that Flem must have brought the horses to the area in order to make money, but the narrator has more information about Flem before he is willing to go on with the story about the horses. He tells about Eula and her young suitors and all the yellow-wheeled buggies along Varner's fence, as well as about the young men leaving for Texas and Flem and Eula being married before going to Texas, too. This part of the story is told rapidly, with humor and a generous acceptance of the ways of the world, light-years away from the melancholic and desperate narration of Eula virtually being sold that we find in *The Hamlet*. The dialect also contributes to making this a tale of everyday life, of something out of the ordinary yet understandable. This is further accentuated through the imagery the narrator employs, which seems fitting and proper in a story told to an audience of country people in an agricultural area. The young men are described as "young bucks setting on the porch, swarming around Eula like bees around a honey pot," and Eula is much more creatively described as "one of these here kind of big, soft-looking gals that could giggle richer than plowed new-ground" (*US*, 166). Suratt also dwells for some time on the baby Eula brought back with her from Texas, mockingly making fun of the fact that the baby is far too big to have been Flem's but without saying that much.[7] Eula has returned with the baby; Flem only returns "last Friday," and so the real story begins, with the arrival of "about two dozen of them Texas ponies" (*US*, 167).

What sort of horses are they? Critics have seen everything from wild, masculine virility to useless commodities in these "cattymounts," whereas others have found them to be another dream of creation represented by these unlikely descendants from Pegasus or to be poetry itself (not symbolizing poetry, but being it).[8] Flem arrives with the horses, but so also does a Texan with "one of these two-gallon hats and an ivory-handled pistol and a box of gingersnaps sticking out of his hind pocket" (*US*, 167). The horses, however, dominate the scene: "They was colored like parrots and they was quiet as doves, and ere a one of them would kill you quick as a rattlesnake. Nere a one of them had two eyes the same color, and nere a one of them had ever seen a bridle" (*US*, 167).

The stage is set for the horse auction on the following morning, and we do not know exactly what to expect, except that we already know that some of the horses got away and are being chased about the countryside. Something must have gone wrong, at least for those who have bought the horses; or perhaps what has happened was only to be expected and of little importance to those who brought the horses to Frenchman's Bend. When the second section begins,[9] there is some doubt as to whether Flem owned the horses, but everyone knows that "they wasn't never going to know for sho if Flem did or not" (*US*, 168).

It is as if the narrator has been warming up to this central portion of his tale, which becomes rapid, vivid, colorful, and dramatic as soon as the Texan gets the bids started. He has to give away a horse to Eck Snopes to coerce him into bidding on the next one, and we get a very detailed and dramatic description of the Texan's fight with one of the horses, a fight which one would think would keep everyone from bidding at all. The horses are not only wild, they are lethally dangerous, and the narrator's choice of comparisons leaves no doubt about this, even if he is also trying to be funny: "Its legs was braced and it was trembling like a new bride and groaning like a saw mill" (*US*, 168). No one bids anything until Henry Armstid arrives on the scene in his broken-down wagon and with his wife in "that ere faded wrapper and sunbonnet and tennis shoes" (*US*, 169). The Texas man finally gets Eck to bid on a second horse after having given him one, and Henry cannot stand there and see Eck get two horses for two dollars. He bids three dollars and raises Eck's four-dollar bid to five, which is all he has, his wife's money, earned by weaving at night and desperately needed for her kids. Henry even threatens to beat up the man who raises his bid.

The rest of the auction is passed over quickly, and instead of the vivid and scenic descriptions of the first part leading up to Henry Armstid's desperate bidding we get brief summaries of how long it took until the horses were all sold, just before sundown. As readers we know that the dramatic confrontation between Henry and his wife is important, and not only because it is given much space and attention but because of the conflict between a stupid man who is more than willing to beat his wife if she protests and a pitiable, hardworking woman who begs for help against the reckless stupidity of her husband. At least this would be a normal reader's reaction at this point of the text, and we do not really know what to do with the author's own explanation of what the horses symbolized:

> . . . the hope, the aspiration of the masculine part of society that is capable of doing, of committing puerile folly, for some gewgaw that has drawn him, as juxtaposed to the cold practicality of the women whose spokesman Mrs. Littlejohn was when she said, "Them men!" or "What fools men are!" That the men even in a society where there's a constant pressure to conform can still be taken off by the chance to buy a horse for three dollars. Which to me is a good thing, I think. I hope that man can always be tolled off that way, to buy a horse for three dollars.[10]

Read in the context of Mrs. Armstid's situation, even before it has developed further in the short story, Faulkner seems to have misunderstood (or perhaps misremembered) how good a thing it was to buy these horses, or perhaps he almost corrected himself when he added "I think." Anyhow, the story subtly changes from an encounter and confrontation between men and horses to a conflict between men and women, for a long time within the limits of the narrative to the exclusion of the original conflict between Flem Snopes and the poor people of Frenchman's Bend who should know better than to spend the little they have on wild horses brought there by Flem.

The horses have been sold, but nobody has been allowed to go in and fetch their horse until all were sold. Henry is impatient, and with the help of his wife he tries to catch his horse. She cannot stop the horse when it breaks free, so Henry hits her with the rope, and the Texas man has to intervene and give the five dollars back to Mrs. Armstid. In the meantime Flem has arrived, and when the desperate and angry Henry Armstid offers the money to Flem, he is not one for not taking it. The Texan, however, promises Mrs. Armstid that she will get her money from Flem tomorrow, but we know that Henry wants his horse. "Hain't no more despair than to buy one of them things" (US, 169), as Mrs. Armstid has said before, and the narrator verifies it: "It was the truth, too. They ain't never made more than a bare living offen that place of theirs, and them with four chaps and the very clothes they wears she earns by weaving by the firelight at night while Henry's asleep" (US, 170).

The narrator has very carefully shifted his perspective throughout his telling about the auction, so that we have had glimpses of Mrs. Littlejohn going about her work, washing clothes, then preparing supper. In the meantime the men who have bought horses have gone to Varner's store to buy rope, Flem and Buck, the Texan, have left, and the narrator is having his supper. Impatient, Henry goes to catch his horse in the lot and is run over by the horses. Then the horses scatter in all directions, frightening the mules, which break loose from harness and wagons and run. The story gains speed again, and the narrator is on top of his dramatic power because he is in the middle of the events that follow, because Eck's horse (probably the one he got for free) enters Mrs. Littlejohn's boarding house. Most of the horse's running up and down in the house, chasing the narrator in his underwear and being hit across the face with Mrs. Littlejohn's scrubbing-board, is pure tall tale, wildly funny, as the horse finally rushes toward freedom and jumping as high as only such stories make possible. But the reader knows, while also rushing through the hyperbolic prose of this part of the story, that the body of Henry Armstid has been trampled on by a herd of horses, and when Eck's horse reaches the bridge over the creek fun and laughter must give in to more seri-

ous thoughts, even if the narrative sticks to its light tone and only qualifies it when the events become too tragic to be made fun of. Vernon Tull
with his wife, three daughters, and Mrs. Tull's aunt are so unfortunate
that they are on the bridge in their wagon when Eck's horse gets there.
A wonderfully detailed and complicated story about horse and mules
and overturned chairs and white drawers in the moonlight is followed by
a more sinister tone:

> The mules jerked Tull outen the wagon and drug him a spell on the
> bridge before the reins broke. They thought at first he was dead,
> and while they was kneeling around him, picking the bridge splin-
> ters outen him, here come Eck and that boy, carrying the rope.
> They was running and breathing a little hard. "Where'd he go?"
> Eck says. (US, 176)

Apparently there is no limit to the stupidity of menfolk in the world of
"Spotted Horses," but the episode with Vernon Tull is not developed
any further in this tale, which is only reasonable, since the narrator just
tells what he knows, has witnessed, or has participated in—or at least
has been told—and since the story is told so shortly after the events that
Tull has not had time to take action against Flem.[11]
    And so, finally, the narrator returns to the wounded Henry Armstid
and can tell from first-hand experience how he helped carry him into
Mrs. Littlejohn's house and later went to fetch Will Varner, who comes
with his "horse-doctoring grip" (US, 177). Mrs. Littlejohn, who now
takes complete command, is tired of male stupidity and uselessness.
When she tells the men to go and fetch Will Varner, her comment is that
a man probably is not much different from a mule—"Except maybe a
mule's got more sense" (US, 177). Having watched the men and the
horses while going about her work, she has good reason to be mad.
"'You men git outen the way,' Mrs. Littlejohn says. 'Git outside,' she
says. 'See if you can't find something else to play with that will kill some
more of you'" (US, 177).
    In the remainder of the story Mrs. Littejohn rules the ground, until
the last encounter between Mrs. Armstid and Flem Snopes, watched by
the men on the porch of Varner's store. The narrator has overheard a
conversation between Mrs. Armstid and Mrs. Littlejohn about the
money Flem was supposed to give back to Mrs. Armstid, but then he
goes on his trip to Bundren's. Returning, he walks up to the store where
Flem is and where Mrs. Armstid finally has decided to ask for the money.
    The narrator has prepared his audience well for this final confronta-
tion by adding bits of information about the Armstid children, who now
must look after themselves: the oldest girl bars the door and sleeps with

an ax in bed, and Henry will not be much of a farmer this year. The narrator talks aloud while Flem listens about what the Texan had promised Mrs. Armstid, but when she asks Flem, we all know the answer, since no other answer is possible for Flem or for a story in which his role and character are so consistent and so obvious. Flem simply says that "He taken that money off with him Saturday" (US, 182). And so we are satisfied, because we are not surprised. Our expectations as readers have been fulfilled; Flem has acted within character, and good people such as Mrs. Littlejohn and perhaps even the narrator have been passive bystanders, unable to prevent Flem from stealing from the poorest among the poor. But Faulkner would not be Faulkner, and his favorite storyteller would have tipped the scale between comedy and tragedy in the wrong direction, if a small, seemingly innocent episode had not passed between Flem and Mrs. Armstid. Flem asks her to wait, politely addressing her as Mrs. Armstid. He enters the store and returns with a nickel's worth of candy, saying, "A little sweetening for the chaps," to which poor Mrs. Armstid says, "You're right kind" (US, 182). At this point we do not know which way to look or whether to cry or to cry out. The narrator knows that only Flem can get away with what he has done and ends his story the way he began it: "Yes, sir" (US, 183).

"Spotted Horses" thus opens and ends on a statement about Flem Snopes, in a story which seems to introduce him to a group of listeners who do not know him.[12] From the long introduction about how Flem came to Frenchman's Bend and what he has achieved so far, a picture of a rapacious, money-obsessed, almost inhuman person emerges from the broader outline of the Snopes clan. It appears that Flem in point of fact stands distinctly apart from his own kind, being much worse than any of the other Snopeses because he is much more shrewd and secretive and knows where to find people's weak spots. When the story about the horses is told in all its hilarious fun and outrageous exaggerations and colloquial similes and metaphors, the final picture of Flem is one of the exploiter *par exellence*. No profit is too small for him, and his vicious cunning and lust for money are rendered dramatically in the story of how he embezzles Mrs. Armstid's five dollars. Despite some scenes and numerous different and additional thematic implications found in the story, Flem's part in it and the interest vested in him by the narrator (and the author) cannot be emphasized too strongly. The whole exposition is devoted to the early phase of Flem's rise to money and power in this backwoods area of Yoknapatawpha. Granted that Flem disappears from the scene time and again, but this is simply typical of Flem's shrewdness and secrecy in all affairs. He has to leave the scene of the horses and the auction so that his complicity in the deal is not too obvious.[13]

Flem's rapid rise to power in the countryside of Yoknapatawpha County, his merciless and relentless exploitation of his poor and illiterate fellowmen, could only be possible in a permissive society where little social control—formal or informal—is present. The kind of human and social evil that Flem represents can only find foothold where stupidity and gullibility join forces with some uncertain wish to ascertain and prove one's masculine strength and male supremacy. The endless struggle to eke out a living from the barren soil may to some extent be responsible for the dream of a better world, which the horses appear to represent, and this may help to explain why the men from Frenchman's Bend waste their money and undertake to catch the horses, putting both themselves and more innocent bystanders in jeopardy. Part of the tragedy ultimately resulting from the horse sale is that pain is inflicted upon people who have done nothing to be so punished. The Tull episode in all its bizarre humor exemplifies this, as does Mrs. Armstid even more poignantly.

The auction, the pursuit of the runaway horses, the suffering but enduring Mrs. Armstid, the seriously wounded Tull and Armstid must all be seen and interpreted in the light of one man's wile and deliberate actions. Even if Flem stays away from the auction itself—which underscores his apartness—he is the central character in the story. Toward the end of "Spotted Horses" he is watched eagerly by all people present, but it is not easy to find out what goes on in his mind. He always acts surreptitiously, and there is nothing showy or ostentatious about him. Everything he does is preposterous. The Texan is deliberately shown to have at least a minimal degree of pity, and this unexpected character trait in such a man is used to put Flem's total lack of any virtue in relief. As R. P. Warren has said, Flem "stands beyond appetite, passion, pride, fidelity, exploiting all these things."[14] Flem shows no signs of regret, and the society shows an apparent unwillingness to halt the all-destructive exploiter's use of Frenchman's Bend for his immediate goals before moving on. The story's conclusion indicates that Flem alone could escape without punishment:

"You boys might just as well quit trying," I. O. says. "You can't git ahead of Flem. You can't touch him. Ain't he a sight, now?"

I be dog if he ain't. If I had brung a herd of wild cattymounts into town and sold them to my neighbors and kinfolks, they would have lynched me. Yes, sir. (*US*, 183)

During the horse auction and the ensuing pursuit of the ponies, Flem indirectly keeps the farmers away from their work on the land, work badly needed to support their families. This is a first, minor illustration of what a force like Flem can do when it is let loose and allowed to function. Natural life becomes corrupted; seen in this perspective, Flem is an avatar and a precursor of times to come that will change the whole system of agriculture and social life in general in Yoknapatawpha County and, for that matter, in the nonfictional world of the South.

"Spotted Horses" points to greed as a primary characteristic of society, "one of such magnitude that the Snopeses can easily exploit it for their own gain."[15] The narrator of the story has been outsmarted twice by Flem Snopes,[16] and among the group of characters not participating actively in the auction, Mrs. Littlejohn—who goes about her work as if nothing had happened—is the only one who can match the horses and, indirectly, not be harmed by Flem. Mrs. Littlejohn and the narrator are passive; they watch, but they do not interfere much, and when they do their protests are too weak, perhaps because they know that they cannot alone stop Flem Snopes. The passivity and noninterference of those not susceptible to Flem's and the Texan's deceit and not subject to the enthralling power of the horses are a prerequisite for the success of the horse auction, seen from the businessmen's point of view.

But, as has been noted a number of times, there is more to be said about the horses and the men's reaction to them. Numerous critics have pointed to the horses as embodiments of masculine vitality and the virility that has forsaken the men of the town. In their impoverished lives, where nothing seems ever to improve their situation, the horses promise a kind of gratification that they otherwise can only dream of. Perhaps they chase the horses that they shall never catch and certainly never put before a plow in the moonlit nights of Yoknapatawpha to keep an elusive dream alive, a dream which they would not even be able to put into words.

John T. Matthews (1992) reads "Spotted Horses" as "a critical, because semi-detached, perspective on the ritual of mass market transaction" (18). It is an interesting reading, even if it tends to become rather farfetched when the magazine context of *advertizements* is his main argument for such a reading. His main points are valid, though, since it is obvious, and telling, that "the lure of the horses cannot be separated from their flashy uselessness—that is, from their status as commodities" (18); yet the salesman and narrator can hardly be said to take a "penetrating look into the heart of the modern mass market" (19).

"Spotted Horses" is, after all, a literary text, and at times a poetic one. A deep understanding of human frailty and misery pervades this story, in which greed and stupidity, vanity and viciousness come quickly to the surface when the poor population of Frenchman's Bend is given the rare opportunity to buy horses at a cheap price. For complex reasons the horses speak to something deep in men of all ages in this farming community. In their hard and relentless work on a soil that barely yields a living, the horses seem to be part of a better world, an easier life, a dream. Flem Snopes knows exactly what he is doing when he brings the Texas ponies to Frenchman's Bend, and he has not miscalculated.

Yet while we watch the seduction of the men of Frenchman's Bend and neighboring areas, we should not overlook the narrator's eye for Mrs. Littlejohn and her activities. Time and again her work is presented, and while the men have fun and bid on horses so that this seems to really be the story, the narrative perspective shifts to Mrs. Littlejohn as many as eleven times. The contrast between men who play and women who work runs through the whole text. The contrast is further developed in subsequent uses of this material, but the many almost identical descriptions of Mrs. Armstid working at night to the sound of her husband's snoring, are indicative of an element in this story that should not be forgotten, even though a reading of the story entitled "Whores and Horses in Faulkner's 'Spotted Horses'" clearly has gone too far in this direction.[17]

"Spotted Horses" is an almost tragic study in poverty, suffering, and human frailty exploited to the utmost by a shrewd and inhuman businessman whose only interest is profit. "Spotted Horses" is certainly also one of the funniest stories Faulkner ever wrote, a classic in American humor, "the funniest American story since Mark Twain," according to Malcolm Cowley's judgment.[18] But the farce of this "frontier trickster tale" (Carothers 1985, 116) is carefully qualified with pathos, its humor tempered by the consequences that the shrewd deals and the funny events have on pitiable individuals. The tone is kept unchanged and at the same pitch all through the story, so that comic and grotesque elements are juxtaposed with elements of suffering and tragedy.

Three Snopes stories from about the same time—"Spotted Horses," "Lizards in Jamshyd's Courtyard," and "Centaur in Brass"—contribute significantly to our understanding of Flem Snopes, as they relate central incidents of his rise to wealth and social position. All the stories are furthermore good examples of man's misuse of man and of one man's exploitation of all virtues and vices while he himself stands beyond and above anything even resembling virtue.

# Chapter 14

# That Evening Sun

## TEXTUAL INFORMATION AND PUBLICATION HISTORY

The textual and printing history of "That Evening Sun" is one of the more spectacular in Faulkner's short story career. The author first submitted the story to *Scribner's Magazine* on October 2, 1930; rejected there, it next went to the *American Mercury* twenty-two days later and was published in the magazine in March 1931, under the title "That Evening Sun Go Down" (Meriwether 1971, 175). The story was featured on the cover of the magazine and was also given the leading place within.[1] It had gone through considerable revision, mostly done by the editor, Henry Louis Mencken, and consented to by Faulkner, who revised it again later on, restoring some of the elements which Mencken's literary judgment had prevented him from allowing in print. The version printed in *These 13* must therefore be considered the final, authoritative text. With minor alterations this text was used in *Collected Stories*.

The prepublication versions of this story include a six-page manuscript fragment entitled "Never Done No Weeping When You Wanted To Laugh," a twenty-six-page carbon typescript entitled "That Evening Sun Go Down," and another typescript with Mencken's editorial alterations and emissions.[2] Although Leo Manglaviti (1972) suggests that "pages four and five have been completely retyped by Faulkner," there is reason to believe that the twenty-six-page carbon typescript in the Faulkner collection at the University of Virginia is the carbon of the very typescript Faulkner sent to Mencken.

Chronologically speaking, there are thus four different stages or layers of "That Evening Sun": the manuscript, the uncorrected carbon typescript, the corrected typescript and the *American Mercury* version, and, finally, the text as printed in *These 13* and *Collected Stories*. In the development toward a final, authoritative text, this order is nevertheless not the correct one. The *Mercury* version, revised to suit Mencken's "best editorial judgment" (Blotner 1974, I:670), represents a rare case of Faulkner's compromise—albeit temporary—with the popular taste that Mencken helped legislate for many busy years, and it is thus a bowdlerized version of a typescript that was originally closer to the final version than the periodical printing is. Proof of this is found in the restoration of the "vine business," which is found in the typescript but not in the magazine, though it reappears in *These 13* and subsequent printings. Likewise, the name of Nancy's husband in the collection once more became Jesus, as it was in the typescript.[3] This being said, one should not overlook the fact that Mencken proposed a number of new paragraph divisions and added the roman numerals to arrange the story in sections. Faulkner later even elaborated upon this by deleting a whole paragraph from the ending yet altogether expanding this part of the story without changing it substantially.[4] After all, the final, Hemingway-patterned dialogue with its open ending had been there in the manuscript,[5] although the evocation of a mood and a special tone had been much strengthened from manuscript to typescript. This close similarity between the concluding paragraphs of the manuscript, the typescript, and the printed versions is not representative for the rest of the text. The whole historical introduction, given by the grown-up Quentin Compson, is not found in the manuscript, and the perspective as well as the emphasis of the story thus changed conspicuously during the process of revision. From being primarily Nancy's story, it becomes much more the narrator's story, and, by implication, the Compson family's story.[6]

All discussions of "That Evening Sun" rest heavily upon the final version, without making use of the interesting prepublication information which might even prove helpful in the reading of the text. Yet the final version should be used, obviously, because it is the result of Faulkner's final effort to perfect his text, including the very careful and conscientious revisions for *These 13*. A significant qualification concerning the final version of the story must all the same be made: there are indications that Faulkner did his final revision on the basis of his early manuscript (or his memory of it) and the *Mercury* text. A line from the typescript has been dropped in the magazine printing, and this line is not restored in *These 13*. If Faulkner worked from his typescript, of which he certainly had a carbon at home, it is unlikely that he would have left out this line, although he might of course have dropped it accidentally.[7]

## READING "THAT EVENING SUN"

"That Evening Sun" is one of the most reprinted and anthologized of all Faulkner stories, and critics generally agree that it is one of the few really great stories Faulkner wrote. Despite the temptation to read it in the light of *The Sound and the Fury* or *Requiem for a Nun,* or even more cautiously in comparison with "A Justice," one should insist on the autonomy of this text. By closely adhering to the text and its subtle and ambiguous dialogues, its beautiful descriptive passages, its dramatic and sympathetic portraits of Nancy in all her desperate fear, one soon discovers how inexhaustible a text it is. More perhaps than for any other of Faulkner's stories one should insist on this autonomy, its singularity as a text in its own right, and refuse to see it as another—illogical and inconsistent—instance in the lives of the Compson children or in the mythological saga of Yoknapatawpha County. To find in the Compson children personality patterns which will be confirmed in later books, especially *The Sound and the Fury,* clearly lies outside the interpretation of this story. Quentin, first-person narrator and character in "That Evening Sun," first and foremost exists within the limits of the tale he tells, and he is clearly a different Quentin from the very troubled young man in *The Sound and the Fury* and *Absalom, Absalom!* James B. Carothers notes that "the narrator of the story projects a calm, dispassionate, mature voice very different from that of the two Harvard Quentins" (Carothers 1985, 12). Though obvious, this apparently needs to be repeated: The Quentin we will deal with in "That Evening Sun" is projected by the story, and so he is not to be equated with the narrator of "A Justice" either, even though the child characters in these two related stories have many things in common.

On the level of narration, the choice on Faulkner's part to have the young man Quentin Compson narrate the opening paragraphs—a late choice in the composition of the story, as we have seen—is the most decisive one for the story's overall structure, for our response to it, and ultimately for the story's meaning. Literature is never simply a question of technical solutions involving narrative voice and perspective, selection of material for narration, and the like. It is always also a question of what the story is about, how character and plot are developed and analyzed, and how emotional reactions and questions of sympathy and irony, as well as more basic questions of attitudes, beliefs, and ideologies are involved. Personal or private idiosyncrasies should be fought back in one's reading, but the critical response to "That Evening Sun" shows that even such a minor requirement is not an easy one to satisfy. I cannot even propose a "correct reading" of this story, although I think it is possible and necessary to point to elements of its narrative structure and thus avoid the most blatant mistakes. At the same time the fashionable pursuit of questions of guilt and responsibility in the racial issues can easily distort discussions of Nancy's guilt or foolishness or of who failed whom. Such questions will only be brought up if and when the text presents them. Nancy's role in Quentin's narrative, her story's impact on his growth and maturation and self-awareness, is perhaps as important as is her role in the plot structure of the story. We should also be aware that Nancy becomes narrator herself, embedded in Quentin's text, and thus analyze also the double nature of her position in "That Evening Sun." Let me just make it absolutely clear that on the level of narration, the disparity between the adult narrator and the childhood voice and perspective he gradually adopts and remains faithful to throughout the text gives an important indication as to what the story is about. This should not mislead us into forgetting the story elements of Quentin's narrative; both those chosen for telling in the poetic and atmospheric opening paragraphs and those in the "story proper" are significant. Hence, Nancy becomes significant, and we shall have to read her as well as Quentin as characters actively participating in the story Quentin tells in his words. Yet we are allowed to listen to dialogue and even to Nancy's futile attempts at storytelling, too. The complexity of this in terms of narrative voice and perspective should perhaps be set aside for a moment, however, since the story is about something, and that something is painful and terrible, whether it is understood to be individual or universal, rooted in Nancy's frailty and weakness of character or in human frailty and the human condition in general terms. In my reading, just because there may be elements in the very transmission of a story about a past experience that lift it above such concrete problems as racial division, injustice, white superiority and supremacy, and lack of understanding in a particular place at a particular time in history, the story should not be reduced to a probing into our frailty or mortality. Not a sociological study, not a bit of realistic history about what it was like in Jefferson some years ago, but a fictional account representing one fictional character's remembrance of a past that through its being remembered and narrated takes on additional meaning, "That Evening Sun" invites the readers to understand it in many ways and on many different levels, which is part of the magic of Faulkner's best stories. Yet there are limits to its possible meaning, too. The best remedy against misreading is to stay close to the text, follow the text, before we sum up our response, consider the sensibility of various contexts, and do our best to suggest interpretations which seem valid, convincing, or persuasive, perhaps even beautiful if not true.

"That Evening Sun" opens on a quiet and detailed description of a Monday morning in Jefferson, based on what can be seen on the streets and expressed in a series of visual images:

> Monday is no different from any other weekday in Jefferson now.
> The streets are paved now, and the telephone and electric companies are cutting down more and more of the shade trees—the water oaks, the maples and locusts and elms—to make room for iron

poles bearing clusters of bloated and ghostly and bloodless grapes, and we have a city laundry which makes the rounds on Monday morning, gathering the bundles of clothes. . . . (CS, 289)

The language is elaborate and has a narrative drive even when this poetic impulse dominates. The repetitive use of "now" creates expectations in the reader of what it was like in the past. The present of the story is shown as a modernized world, and the narrator's very choice of words indicates a skepticism about the present, which the next paragraph supports in the sense that it gives an even more poetic picture of the "quiet, dusty, shady streets" (CS, 289) full of black women carrying people's wash on their heads. In the present of the story, fifteen years later than the past Quentin looks back upon, it seems to be this image of the women carrying bundles of white people's washing high on their heads, Nancy even balancing a black straw sailor hat on top, that is the strongest and most vivid image of change and loss, and it is certainly the visual image he recalls that seems to be the starting point for this whole memory of his own childhood and of a collective past. Modernization and improvement are not condemned or openly criticized. The description of the present scene is quiet and controlled, even if Quentin points to the shade trees that have been cut down. Yet the present is contrasted with the past, and the use of *But* in the beginning of the second paragraph seems to imply a lament, a nostalgia, for that which he remembers. The narrator's interest in the past and his re-creation of it, both in the atmosphere and mood of the scenic descriptions and in the telling of a particular episode from that past, show that the fascination with the past is also personal. The reason for narrating is more or less existential, but there is little doubt that Quentin tells a story in which he is seriously involved himself as a nine-year-old boy. Quentin tells about something that happened to him and his family, and he tells it from the vantage point of the mature and literate young man of twenty-four.[8] But he quickly glides into the language of the child, to remain there for the rest of the story—obviously for reasons of spontaneity and authenticity—so that we as readers can feel and smell and listen to that which he experienced, and if there is a lesson to be learned, it can also become ours. Faulkner is extremely cautious not to let the grown-up interfere with the child's perspective once it has been established. "That Evening Sun" displays consonant narration to an exceptional degree, and some of the revisions of the *Mercury* text may indeed have been undertaken not because they offered explicit and evaluative statements but because they interfered with the narrative perspective which would thus be maintained also through the story's final paragraph. A concluding frame for the story, in which Quentin returned to the initial narrative situation, would probably also have been felt as an intrusion, and the narrative's fictionality, its rhetorical and tropological pattern, and the skillfully arranged illusion of the child narrator would have been laid bare.

To tell a story is to create—or at least suggest—a meaningful pattern for otherwise disparate and chaotic experiences. It is to give narrative form to events of the past to see if they make sense; it is to make the marginal move toward the center, to make the invisible visible, to let voices from the margin support or contradict the master narrative of the narrator, who may retain his control of the whole story. But the very fact that he is telling it reveals that his mastery is illusory, his understanding partial, his knowledge imperfect. Quentin Compson in his early adulthood tells a story within the framework of his own looking back upon what he thinks was a better world, the world of his childhood, but when he lets the story of Nancy and Jesus and himself and his family unfold in the past, he does so through dramatization—dialogue and stage directions—and the commentary or outside descriptions are kept to a minimum. Telling the story of his past is also a means of living through the events of the past once more, perhaps even in an attempt to set things right. Quentin's memories seem to come by way of association, but they are very deliberate. As readers we may wonder why Quentin laments the loss of the old days in Jefferson when the memories that follow are so full of fear and anxiety and even show his own (understandable and forgivable) lack of understanding. A tentative answer may be that Quentin looks back at a period of security and innocence, into which the realities of life only little by little were allowed access. Hence the nostalgia. But it may also be that Quentin relives this story of his past in order to understand what went on and because he is painfully aware that as a mature young man he would have acted differently. One cannot revenge oneself on time or its passing except by returning to past experience and subtly changing it so that it signifies in new and radically different ways for those who listen to the story, or for us as readers of the text. As far as I can see, this is exactly what happens in "That Evening Sun." From a chain of events fifteen years ago Quentin singles out those that he finds important for the story he wants to relay to us, and by a careful narrative handling of the story material and the point of narration the story changes and gains new importance. Repetition and repetition with variation, ambiguities, uncertainties, and an open ending add to the richness and complexity of the story.

After the discussion of the opening paragraphs of the story and extended comments on the narrative situation we shall continue following the story, concentrating on its story elements and plots.[9] Despite the deliberate distinction (or discrepancy) between Quentin as child in character and perpective in the bulk of the story and Quentin as adult and mature narrator in the opening parts of it, one should keep in mind that the borderlines between narrator and character tend to become blurred, so that the image of himself as a nine-year-old participant in the events of the story he now narrates is strongly and decisively influenced by the mature Quentin. The past of "That Evening Sun" is *was,* not only because the time of narration, the present, the *is* of the text, reconstructs, adjusts, and distorts the past, but also because the past of the story is partly responsible for the present situation, of which we know little except what we can infer from the story that follows.[10]

From the panoramic descriptions of Jefferson in the narrator's present and fifteen years earlier, the text focuses on the black women with their bundles of washing on their heads before it narrows and concentrates on one of the women, Nancy. The narrator establishes himself as part of a group who used to accompany Nancy all the way to the ditch that separated Negro Hollow from the white people's world. The identification of the narrator and of his position in the story of past events comes much later, as a natural part of explaining conflicts and responsibilities in the Compson household.

We thus move very quickly from the outside description of Jefferson to a narrative which stays very close to the characters and events and which seems to prove the distance between the narrator's youth and the present. We follow events as they happen, but they are told in the past tense, often in the iterative ("we would go," "we would stop," "every night," etc.). The language subtly changes, especially as dialogue (most often between the children or between Nancy and the children) becomes dominant in the story, and we are almost without noticing introduced to a world of deep conflicts, violence, fear, and anxiety seen from children's points of view, so that their limited understanding and preoccupation with their own small problems underscore and emphasize the selfishness and indifference of the white world.

We notice as we read this memory from Quentin's childhood that Nancy is the central character in something he still remembers vividly and now perhaps has grasped the significance of, but also that the story from the past is not only an episode, a single event, but rather a protracted narrative which includes retrospective glimpses of still earlier episodes in Nancy's life, culminating on the day she talks the Compson children into accompanying her to her cabin because she is afraid of walking in the lane and crossing the ditch alone. Most of Nancy's past is revealed to us as a probable explanation of why Nancy failed to come to the Compson household when Dilsey was sick, even if the children had gone all the way to the ditch and had thrown rocks at her house to get her attention:

So we thought it was whisky until that day they arrested her again and they were taking her to jail and they passed Mr. Stovall. He was the cashier in the bank and a deacon in the Baptist church, and Nancy began to say:

"When you going to pay me, white man? When you going to pay me, white man? It's been three times now since you paid me a cent—." (*CS*, 291)

Mr. Stovall knocks her down and kicks her teeth out—Quentin has already noted that she had a "sad face sunken where her teeth were missing" (*CS*, 290)—and Nancy is lying in the street, laughing. But she was arrested before she met Mr. Stovall in the street, and the story is deliberately ambiguous on the reasons for her being arrested again. "We"— probably referring to what the Compson parents have discussed—mention whisky, but the jailor says she has used cocaine, "because no nigger would try to commit suicide unless he was full of cocaine" (*CS*, 291). Nancy's unsuccessful suicide attempt is accounted for in two ways: She only had her dress to hang herself in, and, with untied hands, she could not make herself let go of the window ledge. She wants to die but clings to life. The whole retrospective story is told in what seems to me a mixture of the child's impressions of what "they told about Nancy and Mr. Stovall" (*CS*, 291) and what the jailer later must have told from the prison, since the first-person narrator would not have had access to this information in any other way, as child or adult. Nancy is cut down, revived, and then beaten by the jailer, who heard the noise she made and found her hanging in her cell, "stark naked, her belly already swelling out a little, like a little balloon" (*CS*, 292). "Balloon" has been used for comparison earlier in the text, describing Nancy's bundle on her head, and is part of the child's vocabulary, as "belly" is. But the observation that Nancy's belly *already* was swelling points forward in time and to the events narrated later on in the story, and is of course a result of the temporal perspective of an adult narrator in control of a string of related events in the past. Nancy's pregnancy leads the story, by associative linking, back to an early phase of her work for the Compsons, when her husband, Jesus, was still around, before Mr. Compson told him to stay away from his house. As we listen to this first prolonged dialogue of the story, we see how the perspective of the child has been adopted and how syntax and diction gradually have changed to give this impression. The children notice Nancy's apron swelling out, and Jesus, jokingly one would think, says it is a watermelon she has under her dress, whereupon Nancy says, "It never come off of your vine though." Jesus, in the first of his two lines in the story, threatens to cut down "the vine it did come off of"

(*CS*, 292), and in the second talks about white men coming to his house and how he cannot stop them, whereas he is not allowed to be in a white man's kitchen. Jesus, with his razor scar on his face, is thus introduced, and even if he is not seen again, the fear of him lies behind the development in the rest of the story. Also introduced for the first time is a pattern that will repeat itself all through the text: adults talking and children not understanding or misunderstanding and therefore asking questions that always seem to focus on the most essential problems of the text: "'Talking what way?' Caddy said. 'What vine?'" (*CS*, 292).

The basic elements of the story seem to be laid down in this early passage, and for a period it appears that Mr. Compson and the children took Nancy home on a regular basis: "Dilsey was still sick in her cabin. Father told Jesus to stay off our place. Dilsey was still sick. It was a long time. We were in the library after supper" (*CS*, 292). The narrative thus moves onward, but even this summary is now given in the child's language and not only from a youthful perspective. This is very carefully done, but the story would have been much poorer if comments that lifted the text above the direct and flat description of events were not included. When Quentin fetches Nancy in the kitchen he finds her sitting there, and the adult narrator and character-narrator of the past seem to share in this emotional reaction to Nancy, who looks at Quentin (the sentence "She looked at me" repeated four times) and says, "I done finished" (*CS*, 292). Quentin seems genuinely concerned, involved, almost desperate: "'What is it?' I said. 'What is it?'" (*CS*, 293).

> She looked at me, sitting in the chair before the cold stove, the sailor hat on her head. I went back to the library. It was the cold stove and all, when you think of a kitchen being warm and busy and cheerful. And with a cold stove and the dishes all put away, and nobody wanting to eat at that hour. (*CS*, 293)

The text then continues, in smooth transitions between different points in time, but in the story line it tells about a long period when they take Nancy home every night. In the telling of this we get a good view into the Compson household, with the complaining and whining Mrs. Compson with her talk of police and taxes and her own need for protection and the well-meaning but apparently weak Mr. Compson and three children of ages five, seven, and nine, as different as they can be and not only because of the difference in age. One line, spoken by Mr. Compson, seems to me more revealing than any other description of the Compsons. When the mother tries to persuade her husband not to take Nancy home, because he would then leave the children unprotected "with that Negro about," Mr. Compson replies: "What would he do with them, if he were unfortunate enough to have them?" This is also the kind of talk children should not be allowed to listen to, and Quentin clearly senses this: "So father didn't look at me. I was the oldest. I was nine . . ." (CS, 294).

Nancy's fear of Jesus is real enough, even if Jesus is in Memphis (as she once says) or in St. Louis (as Mr. Compson suggests). It is discussed time and again, always with lines of children's talk interspersed, Caddy asking questions like "Let what white men alone?" and "How let them alone?" (CS, 295) and Jason insisting that he is not afraid or scared, not even on Halloween. The man with the razor on a string down his back, the sexual affairs of Nancy, the darkness of the lane, and a seemingly irrational fear based on what Nancy can feel as the presence of Jesus and on experience and knowledge of character, all this must make an indelible impression on a young boy's mind. We do not know much about the effects on Caddy and Jason, unless we want to read into "That Evening Sun" the information we have from other texts, which I do not want to do here. The only "later" we know of within this short story is what Quentin tells us from the present point of view, nothing else.

We have followed the text relatively closely through its first part, which is an absolute requirement for a reading of this short story, since everything which happens later must be read against the background information we receive in the first section. And I am not talking about fictional "facts" alone but about the whole narrative machinery, the repetitive use of language, the extensive use of dialogue, and the whole emotional atmosphere thus created. The psychological situation seems to be as important as the sociological one, although one would misread the story seriously if one ignored the question of racism, white superiority, and a system so rigid and evil that a whole race suffers in agony and despair.

We have become acquainted with Nancy's hopeless situation, being "nothing but a nigger," but we cannot do the more extensive character analysis to determine who she is, what she is, and what has formed and shaped her. It is easy enough to say that she brings in laundry and helps in white people's kitchens and is a prostitute, perhaps even drinks or uses drugs, but is she a case of a "bad nigger" or a decent person who is a victim of circumstances beyond her control? In my reading of the story Nancy may well be all of this but can only be understood on the basis of what is said about her in the story, how she acts within the plot of the story, and how the narrator as child and as adult reacts to her. Nancy could be just about anything, but is in many and complex ways "saved" by the very fact that she is the main character in Quentin Compson's childhood memory, told fifteen years later from a mature point of view, told because of an urge, a need, to tell in order to see Nancy in her terrible anguish and pain now because she was invisible to him and everyone else *then*.

As the story continues we hear about the routine of taking Nancy
home, until Mrs. Compson puts an end to it. Then Nancy is allowed to
sleep on a pallet in the kitchen until one night she wakes the whole house
because of her fear and is then allowed to sleep in the children's room.
Throughout this part of Quentin's memory Nancy is described by the
sounds she makes, "like singing and it wasn't like singing" (*CS*, 296);
this sound, coming from nowhere and going nowhere, reverberates
through the text until its conclusion. Quentin's observation that the song
comes from somewhere else, as if from another Nancy than the one looking at them, is repeated numerous times. So are descriptions of Nancy's
eyes. In their bedroom they make such an impression on Quentin that
they "had got printed on my eyeballs" (*CS*, 296). Caddy is aware of the
eyes in the dark, too, and wonders if Nancy can see them like they see
her. Nancy's answer—"I aint nothing but a nigger"—is almost a meaningless standard answer, but in the whole description of eyes and seeing
in the dark, of looking and watching and seeing, the text offers important material for an analysis of sight and seeing, of being visible and
invisible.[11]

The bedroom scene is important for an interpretation of the total
effect of "That Evening Sun," but it is also only preparatory for the concluding and prolonged description of the final events selected for narration by Quentin. Dilsey is well again, but Nancy comes to her in the
kitchen just before dark. From Dilsey's words the children and we as
readers get to know that Nancy has told her that she fears Jesus is back,
even if she has not actually seen him: "'I can feel him,' Nancy said. 'I can
feel him laying yonder in the ditch'" (*CS*, 297). Nancy knows what Jesus
plans to do before he knows it himself, she claims, and so there is no
need for Dilsey's question, "How come you know it's tonight?" (*CS*,
297), with its overtones of fate and finality.[12] Jason, who at the age of
five knows he is not a "nigger," asks Nancy if she is. Her answer has
been used by many critics to center their interpretations on a special
meaning of "nigger" (implying bad, low, evil, worse than those designated "Negro" or "black"): "'I hellborn, child,' Nancy said. 'I wont be
nothing soon. I going back where I come from'" (*CS*, 298).

Nancy reminds the children of the time they played in their bedroom, but when Caddy asks her mother, Mrs. Compson says they cannot have Negroes sleeping in the bedrooms. Dilsey tries in different ways
to get Nancy to go home, but Nancy finally talks the children into going
with her, promising that they will play and have fun. She talks extremely loud, calling Jason Mr. Jason (Mr. Compson's name is also Jason). In

her cabin she builds a good fire and turns the lamp up so much that it begins to smoke. And her storytelling is no good:

> She talked like her eyes looked, like her eyes watching us and her voice talking to us did not belong to her. Like she was living somewhere else, waiting somewhere else. She was outside the cabin. Her voice was inside and the shape of her. . . . (CS, 302)

Nancy is lost in other thoughts, lost to other fears. The story she tells is a fairy-tale version of her own fear and anxiety and is apparently never finished. She tells the story to make the children stay; she tells her story for the same reasons stories have been told since Scheherazade: to stay alive, to keep the darkness at bay, though without much hope that the telling of something has the power to magically change it. The rest of the entertainment for the children does not work either; the popper is broken, and when it is repaired and they start popping corn it all becomes cinder. Jason wants to go home but somebody is approaching, and Nancy makes her strange sound again. In a moving passage the three major characteristics used to describe Nancy through the whole story combine: her eyes, the sound she is making, and her hands:

> Then Nancy began to make that sound again, not loud, sitting there above the fire, her long hands dangling between her knees; all of a sudden water began to come out on her face in big drops, running down her face, carrying in each one a little turning ball of firelight like a spark until it dropped off her chin. "She's not crying," I said.
> "I ain't crying," Nancy said. Her eyes were closed. "I ain't crying. Who is it?" (CS, 306)

Mr. Compson is coming, and he takes the children home after a talk with Nancy, which is of little help, because she knows what she knows. Her only comfort is that she has her coffin money saved up with Mr. Lovelady, and in a fairly long and detailed paragraph the story makes a halt to inform us about Mr. Lovelady. There is little need for this information, except as a relief from the terrible anxiety Nancy describes in images of blood and darkness.

And so she is left there, sitting in front of the fire, "because she was tired" (CS, 309). As Mr. Compson and the children move away from Nancy's cabin and cross the ditch, they cannot see her, but they can hear "the sound that was not singing and not unsinging" (CS, 309), and Quentin must have sensed how futile and hopeless everything is, because he asks a question he may not himself understand the range of: "Who will do our washing now, Father?" (*CS.* 309). Perhaps fifteen years later he relives the whole situation by narrating this story and trying to adopt the child's perspective simply in order to understand the profound and ugly implications of his own question.

Quentin does not tell us what happened to Nancy, and the text is deliberately ambiguous on this point as on many others. The focus of Quentin's tale is not to show what happened and to seek reasons and motivations behind it when looking back from a distance in time and maturity. The story's ending is wide open, and it could not end in a harmonization of conflicting forces and attitudes because that would not have been true to the basic and insoluble conflicts at the heart of the story. It also had to stay true to its narrative principles, and thus Quentin cannot comment from the present point in time, as, in a sense, he does in the *Mercury* text. Faulkner may have sensed strongly that there was so much in the poetic language—the rich imagery, the insistent repetitions, the childish misinterpretations—and in the narrative structure itself that the story should not reach closure but be open for new readers to contribute to the textual meaning of it by rewriting the experience it relays in the context of their own lives.

Having followed the text, and having commented in some detail as we have made our way through it, we need to consider some central aspects of the story in more detail, even if all have been mentioned above. Nancy's "irrational" fear is the first aspect to be revisited. As I noted in the analysis of "Red Leaves," numerous black characters in Faulkner's fiction share an irrational fear of nature, believing that some hidden force may strike and hurt. In some ways nature seems to embody all the oppression and fear they suffer in their daily lives and for which they cannot give the actual explanation or reason, since that would lead to more suffering. Nancy in "That Evening Sun" suffers from such an irrational fear of what the darkness may have in store for her, and she is afraid to be left alone. The distance between Nancy and the Compson household could be described as cultural. The emotional gap between Nancy in her terrible anxiety and suffering and the cold, matter-of-fact Compsons can be measured by their cultural levels. Nancy is still something of the primitive, uneducated, uncultured "noble savage," who has not yet reached a level where superstition has been overcome by information, knowledge, and a hard-won security in the form of a large house, locked doors, and servants. The Compsons have reached a level of success, wealth, and self-assurance where nothing is allowed to interfere with their convictions and beliefs. It is significant that Nancy can persuade the Compson childeren to take her home and stay with her for a while but that the grown-ups refuse to accept Nancy's excuses and explanations. One should be cautious, however, not to condemn a whole white culture because of the whining and moaning Mrs. Compson, who seems to find her own position in the household threatened and accordingly refuses to be left alone "while you take home a frightened Negro" (CS, 296).

The irrational fear of nature, of something inexplicable and unmentionable which may come out of darkness and night and catch up with one for whatever sins one may have committed, also has a basis in traditional superstition and in general gossip and factual knowledge about members of the black race disappearing and vanishing without a trace. When Faulkner places inexperienced and immature people in untouched nature he can demonstrate that fear comes easily and needs not have logical explanations.[13] Such stories also prove how shallow, fragile, and useless our thin layer of culture and civilized manners is when it is put to a test in what Faulkner in one of his stories calls "natural exaggerated situations."[14]

In "That Evening Sun" the irony of a child narrator telling a story about race relations, sex, fear, and death is very important. The discrepancy between the limited point of view of the child narrator and an experience beyond his comprehension is modified by the fact that the child has become an adult at the time of narration. Faulkner is extremely cautious, as we have seen, not to let the grown-up interfere with the memories of a childhood experience by way of commentary, direct statements, or even by letting the narrator tell in his adult language, although the selection of story elements and some of the imagery definitely belongs to the mature Quentin.

We should nevertheless not overlook the most obvious fact of the narrative pattern in "That Evening Sun," namely that the whole story is told by a twenty-four-year-old Quentin.[15] Every word, even those spoken by other characters, are Quentin's words as he recollects them at the time of narration. The postponement of narration is extremely important. The obvious gain is the opportunity to analyze and comment upon the story proper, which may either be done directly or simply be an indivisible and indistinguishable part of the narrative. The adult narrator unconsciously but inevitably comes to put his mark on the child's story. The child's feelings, reactions, and impressions are remembered such a long time afterward that memory has necessarily distorted some of the events about which he tells.

In order to sort out the problem of explicit commentary in the story, let us briefly look at the paragraph from the *Mercury* printing that Faulkner excised from the story—perhaps the most crucial change in the text from the magazine version to the one in *These 13* and *Collected*

*Stories,* although the text is changed substantially also in details of story elements, especially in the plot structure. The paragraph in the *Mercury* text reads:

> Then we had crossed the ditch, walking out of Nancy's life. Then her life was sitting there with the door open and the lamp lit, waiting, and the ditch between us and us going on, the white people going on, dividing the impinged lives of us and Nancy.

It is easy to think, as those critics who have commented on this paragraph have, that Faulkner left it out because it is too explicit a commentary on what the story otherwise shows us, albeit indirectly and at times ambiguously. But the deletion of this paragraph is only part of a very detailed and substantial work of revision, which also established a final, sixth section. This section describes Mr. Compson and the three children leaving Nancy behind in her cabin with the door open and establishes the distance between the two worlds as directly and concretely as the excised paragraph. Also, there is no doubt that the narrator slips from his untenable position of being adult narrator and keeping the perspective of himself as child character and observer, so that the distance between the two seems to collapse entirely. The narrator's last attempt to maintain his perspective or return to it for a last time is when he, as the nine-year-old character in the past events, asks his father, "Who will do our washing now, Father?"—which seems to be a very subtle comment on an experience not at all understood in its complexity then but, in the narrative irony of the very same sentence, seems to indicate that he now knows what kind of experience he partook of and how utterly helpless and useless they all were in relation to Nancy's plight, regardless of whether her fear was based in reality or just something she imagined.

The narrative pattern in "That Evening Sun" has striking similarities with the pattern in "A Justice"—also a story told by Quentin Compson. The main difference is found in the position in the text of the grown-up narrator's description of the present moment. In "A Justice" Quentin comments in the very last part of the story that he did not see where the story took him but that he would understand its implications later on. In "That Evening Sun" the story to come is defined in the opening paragraphs as a memory from a time that can never return, from a childhood that was secure and innocent, into which death, sex, and fear were not allowed access. The innocence of Quentin's childhood was possible simply because he lacked understanding of other aspects of life, which in its turn may be seen as a result of his upbringing, which included protection, exclusiveness, membership in a superior race, and lack of emotional capacity. In "A Justice" there is no internal evidence to refute the impression that Quentin tells his story as a grown-up looking back with some nostalgia upon the Sundays of his childhood world, and the same, as we have seen, is in complex ways true for "That Evening Sun."

A final point about "That Evening Sun" may be mentioned. If this story demonstrates the child reporting on something he does not grasp, the elements chosen for narration would most likely have been totally different. Only a storyteller with a keen sense of dramatic effect would juxtapose Jason's fear of the Halloween pumpkin with Nancy's fear of a waiting murderer. No one but a skilled artist would let the black characters call Nancy's place a "house" while all the white characters use "cabin." A similar case can be made of the effective description and recurrent use of Nancy's hands and of the very perceptive description of Mr. Lovelady.

By using representatives of other races—black and Indian—in the two stories with Quentin Compson as child character and adult narrator, Faulkner was able to fuse the meaning of legend and myth to Quentin's own life. The significance of Quentin's experience (some critics would call it his initiation) is suspended and cannot be fully grasped either by the narrator himself or by the reader. The change from the collective consciousness and the use of "the best of gossip" in some of the village stories to individual consciousness and the use of legend and myth in "That Evening Sun" and "A Justice" proved to be a very productive and effective one. It is not only another example of the wide range of storytelling techniques in Faulkner's short fiction. "That Evening Sun" is an example of the short story genre at its best and fullest—a text to be returned to over and over again, to find new layers of meaning, new combinations of images and fictional facts, new angles of approach. In my understanding it is both a simple and straightforward short story and one of the most inexhaustible of all the stories Faulkner ever wrote.

# Chapter 15

# Victory

## TEXTUAL INFORMATION AND PUBLICATION HISTORY

"Victory" is not mentioned on Faulkner's sending list nor in his known correspondence. It is thus a story whose actual date of composition we can only guess at. The number of typescripts and manuscripts indicates work on this story over some time. There are four different incomplete manuscripts and typescripts extant, but apart from the fact that they show that Faulkner worked on and off with "Victory," they offer no evidence as to when the story was actually written. Blotner states that "Victory" is much earlier than 1931, when Faulkner worked to expand the planned collection of short stories. Blotner's assumption is apparently based on the similarity between the last scene of "Victory" and a letter Faulkner wrote home from England in 1926.[1] The germ of the story lies probably here somewhere; the first drafts possibly, too, since the prepublication material indicates that they belong to a very early phase of Faulkner's short story career. Including "Crevasse" as an episode in its early versions, "Victory" was a very long story that could hardly be published unless its length was reduced. But in his work on this story, Faulkner demonstrates both his thriftiness and his acute awareness of how old material might be revised and reused.[2]

In "The Short Fiction of William Faulkner" (Meriwether 1971, 310), James B. Meriwether describes the prepublication versions as "MS., 9 pp. (incomplete); TS., 56 pp. (incomplete); TS., 49 pp. (incomplete)." Blotner (1974) assumes that the nine manuscript pages belong to two different fragments, four and five pages long respectively, and that they are later than the two typescripts (I:100–1, 692). This seems more than likely. A close study of the manuscripts indicates that they are indeed attempts to work out new elements for the story in typescript and that they, in accordance with Faulkner's inconsistent practice, represent new attempts at improving already completed and typed stories. The five-page manuscript represents a new introduction to "Victory," describing the stay in France, whereas the four miscellaneous pages include an opening paragraph which is very close to the printed story's opening. The sequence of the four texts, with corrections for the lengths of the two typescripts, is, in my understanding: fifty-one-page typescript; fifty-four-page typescript (numbered 3–56, incomplete); five-page manuscript, incomplete; four-page manuscript, miscellaneous pages. How the author proceeded from this mixture of typed and handwritten material to type the version which was printed in *These 13* is something about which we can only speculate. Probably in the spring of 1931 Faulkner excised "Crevasse" from the longer story, and this left him with two very different stories. The final version of a rich, varied, but not too effective story is certainly a much later work. "Victory" is nevertheless a more competent and a better story than Faulkner critics—to the extent that they have paid attention to it—have thought. My own opinion of the story has changed gradually over the years, until I now am willing to include it among Faulkner's dozen best works of short fiction.

"Victory" appeared originally in *These 13,* as did two other war stories, "All the Dead Pilots" and "Crevasse." Only "Ad Astra" was printed before it appeared in the collection, and they all received indifferent treatment by the reviewers of Faulkner's first collection of stories. The "war is hell" school of fiction was out of vogue, and Faulkner's inability to sell these stories is a clear indication that there was little demand for stories about disillusioned young men who were unable to adjust to a world at peace.

The generalizations about the sad and undeserved fate of the soldiers who served their countries in the three other World War I stories in *These 13* are made concrete in the description of Alec Gray's destiny in "Victory," which in many respects is Faulkner's most successful World War I story. "Crevasse"[3]—excised from "Victory" in an earlier vesion— may be a more condensed and hence more forceful brief narrative, and "Turnabout," which joined the four other stories in "The Wasteland" section of *Collected Stories,* has more excitement and color and courage but is also much more in the popular vein, albeit not formulaic.

The critical attention given to Faulkner's war stories tends to be of two kinds. Critics who have treated these stories as a unified group have lost many implications and significant levels of meaning in the individual stories, but most often the stories have been dismissed with a passing remark of dissatisfaction. "Victory" has been read in relation to such noble terms as endurance, duty, and pride, but such interpretations seem to be abstractions from the story proper and too general, if not wrong, in what they say about Alec Gray and his rise and fall. Critics who have dealt with individual World War I stories also seem to have forgotten that these stories are war stories more than anything else, even if they share their descriptions of the world as a wasteland with numerous other Faulkner texts from the same period.[4]

## READING "VICTORY"

"Victory" as a title is blatantly ironic, in more than one sense. The protagonist comes out a loser despite his contribution to the victory in the war. He is a loser also in relation to his class, his family clan, society, God—and himself. And even the victory over the Germans which put an end to World War I is shown to be more than problematic for those who survived the war. They cannot find employment, and they often think that those who were killed on the battlefields are really better off than those who live in poverty in a wasteland world in the aftermath of the terrible fighting and bloodshed.

It is important to be aware of the irony implied in the term *victory,* because it enables us to avoid misreadings where the text is ambiguous or where the shifting perspectives may heap too much blame and responsibility for his situation of loss and deprivation on Alec Gray himself. There is no doubt in "Victory" that the kind of victories offered by a war do not change a rigid class system, and the possibilities of rapid rise to the officer class in the hierarchy of the military system do not exist in a class-conscious society after the war. People like Alec Gray may happen to think that they have made the transition to a different class, so that their plain and simple background can be left behind and forgotten, but Faulkner's text establishes a structure in which each and every man looks after his own, and the democratizing effect of the war is almost ridiculed. The story is not about these structures, even if it is critical of them by implication, but it is vital for an understanding of Gray's story to be aware of the framework of history, society, and power, of the rules, traditions, and customs against which it is played out. The story is explicit in its negative and pessimistic picture of postwar Europe, even the restoration of it that slowly takes place, and the only promise within the text of a better life with hopes for the future seems to be in the portrait of Walkley, who knew what lay in store for him after the war and therefore emigrated to Canada. But the story is first and foremost a long, at times slow-moving, at times rapidly dramatic, tale of a young Scottish shipwright's career in the war and his rapid decline and fall in the years afterward. An important interpretive question is why Alec Gray cannot go home again, and since he falls so low, what sort of motivation is given in the text for his fall, because his destiny is defined within the context of postwar Europe but not sufficiently explained by it. If it were, the story would be of only limited interest.

Our first encounter with the protagonist of "Victory" happens as he descends from the train at the Gare de Lyon, and we follow him to the Gare du Nord, and then in a hired car across a war-scorched landscape with scars still fresh from the fighting to a village of new brick and iron which only adds to the bleakness of the landscape. We see him as a tall man with spike-ended moustaches and almost white hair from the perspective of "those who saw him," either in a general sense or particularly, as is the case of two women on the train from Arras. The narration is omniscient, and the narrative voice remains the same throughout the story, while the perspective changes time and again. Gray is always seen from an external point of view, and what we see and get to know about him is very often misunderstood, a false interpretation, a misreading. At the same time it indicates that Gray from the outside may pass as a "milord military" (CS, 431), and the French observers therefore place him in the high class of officers and imagine that he will be "in a carriage with the fine English ladies in the Bois" (CS, 431). As readers we suspect that such observations are false, and as we follow Gray on his visit to the war scenes the narrator makes it clear that he is not of the wealthy upper-class officers. We see the colors of a Scottish regiment; we watch him go to the cheap hotel in the new village of "harsh new brick and sheet iron and tarred paper roofs made in America" (CS, 432); and we watch him among peasants with "baskets of live or dead beasts" (CS, 437) in a third-class carriage from Arras.

We get numerous descriptions of the yet unnamed protagonist from the outside, either as direct characterizations by the narrator or indirectly as the narrator reports what others saw and what they made of it. We do not get close to Alec Gray, since every observation is an outside one, and since we hardly ever, and then only by indirection, hear or see his reactions or thoughts. Some of the elements in the portrayal of Gray are close to being formulaic or at least prejudiced; he is understood to be British by the French observers, and so they equip him with what they find to be typically British traits. Let us look a little more closely at Alec Gray as he emerges from the opening and expository section, which chronologically belongs somewhere in part 6 of the story in seven parts, followed only by the descriptions of Gray's steady and rapid decline.

Alec Gray is tall, a little stiff, with white hair and spike-ended moustaches. Everything about him seems to be correct, and so the observers see in him a military man. Something is wrong with his eyes, but he appears to be purposeful and assured, knowing what he wants. He carries very little luggage but, typically enough, always a stick. His moustaches gleam "like faint bayonets," and his cravat is striped with "the patterned coloring of a Scottish regiment" (*CS*, 433). The host and a woman in the hotel where Gray stays think he is too old to have been to the war himself, and so they imagine that he may have come to look at the grave of his son. Yet they seem to agree that he is too cold to ever have had a son, and this understanding is repeated by two women on the train somewhat later.

Gray is, then, characterized by his stiffness and correctness; "the stiff, incongruous figure leaning a little forward on the stick" (*CS*, 436), by his moustaches and by his eyes. He does not seem to be much for conversation and keeps to himself. Gray is reading all signposts along the train route, and the French ladies think that he has at least heard about the war, so he might as well look at it. As readers we are led to understand that the white-haired and stiff gentleman has actually fought in the war and can deduce that war must have changed him considerably, so that he looks much older than he actually is. The obvious irony of the misinterpretations of all observers also prepares us for a story about the protagonist's active participation in the war, the scenes of which he now returns to.[5]

Apart from describing the protagonist and the tour through what still appears to be a wasteland four years after the war, the opening section gives extended descriptions of postwar Europe. Not only the scars of war are singled out for description. The narrator is even more pessimistic when he depicts the results of restoration. Europe is still in ruins, and what has been rebuilt is described as harsh and cheap. The description of Gray's bedroom in the hotel leaves no doubt about the narrator's attitude to the new and modern, the rebuilt Europe among the ruins of war:

> They mounted, thrusting their fitful shadows before them, into a corridor narrow, chill, and damp as a tomb. The walls were of rough plaster not yet dried. The floor was of pine, without carpet or paint. Cheap metal doorknobs glinted symmetrically. The sluggish air lay like a hand upon the very candle. They entered a room, smelling too of wet plaster, and even colder than the corridor; a sluggish chill almost substantial, as though the atmosphere between the dead and recent walls were congealing, like a patent three-minute dessert. (*CS*, 433)

The fact that the story opens with Gray's visit to France four years after the war's end is important in light of what follows, which, not unexpectedly, are scenes from the war. The introductory part gives explicit as well as implicit comments on the war and its long-term effects on people and landscape, and it foreshadows and even prepares much of what comes later in the text.[6]

Section 2 takes us straight into the war. A batallion stands at ease in the rain, and a young man arouses the officers' outrage by not having shaved and by not using "Sir" whenever he addresses his superiors. A sergeant-major is told to take the soldier's name; he asks his Sergeant to do it; and, finally, moving in correct lines through the hierarchy of the officers, 024186 Gray's name is taken for "insubordination" (*CS*, 440). Gray seems almost unaffected by the whole episode. He admits to not having shaved because he does not shave, since he is not old enough to do so. Gray answers "doggedly and without heat" (*CS*, 441), but also patiently and stubbornly, without excuses, without attempting to get away from the penalty for this minor neglect. His refusal to say "Sir," and his apparent unwillingness to do so even after he has been reprimanded and reminded to also tells of stubbornness and self-reliance. Young Gray seems utterly incapable of adjusting to the set of what he must experience as inexplicable and useless rules and regulations within the military system, and in telling this minor episode from a parade of a battalion, the narrator clearly wants to show the rigidity and stupidity of the system, since Gray has done little wrong except embrace his inferiority and low status without hesitation or question.

Young Gray, enlisted and trained as a soldier, should know the rules, and the noncommissioned officers seem almost unwilling to take down his name, as if they were on his side. Being young and inexperienced, Gray obviously must have brought with him most of his attitudes, his strong will, and his self-reliance from home, and in section 3 we are allowed to visit among the plain people of Clydeside in Scotland. In an uneven narrative which covers many areas and events and spans many years, the descriptions of Alec Gray's family and their lives are among the story's magic moments. Not only because we meet good, hardworking people with high and unchanging ethical standards, God-fearing and proud, ready and willing to serve country and nation if need be, but also because we see them as reluctant to let others decide how they serve best. As shipbuilders for two hundred years, they have most certainly served their King or Queen and Country, even though they may think that they not always served their own country and that going to war would be to fight and risk one's life in somebody else's battles. Loyalty, family pride, and stubborn endurance, based solidly in a long and unbroken tradition of building quality ships, characterize these relatives of the plain people of Yoknapatawpha. In contrast, the American cousins in stories like "Two Soldiers" and "Shall Not Perish" seem exaggerated, incredible, and sentimentalized where the Grays are believable, trustworthy, and absolutely reliable in their Protestant ethics and adherence to the old ways.

In section 3 we are present at a family council, obviously being held because young Alec has expressed a wish to enlist and participate in the ongoing war. His father, Matthew Gray, is heard as he argues why Alec should not leave the shipyard to become a soldier:

> "For two hundred years," Matthew Gray said, "there's never been a day, except Sundays, has passed but there is a hull rising on the Clyde or a hull going out of Clydemouth with a Gray-driven nail in it. . . . And now, when you are big enough to go down to the yards with your grandadder and me and take a man's place among men, to be trusted manlike with hammer and saw yersel." (CS, 441)

There is much pride involved in what Matthew Gray says—the narrator calls it "dour pride"—but there is also a sense of tradition and perhaps even the working man's reluctance to let go of a good worker, even if only temporarily. The grandfather, old Alec, is less concerned with the immediate problems if young Alec leaves. He knows that the young man is a competent shipwright already and boasts that he himself can go on working, being only sixty-eight, while young Alec does a little fighting, since the war will soon be over, anyhow. Matthew Gray is still more concerned about the needs of the shipyard and mentions his other children, who are still too young to help him build ships. But his final statement seems independent of everything else he has said and is likely to represent what he really thinks and means: "a Gray, a shipwright, has no business at an English war" (CS, 442).

But it comes as no surprise to the reader when we discover that the grandfather has the stronger argument, because we would have been disappointed if this proud Scottish family had not done their duty before and sent soldiers off to "save the Queen." Old Alec produces a box within which is another, smaller jeweler's box, with a "bit of bronze on a crimson ribbon: a Victoria Cross" (CS, 442). It had been given to Uncle Simon (Matthew's uncle) while old Alec kept the hulls going out of Clydemouth. As readers we may want to intervene and say that wars have changed; the fact that Simon returned from his service does not mean that young Alec will return from the hell of modern warfare. The persuasiveness of the tradition and a strong sense of duty, no matter whose war it is, finally seem to convince even Matthew Gray. "Nay, Matthew; dinna thwart the lad; have no the Grays ever served the Queen in her need?" (CS, 442) are old Alec's final words. Perhaps as an indication of how wrong a decision this was after all, we are told that the day young Alec left was also the last day of work for old Alec, who spends his days in a chair on the porch, listening for the sound of guns going off.

Alec Gray left to enlist with the New Testament and a loaf of homemade bread. The book must have been a Bible if we are to trust the quotations and references later on in the text, but the Book is important as a symbol of his heritage, even though it is given an unsuspected role in the development of Alec's life as a soldier. Alec leaves home for soldiering, which he finds very different from shipbuilding, as he says in first letters. And as long as we are allowed to follow Alec Gray through the years of war and in four or five years following it, excerpts from letters, printed in italics, are our source of information about the family at Clydeside. Alec keeps quiet about many things, but the letters function well as a technical device within the structure of a narrative. We need to know something about the world Alec left behind, and the letters make it so much easier for the narrative to maintain its perspective close to young Alec and still inform us about his family, merging the two perspectives by letting Alec read the letters and react to them.

For seven months Alec does not answer his parents' letters (his mother and father write joint letters to him on the first of every month), but he receives one of the letters, asking if he still has the Book, during the period he spends in the penal colony for insubordination, and his answer is integrated in the narrative as follows:

> *I am well. Yes I still have the Book* (not telling them that his platoon was using it to light tobacco with and that they were now well beyond Lamentations). *It still rains. Love to Grandadder and Jessie and Matthew and John Wesley.* (CS, 444)

His mother had clearly thought of a different use for the Holy Book, but we learn later on that he opens the book at "the jagged page where his life had changed: '. . . *and a voice said, Peter, raise thyself; kill—*'" (CS, 448). This is vitally important for our interpretation of the text, since it indicates that Alec has acted in accordance with words received from the Holy Scripture and not only to revenge himself on his sergeant-major. It may not change much, but I think we should keep in mind the religious background of his family and the significance of the Bible as the only object from home still with him in the trenches and afterwards.

Back in ordinary duty Alec begins to shave because he is old enough, and when he asks about the old sergeant-major, he is told that he is still in the same battalion. They move up to Arras, and Faulkner includes one of his many scenes in the war stories where the generals act stupidly and demonstrate their power and lack of consideration for the soldiers. The general stands waving beside his car on the road while each man in the battalion must wade deep in the mud of the ditch to pass him and then heave himself onto the road again.

In combat action in the trenches Alec uses a moment when he is alone with his sergeant-major to murder him with his bayonet. He may have seen an omen in the text from the Bible, and life in the penal colony has most certainly been terrible, yet his murder is both brutal and premeditated, and the text leaves no doubt about the bestiality of the murder and of the cold-blooded control with which it is carried out:

> He frees the bayonet [from the sergeant-major's throat]. The sergeant-major falls. Gray reverses his rifle and hammers its butt into the sergeant-major's face, but the trench floor is too soft to supply any resistance. He glares about. His gaze falls upon a duckboard upended in the mud. He drags it free and slips it beneath the sergeant-major's head and hammers the face with his rifle-butt. Behind him in the first traverse the Officer is shouting: "Blow your whistle, Sergeant-major!" (CS, 446)[7]

This murderous act is shown to lie behind Alec Gray's temporary rise and ultimate downfall, since he takes command now that his sergeant-major is dead and leads a charge with great bravery. He is decorated and spends time in hospital healing his war wounds. He can write home that he has *"a ribbon like in the box but not all red. The Queen was there"* (CS, 447), and in his next letter he tells that he is going to a school for officers. This message is so important that the narrative changes perspective so that we follow Matthew Gray's thinking and pondering over this letter before he writes it, "slowly and deliberately and without retraction or blot" (CS, 447). Matthew Gray has made up his mind, and he speaks his mind freely and directly to his son. Matthew's letter represents traditional wisdom, and it tells Alec not to forget who he is and where he belongs. Clearly the father would not object to his son's chances of rising in the world if he did not sense that Alec wants to do this for the wrong reasons. Matthew also fears that his son is being fooled into believing that he shall become a gentleman among other gentlemen and that his son is bound to suffer from this mistake. Much of the power of the story lies in this conflict, which is reiterated and specified even more clearly much later on, during Alec's final visit to his home. In a letter Matthew writes:

> . . . *your bit ribbon . . . for that way lies vainglory and pride. The pride and vainglory of going for an officer. Never miscall your birth, Alec. You are not a gentleman. You are a Scottish shipwright. If your grandfather were here he would not be the last to tell you so . . . We are glad your hurt is well. Your mother sends her love.* (CS, 448)

Life goes on at Clydeside, a new sister has been born, the grandfather has died, ships are being built, letters written, and the Bible consulted when the acquired wisdom of the tribe becomes insufficient. But Alec, for reasons on which we can only speculate, does not listen, and as readers we are not surprised. Perhaps we expect Alec to become a "good" officer, in the sense that he behaves differently in front of his men than the many we see with upper-class backgrounds. I do not think we do; our suspicion is that Alec has made a decision to climb and rise and become like those who had the power to penalize him, and Faulkner creates a scene which is a clear parallel to the earlier one with the unshaven young Alec, in which Subaltern-Captain Gray orders his sergeant to take down the name of 010801 McLan because his rifle is filthy (*CS*, 449).

One of the best war scenes of combat and desperate fighting, including acts of heroic folly, in all of Faulkner's stories then follows to complete and round off section 4. Alec Gray appears to be more dead than alive when he is found, and again he is decorated. His father reads the citation in the *Gazette*, but is weary of the long war: "*When a war gets to where the battles do not even prosper the people who win them, it is time to stop*" (*CS*, 452). And for Alec, war has come to an end. He is in hospital with another "gas case," a subaltern who dreams of going to Canada after the war. Gray stays in the hospital through Armistice Day, but seems to be well again around Christmas. The medical officer tries to joke with Gray, telling him that the murmur in his chest may "keep you from getting in again" (*CS*, 453), but the text tells us that Gray did not laugh. We also know that he has been asked to come home, because ships will be more in demand than ever before, but we suspect on the basis of his not being interested in the suggestions about Canada, not wanting to go home, not pleased that he may be unfit for enlistment in a new war, that he has become a professional soldier and thinks of himself as a soldier. His *Kriegserlebnis* has changed him completely, and the rest of the text will provide few surprises, since the textual signals are so clear. We do not know how long Gray will keep his form, keep up appearances, although we know that he seems to be doing fairly well four years after the war on the basis of the opening section. But we have been prepared by the narrator's attitude, by his juxtaposing of letters, by his comments on Matthew Gray's words of wisdom, that Alec is lost, doomed, dead if he does not return home. He has been allowed entrance into a world which is not his own, and soon there will not be room for him in this world, if we have interpreted the textual signals so far correctly.

Having followed the text closely to this point, in an attempt to understand the motivations behind Alec Gray's behavior as well as to explain the most important story elements in the narrative (its plot), there is little reason to read on as slowly through the long and tedious descriptions of Gray's gradual downfall in London. The details are needed to demonstrate how it happened and why it finally became inevitable, and the slow narrative also seems to mirror the boredom and futility and absurdity of Gray's life.

But he pays one visit more to his parents and has a long conversation with his father, before beginning his life as a retired officer in the capital of the British Empire. The conflict between father and son, between two ways of looking at the world, or perhaps now between two kinds of experience, is summed up in this simple phrase by the father: "the proper uniform for a Gray is an overall and a hammer" (CS, 454). Alec seems to accept this statement but apparently thinks that he has been given a chance, a golden opportunity, that he cannot relinquish. He knows that he is a Gray by birth and tradition and even profession, but also that he has been given a chance to rise in the world by accident. The narrator's explanation of why Alec seems to accept his father's statement about his proper uniform is otherwise difficult to explain: "'Ay, sir,' Alec said, who had long since found out that no man has courage but that any man may blunder blindly into valor as one stumbles into an open manhole in the street" (CS, 454).[8]

Matthew warns Alec about his new friends, officers and such, and at the same time supports our feeling that Alec has made a terrible choice and stands few chances of having a good or decent life. Matthew knows that "only them that love you will bear your faults. You must love a man well to put up with all his trying ways, Alec" (CS, 455), and when he opens the heavy, brassbound Bible, he finds a paragraph concerning pride and knows that he has lost his son: "You will go to London, then?" (CS, 455).

Alec has a position waiting in an office, rooms in the proper quarter, cards made, and walks with his stick as the gentleman he pretends to be. With the last of his money he sends gifts home, including a black silk dress for his mother. He makes the trip to France we have already read about, and upon his return his position is gone. The rest of the text delineates a steep and quick downward movement, until we finally see him selling matches on the streets around Piccadilly Circus. He is discovered there also by Walkley, the subaltern who shared a room with him in the hospital and who wanted to go to Canada. The final section is told from Walkley's perspective, but even if he approaches Gray and Gray admits that he knows him and tells his name, he wants to be left alone: "Let me alone, you son of a bitch!," Gray says, "with a kind of restrained yet raging impatience" (CS, 464). So Walkley moves on swiftly, nauseated by the experience.

Alec Gray is caught in the spider web of urban life, based on false pretensions. When he has begun this new life his pride prevents him from changing its course, even when he becomes a beggar on the streets. The narrator takes time to relate small stories about other destinies near the end of the story about Alec Gray, among them a long-winded tale about a blind man fooled by his girl, and the text thus seems to indicate that the other bums and beggars have reasons for their circumstances that Alec Gray does not, having chosen his life as he has and being unable to escape from it because he has made it impossible for himself ever to go home again. A coincidence of time, place, and people which only a war could provide combines with character traits and his own choices so that it becomes imperative to become an officer and, later, to belong to this class at any cost. And even if we see the forces that shaped his course, we know that he has had other options and is completely lost because he has settled for new values of little worth to replace the lasting, traditional, and life-giving norms of family and home. All through the narrative Alec Gray and the readers are reminded of these values, so Alec's failure to correct his course and readjust to a life for which he was well equipped is something we have a constant awareness of. War is depicted as destructive on all levels, and the destiny of the God-fearing young Scot[9] must be interpreted within the framework set by the great catastrophe of World War I. And one should be very careful and reluctant in applying one or more of Faulkner's Nobel prize keywords in an interpretation of this story. The endurance theme is not at the center here, even if some stable values seem to be endorsed in the descriptions of the Grays of Clydeside.[10]

Alec Gray's story proves that not only Sartorises or other people of more or less aristocratic birth are lost and condemned; also the humble people who during a war rise to a pseudo-aristocracy (the officer class) will ultimately fall. The tragic results of Alec's break with his family and the traditional values it represents may also indicate that the plain people's values are normative: they set a standard against which other characters' actions and ideals may be measured.[11]

In "Crevasse" the world of the living outside the cave cannot offer any hope of rebirth; and if the soldiers have any dreams, they are dreams of survival. The war-scorched landscape is moribund, and summer seems far away. This picture of the wasteland of war demonstrates better than the sentimentality, lost-generation gibberish, and quasi-philosophical assumptions of "Ad Astra" and "All the Dead Pilots" what kind of reality the dreams had to be tested against. In "Victory" the waste, futility, and cruelty of war are extended into postwar Europe, where unemployment and dishonor face those who helped win the war so that everyone could maintain at least one dream, the most important of them all: the dream of peace in our time. This theme links "Victory" with "Mountain Victory," another powerful tale of war and the longing for peace.

# Chapter 16

# Wash

## TEXTUAL INFORMATION AND PUBLICATION HISTORY

Faulkner probably wrote "Wash" during the summer of 1933, in a period when his short story production was irregular and low. "Wash" was only the second new story in 1933 (preceded by the Indian story "Lo!"). This was an enormous decline in short story production compared to the previous two or three years. With few exceptions his short stories would from now on stand in close and significant relationship to his novels, either because they later were integrated into the longer narratives or because a number of stories with thematic and formal elements in common would, in revised shape, make up volumes such as *The Unvanquished* and *Go Down, Moses*. "Wash" is one of the germs of what some consider Faulkner's greatest novel, *Absalom, Absalom!*, although "Evangeline," unknown for a long time and not published until 1979, shows an even earlier interest in this material (Skei 1981, 71–72). There is no trace of "Wash" in Faulkner's correspondence with his agent, but he must have sent it to Morton Goldman, who sold it to *Harper's Magazine* on November 2, 1933 (Blotner 1974, I:819). The story was published by *Harper's* in February 1934, and it was collected in *Doctor Martino and Other Stories* a few months later. "Wash" was also included in *Collected Stories*, which is surprising, since Faulkner had used the story, albeit in substantially revised form, in *Absalom, Absalom!* (1936). As we know, he did not include "The Hound" or "Spotted Horses," both reused in *The Hamlet*, in his major short story collection. It is tempting to suggest that "Wash" was included in *Collected Stories* because many people were involved in the process of publishing this collection, yet we also know that Faulkner's practice was inconsistent in matters of this kind. The author may simply have felt that

"Wash" had been so completely suffused in the text of the novel and so seriously revised to suit the narrative techniques employed there that the story might just as well live on as a short story in its own right. Or he may simply have thought so highly of this short story that he wanted to use it in his *Collected Stories*.[1] Yet the strange fact remains that this story about Wash Jones and Sutpen is the only story that was both reused in a novel and retained as a short story in *Collected Stories*.[2]

In a famous letter to Malcolm Cowley, Faulkner explains how *The Hamlet* was written, thereby giving an outline of how he created the Snopeses and how they grew and developed over the years. Surprisingly, "Wash" is mentioned in this connection: "So I wrote an induction toward the spotted horse story, which included BARN BURNING, and WASH, which I discovered had no place in that book at all."[3] What this tells us is that the story somehow came out of Faulkner's year-long work with many aspects of the Snopes material, which he was unable to bring together in a novel until *The Hamlet*. The changes from manuscript drafts to typescripts of "Wash" show that the basic elements of the story's plot were kept unchanged, although the story was considerably altered during the process. For such a brief story with an unusually dynamic drive toward the ending, it is only reasonable that the author experimented with openings as well as with endings and discarded attempts at showing Wash in hiding or focusing on Sutpen. The final solution—Sutpen's rejection of Milly and the baby daughter—brings in Wash's terrible situation immediately, and the story's apocalyptic ending is prepared in its very opening (*William Faulkner Manuscripts 15 [Vols. I & II]: The Hamlet*, xi; Jones 1994, 387). Beginning the story with Milly and the child forces the storyteller to move back in time through retrospective flashbacks to portray character, tell the story of Wash's sordid life and Sutpen's bravery in the war, and thus by retarding the speed of the narrative give added intensity and increase the dramatic tension of the story when the narrative returns to the present.

## READING "WASH"

"Wash" is one of Faulkners's taut and forceful short narratives, self-contained and complete in itself despite its close relationship to *Absalom, Absalom!*. It is one of Faulkner's best short stories, and its strength is completely different from the function of the same material in the technically very complex narrative of the novel, in which Quentin's "reconstruction of Sutpen's effect on those who knew him" (Carothers 1985, 38) obscures the facts surrounding Sutpen's murder as well as the character of Wash Jones. The story has received surprisingly little critical attention as a short story, and even those who insist that it must be regarded as an autonomous story and treated as a separate work of art in its own right tend to discuss its relationship to *Absalom, Absalom!* rather than the structural simplicity and narrative power of "Wash" (Carothers 1985, for example, and Ferguson 1991).[4] The very title of the story points to its sharp focus on Wash Jones, and the story centers on his disillusionment upon discovering how callous and inhuman is a man whom he for years and years has idealized. Everything in the story evolves from this disillusionment, this sudden moment of revelation and insight, which also includes a discovery of how strong and stubborn Wash's pride is, contrary to what Sutpen had thought. Wash discovers that his basic mistake has been to think that Sutpen was born a superior human being, and Sutpen discovers that he has made a fatal mistake in assuming that Wash always and in all circumstances will bend and yield and be subservient. Even if Wash concedes that women are a mystery to him, it may well be that his discovery of Sutpen's evil is related to a vague understanding that he has to defend the honor of a woman—his own granddaughter (Carothers 1992, 51).

In the story's middle section we see Sutpen ride off to fight in the Civil War, and we follow Wash through the years of Sutpen's absence, but basically the section introduces us to the world of Sutpen's Hundred in the years after the war, a world characterized by loss and poverty and decay. In this part of the story we follow the endless conversations between Sutpen and Wash as they drink inferior whisky in the rear of the "store" Sutpen has set up, and we watch the beginning of Sutpen's seduction of Wash's granddaugher, Milly. The story resumes in the present time established in the opening section but also continues from the middle section after a lapse of two years, which we know have also been filled with the same talk about having lost the war but not being whipped, even if the middle section ends on Wash's attempts to get insurance from Sutpen that he will treat his granddaughter well. (She is fifteen; two years later she gives birth to Sutpen's child at the age of seventeen.) The whole story describes the development over a long period of time, and then quickly, inevitably, and urgently in the course of a single day, of a strange triangle, culminating in a tragic, apocalyptic drama when Wash suddenly sees and understands what Sutpen is and has done. It is a story about disillusionment, and violence is Wash Jones's only means to preserve some of the pride he has vainly and falsely asserted all his life by apotheosizing Sutpen.

Despite the story's apocalyptic horror, Faulkner refuses to describe the violence directly, and the omniscient narrator moves aside and looks in another direction when Wash lifts the scythe, and, later, the butcher's knife. In its slow development from apparent friendship and admiration to revealing insight and conflict, "Wash" may be seen as a "concentrat-

ed parable of Southeren degeneracy in the aftermath of the Civil War"
(Stewart 1969, 588).

"Wash" is set on the Sutpen plantation, and the scenes of violent
action take place some time around 1870,[5] between dawn and sunset of
a sunny Sunday. The middle section, falling between the narration of the
events at dawn and those that precede the opening scene and the violent
and horrifying actions which follow just before sunset of this sunny and
bloody Sunday, lets us see Wash in all his prejudice and pride, including
his limitless worship of Sutpen and his frantic belief in his own superiority to the Negroes on the plantation. All of this lends credibility to
Wash's emotional reactions when he finally discovers what Sutpen is
worth.

The first scene in "Wash" is one of Faulkner's marvelous frozen
tableaux, with Sutpen standing above the pallet bed with mother and
child. His legs are straddled, the riding whip is in his hand, and the long
pencil strokes of the sun fall upon him and on "the still shape of the
mother, who lay looking up at him from still, inscrutable, sullen eyes"
(CS, 535). The black midwife is also present and can hear Sutpen's
words to his young mistress: "'Well, Milly,' Sutpen said, 'too bad you're
not a mare. Then I could give you a decent stall in the stable'" (CS, 535).
As readers we listen to these incredible words, and even if they cannot be
excused no matter what we get to know later in the text, they become
explicable because we understand that Sutpen has watched his mare,
Griselda, foal earlier this morning. Milly does not react at all; she is
described as sullen and inscrutable once more, and this may be taken as
an indication that she does not have much faith in Sutpen and has a
much more realistic appreciation of him than her grandfather does. The
midwife becomes involved in the brief talk with Sutpen, so that he can
tell about the colt Griselda foaled and also get confirmation that the
baby on the pallet bed is a "mare" (CS, 535). Sutpen seems totally unin-
terested, and the newborn colt reminds him of his old horse, Rob Roy,
when he "rode him North in '61" (CS, 535). His terrible remark to Milly
is clearly based on his knowledge that the baby is a girl, a knowledge we
as readers come to much later in the story, after the middle section has
come to an end and we return to the events of the Sunday in 1870—even
to a point somewhat earlier than the sunlit opening tableau. This comes
later, and even if we as readers experience the text differently on second
reading, it is a deliberate choice on the part of the narrator (and the
author) to withhold information until we have learned more about Wash
Jones's character, his unlimited admiration of the "Kernel," and the
strange companionship they share in the dreary years in the aftermath of
the great war. But the opening scene, moving from the initial tableau
through the brief conversation about colts and mares to the outside of

the shack, where Wash is holding the reins of his waiting horse and a rusting scythe is leaning against the corner of the porch, among the rank weeds that should have been cut with the very same scythe by Wash months ago.

The brief opening section of the story (which has no section divisions but open space to indicate shift of scene, time, and perspective) very effectively prepares for the narrative to come. The reference to Sutpen riding off to fight in 1861 is one of many foreshadowings or anticipations of what the narrative will bring as we read on. The introductory paragraphs show us Sutpen's arrogance and cynicism; the rank weeds and the scythe seem to be bad omens. We have seen births, but we also have a foreboding of the grim reaper. We are at dawn of a bright morning, but everything in the opening section seems to point toward a day when we shall watch the sun rise and set over the Sutpen plantation and the people living there. Seldom, if ever, did Faulkner create dramatic tension and expectations so convincingly in the opening of a short story. The tableau with the sixty-year-old man, horsewhip in hand, above the young girl with a newborn baby, the dilapidated building, the weeds, the scythe, the midwife calling Sutpen "Marster," and Wash also in the position of servant—all this gives an impression of something terribly wrong, utterly bad, with enormous potential for death and destruction. We do not know the relationships between the different characters, but we have a sense of what they may be, and as we read through the middle section's account of the times and affairs leading up to this point in time tension does not diminish even if the pace of the narrative slows down. On the contrary, tension builds, and the decisive moment, the critical point, the denouement of a tragic development, is when we get confirmation that Wash, waiting outside with the horse, has actually heard the words Sutpen spoke to his granddaughter. But we shall have to follow the text through its middle section before returning to a point in time just before the opening tableau.

The middle section of the story falls roughly into two parts. The first one deals with Wash Jones's life and thoughts in the years when the "Kernel" was away fighting the Yankees. This part is important since it conveys the impression that Wash looks upon Sutpen as God. He virtually fuses his image of Sutpen on the black stallion with his conception of God: "If God Himself was to come down and ride the natural earth, that's what He would aim to look like" (CS, 538). He does so in a desperate and vain attempt at asserting his own superiority to the Negroes. Wash did not go to the war when the colonel left, and he tells everyone who asks—and even those who do not—that he is taking care of the plantation and the Negroes for the colonel, which everyone knows is not true; it may well be that he is the only one who believes it. Wash seems to live under the illusion that he has a particularly close, or at least different, relationship to Sutpen than a Negro could ever have, and even though he is worse off than the plantation Negroes, he has to cling to some sort of pride, be it false or not, and he seems always to be in a state of impotent rage because of a self-understanding laughed at by everyone around him, including the blacks. Black laughter seems to surround him, but Wash knows intuitively that he is better than the blacks even though worse off than they, and it is the pride and satisfaction of knowing Sutpen, combined with an exaggerated admiration for him, that keep Wash going through the terrible war years. He is really nothing more than a squatter in a corner of Sutpen's plantation, with a dilapidated shack, and we are left in no doubt as to his poverty and also his marginality:

> . . . his sole connection with the Sutpen plantation lay in the fact that for years now Colonel Sutpen had allowed him to squat in a crazy shack on a slough in the river bottom on the Sutpen place, which Sutpen had built for a fishing lodge in his bachelor days and which had since fallen in dilapidation from disuse, so that now it looked like an aged or sick wild beast crawled terrifically there to drink in the act of dying. (CS, 536)

The reason why Sutpen has allowed Wash to live on his property for so long is one we only can guess at in the short story, but even if we are told that they spend some Sundays drinking and talking together when there is no company in the house, we sense what we get to know in *Absalom, Absalom!* that Sutpen comes from the same background of poor farmers without property. Wash seems to have been accepted as a drinking partner on rare occasions before the war; after the war, when property and slaves and everything are lost, this becomes a ritual and a habit, and it is made abundantly clear by the text that Sutpen accepts Wash because of loneliness and because of the need for someone to take care of him and bring him to bed when he drinks himself into delirium. During the long years of war, when Wash seems to hear the echoes of black laughter all the time, he remembers "the fine figure on the black stallion, galloping about the plantation" (CS, 538), and this enables him to think of the real world of Negroes laughing and being better housed and clothed than he as "but a dream and an illusion" (CS, 538). The actual world would then be "this one across which his own lonely apotheosis seemed to gallop on the black thoroughbred" (CS, 538). Wash even seeks comfort in his own misinterpretations of the Bible to feel superior to the Negroes.

Before Colonel Sutpen returns in 1865, the plantation is completely in ruins; Sherman has gone through it, and most of the slaves left with him. Sutpen's son had been killed in action the same year his wife died.

He returns on the black stallion, with a citation for gallantry from General Lee, to poverty and deprivation, to a daughter who now subsists "partially on the meager bounty of the man to whom fifteen years ago he had granted permission to live in that tumbledown fishing camp whose very existence he had at the time forgotten" (CS, 539). We do not know if Wash was present when the Colonel left for the war, but he is there when Sutpen returns, unchanged: "still gaunt, still ageless, with his pale, questioning gaze, his air diffident, a little servile, a little familiar. 'Well, Kernel,' Wash said, 'they kilt us but they ain't whupped us yit, air they?'" (CS, 539). In this description of the unchanging Wash—the Colonel seems to have aged ten years—and in the catalog of character traits and attitudes, our picture of Wash seems to be complete. This is the man, father and grandfather, poor, shiftless, who seems to have endured and survived years of hardships because of a strong personal pride, based on as serious a misjudgment of character as can well be imagined. The fact that Wash did not go to the war, for which the Negroes tease him, is not brought up in any other way in the text, but Wash has no other excuse than a daughter and family to keep and no Negroes to look after them.

For the reader who remembers the defeated plantation owner and Confederate officer on his way home in "Mountain Victory," Colonel Sutpen appears to be the exact opposite. War has not changed him much, and he is unable to keep up appearances and live according to the rules of the plantation aristocracy. His failure indicates his background and his real—if not exactly natural and inborn—character traits. And, thinking of the officer who never made it back home to Mississippi but was killed in the Tennessee mountains ("Mountain Victory"), the reader may also come to think that Wash's servility and stupid admiration supersede that of Captain Weddel's black servant, even if the latter is much of a caricature.

David Minter (1992) has written of the world of Sutpen's Hundred in the aftermath of the Civil War that it is a "world of class and caste in which race and gender loom large as shaping forces, though not always in completely predictable ways, since neither Wash Jones nor the slaves nor the former slaves can ever quite be sure which of them is lower and which, higher. Only Sutpen's status seems assured" (94). This seems an apt description of the situation before the war came to an end; afterwards the conflicts of class and caste are still there, still unsolved, but they are not central in the text, nor do they appear to be of particular importance for the further development of the basic and tragic conflict in the story's present: Milly's baby and Sutpen's reaction. Yet there are some basic forces shaping everything and everyone within the limits of the story, and Minter may have pointed at the two dominant ones:

"Wash Jones and Sutpen are conscious of two big facts: that neither of them is black and neither of them is female" (94). Sutpen has his arrogant ways with women, but the sixty-year-old war veteran's seduction of Wash's granddaughter cannot be much to be proud of. Wash does not understand women, and, thinking of his wife and his granddaughter, he says, "Women. Hit's a mystery to me" (CS, 546).

As we read on through the middle section of the story, we move away from the descriptions of how Wash endured black laughter and all other hardships while the Colonel was away simply by imagining himself to live in a different world and belonging with his ideal, Colonel Sutpen, in this imaginary world. The world has not changed much in the second phase of the story of the past leading up to the bright Sunday of the story's opening, but Sutpen is back, and he and Wash seem to form a strange alliance in a situation where both of them may well have felt that any company was preferable to no company. Sutpen is marked by the war, but particularly affected by his downfall and degradation from rich plantation owner to storekeeper. For five years—and they must have been long years—Sutpen and Wash drink bad whisky and talk about having lost the war yet not being whipped. Sutpen must deal with Negroes and poor whites who come to the store "to haggle tediously for dimes and quarters with a man who at one time could gallop . . . for ten miles across his own fertile land and who had led troops gallantly in battle" (CS, 539).[6] Sutpen is in the habit of emptying his store in a fury, closing it up, and drinking with Wash until Wash somehow has to get him back to the house and into bed. Sutpen's daughter, Judith, is there, but Wash always takes care of Sutpen when in coma or delirium he reaches a stage of "impotent and furious undefeat" (CS, 539–40) and wants to kill Lincoln and Sherman.

During the five years after the war which the story of Wash and Sutpen covers, a change in their relationship occurs and is reflected in the text. It is occasioned by Milly's growing up, the sullen, inscrutable mother of seventeen whom we meet in the opening paragraphs of the story. When she is fifteen her grandfather sees a ribbon around her waist and knows where it comes from. When later she appears in a dress which Judith Sutpen has helped make, Wash approaches Sutpen and is "quite grave": ". . . she ain't nothing but a fifteen-year-old gal" (CS, 541). Wash then goes on to explain that the only reason he lets Milly keep the dress is that it comes from Sutpen and because he is different. Sutpen wants to know how he is different but also claims that he now understands why Wash is afraid of him. Wash seems to have become different now that he takes on a grandfather's responsibility for a child; his gaze is described as tranquil and serene, and he explains why he thinks Milly is safe with Sutpen:

I ain't afraid. Because your air brave. It ain't that you were a brave man one minute or day of your life and got a paper to show hit from General Lee. But you air brave, the same as you air alive and breathing. That's where hit's different. Hit don't need no ticket from nobody to tell me that. And I know that whatever you handle or tech, whether hit's a regiment of men or an ignorant gal or just a hound dog, that you will make hit right. (CS, 541–42)

Wash does not have to meet Sutpen's arrogant stare after his unusually long speech; Sutpen seems embarrassed: "Now it was Sutpen who looked away, turning suddenly, brusquely" (CS, 541). He knows what he is doing, and he knows that Wash errs completely in his judgment of character. But it is also quite obvious that he cannot admit it, and the two men turn to the jug of whisky instead, and life goes on for two more years while the narrative pauses. It resumes on "that Sunday two years later," but the narrative adopts Wash's perspective and starts before the tableau in the opening paragraph.

Wash has fetched the midwife for Milly, and he waits outside, "quiet though concerned" (CS, 542). His mind wanders to what people, black and white alike, have been saying about the strange triangle made up by himself, his granddaughter, and Sutpen, who are described as being "like three actors that came and went upon a stage" (CS, 542).[7] People have whispered and gossiped about Wash, who has finally, after twenty years, "*fixed old Sutpen at last*," but Wash does not at all think in such terms. He is proud, and, listening to his granddaughter in labor, "thinking went slowly and terrifically," involving the sound of galloping hooves and the proud figure of a man on a fine stallion. Wash's thoughts break free, and he finds words for his image of Sutpen "as the apotheosis, lonely, explicable, beyond all fouling by human touch" (CS, 542). More important than the exaggerated description of Sutpen, who to Wash is bigger than everyone and everything, is the understanding that this must somehow have put its mark on Wash himself:

. . . And how could I have lived this nigh to him for twenty years without being teched and changed by him? Maybe I ain't as big as him and maybe I ain't done none of the galloping. But at least I done been drug along. Me and him kin do hit, if so be he will show me what he aims for me to do. (CS, 543)

This is a statement, if not a prayer, for someone who wants to serve, who asks for guidance in a language with religious overtones. His thoughts of the galloping hooves and his vain self-delusion of having been "drug along" brings the text to the dawn we have been told would come after a while. Milly's baby is born, and Wash is told that it is a girl, and again, repeatedly, he hears the galloping hooves and sees the galloping figure again, galloping "through avatars which marked the accumulation of years, time . . ." (*CS, 543*). Wash is pleased to be a great-grandfather. He is ordered by the midwife to go and tell Sutpen, but he is there, on his old stallion, right where the scythe leans, not yet used to clear away the weeds Wash wades through. Wash is pleased that Sutpen is there, but the text warns us that he may not be there because of Milly's situation by referring to Wash, who "took it for granted that this was what had brought the other out at this hour on Sunday morning" (*CS, 544*). Wash is triumphant, telling Sutpen that it is a girl, but Sutpen is on his way to the pallet. We have heard the words, and we may have had the suspicion that Wash, holding the reins of the stallion just outside the wall, heard them, too. Now the text tells us that our suspicion was indeed correct: "He heard what Sutpen said, and something seemed to stop dead in him before going on" (*CS, 544*).

Wash cannot believe what he has heard, because it so totally undermines everything he has thought, dreamed about, forced himself to believe, needed to endure hardships and pain. He cannot give up his illusions without thinking through what he has heard: "'I kain't have heard what I thought I heard,' he thought quietly. 'I know I kain't.'" But then he listens to Sutpen talking to the midwife about the colt, and he knows that Sutpen has been up early because of a horse and not because of Milly—"Hit ain't me and mine" (*CS, 544*).

And so Wash has passed a point of no return; dawn has broken, it is daylight, and as actors on a stage, with the instruments of power and command and of death close by, the text chooses to look in another direction after Sutpen has used his whip and brought Wash down on his knees. He rises, scythe in hand, as the grim reaper, and the text does what the tragedies of old used to do for decorum's sake, narrates by indirection: "When Wash rose and advanced once more he held in his hands the scythe which he had borrowed from Sutpen three months ago and which Sutpen would never need again" (*CS, 545*).[8]

With the body of Sutpen lying in the weeds outside his house, Wash Jones sits down and waits "through all that long, bright, sunny forenoon" (*CS, 546*), and he is still sitting at the window when a white boy comes by and discovers the body, so he knows that they will be coming for him soon. Wash talks a little to his granddaughter, gives her water, cooks for her even though she does not want any food, and reflects on the men whom he knows will be coming to get him. With his new understanding of Sutpen and his class of people, Wash knows that he cannot escape, because fleeing from a dead Sutpen would only mean running into all the living Sutpens, who "set the order and the rule of living."

Wash senses that he cannot escape "the bragging and evil shadows . . . since they were all of a kind throughout all the earth which he knew" (*CS*, 547). He knows that people will think that he killed the Colonel because he expected Sutpen to marry Milly and Sutpen refused to do so. Wash knows that he never expected anything from Sutpen and never asked him for anything, because he did not think he needed to. Wash also understands how the brave and gallant Confederate heroes of Sutpen's kind could be beaten in the war, and he comes to think that it would have been better if they never returned home from the war.

Wash does not try to escape; he sits through the long Sunday, waiting, paying attention to his granddaughter, and acting friendly toward her. He has clearly made up his mind not to be taken alive, but whether the rest of the plan he carries out is premeditated is a different question. When the horses and the men come for him, and a major calls "Jones," he answers but tells them that he wants to see his granddaughter. This time the narrative gets closer to the actual killing, as we watch Wash fumble for his granddaughter's throat, his razor-sharp butcher knife in hand. Spreading kerosene all over the crazy building, he runs out of the glaring blaze, bearing down upon the men with his lifted scythe

> "Jones!" the sheriff shouted; "Stop! Stop, or I'll shoot. Jones! *Jones!*" Yet still the gaunt, furious figure came on against the glare and roar of the flames. With the scythe lifted, it bore down upon them, upon the wild glaring eyes of the horses and the swinging glints of gun barrels, without any cry, any sound. (*CS*, 550)

David Minter (1992) describes "Wash" as "grim, taut, and powerful," and most critics have used similar words to describe this story. Minter states that "only Faulkner's refusal directly to present its several deaths saves it from becoming horrific" (95). The story is tough on a reader anyhow, even if explicit descriptions of three or four killings are avoided. The emotional impact may even have been stronger than if we had witnessed the killings in explicit detail, which would have rendered them as more cold-blooded than they seem to be now, when Milly and her baby seem to be killed for mercy. The motivations behind Wash's action appear as valid within the strange world and personal relationships the text draws up. We may not get close enough to understand Wash's character, his psychology, but the story does not really emphasize a distorted or disturbed sense of reality in which life has become of little value. The motivational forces behind Wash's new understanding and the actions that inevitably follow must be described as social and historical. When Wash understands that there is nowhere he can escape, he has given up the dream of freedom, the dream of freeing himself and his granddaughter and her child from poverty, oppression, circumstances, hopelessness. Faulkner tells the story of Wash Jones calmly, deliberately, slowly. It is hard not to imagine that he has concluded that Wash may be right when he thinks, *"Better if his kind and mine too had never drawn the breath of life on this earth. Better that all who remain of us be blasted from the face of earth than another Wash Jones should see his whole life shredded from him and shrivel away like a dried shuck thrown onto the fire"* (CS, 548–49).

It is not always pleasant reading to follow a Faulkner short story, and "Wash" is in many ways disturbing and unpleasant as well as very convincing in its telling of human misery, loneliness, illusion, and despair leading to disastrous actions when everything a man believes in and has lived for suddenly is revealed as false, as lies, as deceit. It does not change much that he at times has forced himself to believe in something he was the only one who believed. Assaulted by the power of this telling, we may not notice all the details of language and symbol.

While the opening scene focuses on Sutpen as he comes to see Milly and their daughter at dawn, the last scenes are basically seen from Wash's point of view. The cyclical movement of the day from sunrise to sunset is used very deftly by Faulkner, primarily to give an additional symbolic touch to the scenes in which descriptions of the sun are found. Dawn not only represents the beginning of a new day, it is also the time when a new life begins, and it is the time of dawn—understanding, insight—in Wash's mind. When Wash suddenly and almost reluctantly grasps the meaning and the intention of Sutpen's remarks, the sun is said to be up. He kills Sutpen in broad daylight, and his vigil for the law enforcers lasts through a long and sunny Sunday. When the long waiting comes to an end, sunset is there, and in "Wash" the evening sun really goes down, more so than in the short story of that title. Wash kills his granddaughter, probably also the baby, with a butcher's knife, and he sets fire to the shed. He has been forced to give up Sutpen as his God, and now that he has set out upon his tragic path he acts as if he were not only jury and judge but actually God himself. He has shown the masters that not only they possess the power of revenge, as they may have thought previously, and which clearly is the reason why Sutpen cannot even understand it when Wash finally rises up against him.

Wash Jones's horrible actions are not only a result of his rage and despair when he discovers that he has misjudged Sutpen completely. Wash also reacts against the whole code of conduct that Sutpen represents, against a whole social order in which he himself is placed at the bottom, even though he insists that the Negroes are inferior to him in all respects. After Wash has killed Sutpen and awakens from the trance he has been in, he has a vision in which he sees Sutpen, Milly, himself, and the whole society of which they are a part as the results of men who are nothing more than bragging and evil shadows who have set the order and rule of living. There is thus no place for him to go. His chief concern is not with the dead Sutpen; his problem is all the living Sutpens from whom men like Wash Jones can never escape. After Wash has had his epiphanic insight he knows what life has in store for him, and he therefore refuses to remain in the world of the living. The figure on the galloping horse, one of the dominant figures in the story, gives way to a different horseman—one of the horsemen of the Apocalypse. Wash for long years only saw the image of Sutpen on his stallion as a glorious figure, representing chivalry and gallantry, and did not really think of Sutpen as a representative of the warriors, those spreading death and destruction and the smell of sulphur (mentioned twice in the story) where they rode. Horse and rider have thundered on through history not as saviors but in an ongoing chain of aggression and destruction to claim and secure power and position. Wash only senses what must be done, what cannot be avoided, what he cannot bear and still be alive. It takes a Wash Jones to completely misunderstand the components of a figure like Sutpen, and he glorifies that which he does not understand and thinks that what they seem to share makes them more alike than they could possibly ever become.

In the technically flawless and thematically brilliant story of Wash Jones, Faulkner gives one of his most convincing pictures of the past as "the source of dynamic evil" (Warren 1968, 269). "The hard-edged unity of the short story" (Stewart 1969, 586) makes it "unsurpassed of its kind" (Waggoner 1966, v).

# Notes

## CHAPTER 3: THE SHORT STORY GENRE

1. Meriwether and Millgate 1968, 59.
2. Gwynn and Blotner, eds., *Faulkner in the University*, 207.
3. Michael Millgate, "Was Malcolm Cowley Right? The Short Stories in Faulkner's Non-episodic Novels." Millgate 1997, 164–72.
4. When answering questions at the University of Virginia and in other interviews, Faulkner himself contributed to such an understanding of his short story achievement. See *Faulkner in the University*. For a negative evaluation of Faulkner's short stories, see Dorothy Tuck (1964). See also the introductory chapter to my *William Faulkner: The Novelist as Short Story Writer*.
5. Related problems are discussed briefly in Hans-Wolfgang Schaller's dissertation, *Kompositionsformen im Erzählwerk William Faulkners: Entwicklungszüge von der Kurzprosa zum Roman* (Göttingen 1973), see in particular chapter 4, page 1.
6. Very sensible discussions of genre theory, based on a study of the most important genre discussions of several decades, can be found in Paul Hernadi, *Beyond Genre: New Directions in Literary Classification*.
7. Brander Matthews, "The Philosophy of the Short Story," 52.
8. Poe's definition of the short story appeared in a review of Hawthorne's *Twice-Told Tales*. See e.g. Hollis Summers, ed., *Discussions of the Short Story*.
9. See the discussion of this in Robert Scholes, *Structuralism in Literature: An Introduction*, 85–86.
10. It is important to note that I distinguish between a subgroup of short stories and the short story genre here, so that Faulkner's best or most competent stories to me appear to belong to the subgroup which most often deal with existential experience. Charles May (1984) insists that the genre should be defined on the basis of the special kind of knowledge found in the stories, which he finds to be closely related to the question of length.
11. Heide Ziegler centers her study on the "frozen moment" as the agent for bringing about existential experience, but is also aware of the problems in using such a term when *growth* and *maturation* often are key thematic components of the text.
12. Ziegler's arguments also tend to go in this direction: what she calls the *exemplary* nature of the existential experience is related to its inherent universality. May would probably prefer terms such as *basic* or *more original* rather than anthropological or universal.

13. It is dangerous to present a theory of different attitudes and interests in certain phases of Faulkner's career; from the "outrage of a potential believer" in his early years to a much more balanced acceptance of man's capacities in his post-Nobel prize years. A number of interesting discussions of trends in the late career can be found in Gresset and Ohashi, eds., *Faulkner: After the Nobel Prize*.

## CHAPTER 5: BARN BURNING

1. See Tom McHaney's "Introduction" to volume 1 of the manuscripts of *The Hamlet*, xi. See also my discussion in *William Faulkner: The Short Story Career*, 92–93.

2. Ober sent the story out five times (beginning with the best-paying publication, the *Saturday Evening Post*) before it was sold to *Harper's* on the sixth attempt on 31 March 1939 and published in the June issue (Skei 1981, 93). Ober also records that the story was sold to the *Pocketbook of O. Henry Prize Stories* for fifty dollars.

3. *Selected Letters of William Faulkner*, 108.

4. James Ferguson (1991) finds in "Barn Burning" an "authorial voice" which gives "the reader insights far beyond the capabilities of the youthful protagonist" (95). This authorial voice clearly belongs to the narrator of the story, yet it in some instances includes knowledge of what Sarty's mature understanding would be. The authorial intrusions are called "additions," and Ferguson thinks the story has become "incomparably richer" because of them. To use terms such as *addition* or *digression* when talking about literary texts for me implies an understanding of "model texts" (genre conventions) that modern literature should have taught us not to rely on.

5. Page references to the *Collected Stories* are hereafter designated with the abbreviation *CS*.

6. Phyllis Franklin, "Sarty Snopes and 'Barn Burning,'" discusses the few studies of the story that had been written by that time and takes arms against George Marion O'Donnell's distinction between Snopeses and Sartorises, as well as against those readings that find Ab to be at the center of the story, for example, Elmo Howell's (Howell 1959, 13–19).

7. Joseph W. Reed (1973) thinks that the story's argument that "trust in society is a natural sense is perhaps unbelievable" (46), but the narrator also reflects on what Sarty has inherited from his mother, apparently other qualities than those bequeathed to him "willy nilly and which had run for so long (and who knew where, battening on what of outrage and savagery and lust) before it came to him" (*CS*, 21).

8. At one point in the story the narrator reduces or undercuts his omniscience. This is when Sarty meets Mrs. de Spain and says of her, "a lady—perhaps he had never seen her like before either—" (*CS*, 11), the uncertainty of which seems a bit unwarranted since we as readers are certain that Sarty has not seen her like before. The text's insistent half-mockery in repetitive descriptions of the womenfolk of Sarty's family (two pairs, two generations of sisters) also seems to support this argument.

9. Ab's horse trading is said to belong to a period before the older brother

was born, but it hardly refers to his wartime experience as it is described in *The Unvanquished*. The story implies that he has been beaten severely in the trade, which both explains his present impoverished situation and his violent ways. The horse trading story that Ratliff tells in *The Hamlet* is not about Ab as a professional trader but rather about his being "a fool about a horse" and is used to explain his meanness. Ab has not always been the way he is, according to Ratliff, who grew up as Ab's neighbor, he has just "gone sour." Within "Barn Burning" we get no such information, however, and Ab's nature is even more perplexing within the framework of the story.

10. Little attention has been paid to the fact that Ab spends the rest of the Saturday after the court session with de Spain with his two sons in relaxed conversation with other people, having his wagon repaired, eating cheese from the store, visiting a horse auction—acting, in short, *fatherly*. Upon returning home he immediately goes about the business of preparing to set fire to de Spain's barn, and there is nothing pleasant or relaxed about him anymore.

11. Faulkner is not consistent, however. Even though it is clear that the boy later might have thought this or that, the next paragraph opens by stating "But he did not think this now"—apparently indicating not only that he might think this later but that he really had such thoughts. Such distinctions are vitally important to an understanding of the adult Sarty Snopes. Did he ever reach this kind of insight or did he always "intuitively" feel what was right or wrong?

12. See Wayne C. Booth's discussion of the uses of "explicit judgment" in "Barn Burning" (Booth 1961, 308) and Carothers's appropriate comments on this aspect of the story. Carothers calls the comments for "authorial asides," but they are very much part of the narrator's handling of the story he is telling, and reference to an outside author—or even to an implied one—is not called for here.

13. Carothers seems to think that he is tied up and then unties himself and runs away. The story is, however, explicit on this point, while it is rather vague about Sarty's running away from de Spain in the direction of the barn to warn his father and brother. The phrase "knowing it was too late yet still running even after he heard the shot" (*CS*, 24) indicates that Sarty even at this point is still being "pulled two ways."

## CHAPTER 6: CARCASSONNE

1. See Meriwether, "Faulkner's Correspondence with *Scribner's Magazine*," 265, and Skei 1981, 38.

2. See Stephen Ross, "'Lying beneath Speech': Preliminary Notes on the Representation of Thought in 'Carcassonne.'"

3. Noel Polk's reading of "Carcassonne" (1984), by far the most extensive and detailed of all interpretations of the story, is based on the assumption that the story is written as a conclusion to the volume and that it must be interpreted in the light of the volume as a whole.

4. One of the best, if not the best, commentary on "Carcassonne" is David Minter, "'Carcassonne,' 'Wash,' and the Voices of Faulkner's Fiction." See also Minter 1980, especially pages 60–61.

5. One of the sources for this use of "skeleton" is clearly Housman's poem

"The Immortal Part." See Polk (1984) and Brooks (1978b) for further discussions of how Housman was a decisive influence on "Carcassonne."

6. There are references to "tarred paper" also in "Victory," the first story in *These 13*. There it is used in descriptions which contribute to a picture of the post–World War I scene as a kind of wasteland; it has none of the productive, dream-making functions which it is given in "Carcassonne." Even "tarred paper" is an ambiguous term, carrying opposite implications. It is both as bad a blanket as one could wish for, but it serves as "a pair of spectacles through which he nightly perused the fabric of dreams" (*CS*, 896).

7. The two "worlds" do not exist alone and without influencing one another. On the contrary, the outside world is very much responsible for what goes on in the inner world, while the fantasy world of the imagination also determines the artist's perception of the outer world. The contrast is continued in the opposition between Standard Oil Company, Mrs. Widdrington, and Luis in the cantina on one side and *"him of Bouillon and Tancred too"*—glorious figures from the early crusades—on the other side. The final pair in the series of contrasts is a body-soul dichotomy: "he himself" and "his skeleton" are presented as if they were actually separate beings, even to the extent that they discuss and quarrel with each other. This dialogue is a part of the total conflict of the story: a conflict between a young man who wants to follow his dream and calling and an environment that remains hostile or at best indifferent.

8. The Spanish meaning of *rincon* is corner. See Minter 1992, 88.

9. Gwynn and Blotner, eds., *Faulkner in the University*, 22.

10. *Faulkner in the University*, 136.

11. Cowley, *The Faulkner-Cowley File*, 115–16.

12. The "one pitch" and the contrapuntal integration of *Doctor Martino* would, as far as I can see, be very difficult to demonstrate. Faulkner clearly referred to *Collected Stories* and not to the two collections from the 1930s in his letter to Cowley.

13. One reason why I have not read the story in the context of the collection is that I am doubtful as to the unity and interdependency of a volume of separately published stories. Another reason is that Noel Polk (1984) has done this contextual reading so well and in such great detail that it does not have to be done again.

14. From Faulkner's "Address upon Receiving the Nobel Prize for Literature," in *Essays, Speeches and Public Letters*, 119.

## CHAPTER 7: DRY SEPTEMBER

1. See Meriwether, "Faulkner's Correspondence with *Scribner's Magazine*," 260–61.

2. Noel Polk, in his introduction to volume 9 of the William Faulkner manuscripts, does not agree; he thinks the carbon typescript is a "composite of two different typings." My notes about the original papers show that pages 5, 10, 11, and 12 are on much thinner paper than the others, which either shows that Faulkner used different paper more or less at random or that he retyped some of the pages (further suggested by the fact that the pagination is crossed out and

corrected on some of the pages). The name *Scribner's* is added in ink by the author on the typescript. The notes end by stating that "TS.: indubitably copy of the one sent to Scribner's as setting copy," which proves nothing, of course.

3. Most important is perhaps that the name of the leader of the lynching party is changed from Plunkett in the prepublication versions and the *Scribner's* text to McLendon in *These 13*. See Millgate 1966, 263. Manuscript and typescript are in the Faulkner collection at the University of Virginia, but also available (in photocopied form) in *The William Faulkner Manuscripts*.

4. The omitted paragraphs may be responsible for some of the pagination corrections in the carbon typescript in the Virginia collection. In a single typescript page among the Rowan Oak papers (page 10), the paragraph from which Millgate quotes the opening lines is found (lines 6–16): "Life in such places is terrible for women. Life in all places is terrible for women. . . ." The paragraph ends by stating that the monotony of the days and nights of these women "lay like gunpowder in a flimsy vault."

5. Only in stories such as "Mistral" and "Divorce in Naples" do abstractions about women seem to be so closely associated with central elements and attitudes in the stories that they could not be left out without seriously changing the stories and perhaps even reducing their impact and value.

6. Hawkshaw (or Henry Stribling) is also a character in a much less successful short story set in Jefferson, "Hair." Critics have accused him of being too weak to match the likes of McLendon, but Hawkshaw is nonetheless the only person who tries to stop the lynching, even though he is forced to back out. He is not a hero in the popularly accepted sense of the word, although Faulkner drains heroism of meaning in the story by relating that McLendon has been decorated for valor in World War I.

7. Critics have used terms like "limited" omniscience for some of the narrators in Faulkner's stories. This is a contradiction in terms, since omniscience is of course not limited, but the narrator still has to select which scenes, events, and characters in a story to present at different times. The narrator in "Dry September" is, technically speaking, extradiegetic, not present or manifest in the text. There is no limit to his knowledge, as far as the text indicates: he chooses to follow one line of action and not return to what happened elsewhere at that time, not because he does not "know it all" but because it is vitally important in this kind of narrative to let the story tell itself in a straightforward, chronological fashion, so that the presence of the narrator can only be detected on the basis of such narrative features as character descriptions and evaluative statements.

8. Joseph W. Reed, Jr., *Faulkner's Narrative*, 55.

9. Ralph Haven Wolfe and Edgar F. Daniels, "Beneath the Dust of 'Dry September,'" write that the actual lynching is not a community action. Even if this is true, the story leaves no doubt about the community's involvement and responsibility.

10. James Ferguson (1991) finds this tendency to let a final scene sum up the story to be one of Faulkner's more common ways of reaching closure in a story (134).

11. Ferguson discusses Faulkner's use of the leitmotif with particular emphasis on "Barn Burning" and "Dry September" (137–39). I am not altogether convinced

that dust should be considered a leitmotif or that its connotations are stable enough to indicate death and sterility all the way through the text. Dust functions on many levels in this story, and its strength as an image lies in this flexibility.

12. Zilphia, Elly, Emily, and Minnie share the fate of being women in what is definitely a man's world, and what is also a very class-conscious, gossipy small town. They are all let down by the men with whom they have close relationships and feel uneasy about the limitations put upon a woman's life by tradition, expectation, and common consent.

## CHAPTER 8: THE HOUND

1. See Faulkner's introduction to the Modern Library edition of *Sanctuary,* reprinted in *Essays, Speeches, and Public Letters,* 178.

2. The clerk in Varner's Store in the magazine version of "The Hound" is a Snopes; but that, of course, does not make it a Snopes story.

3. The story of Mink's murder of Houston is indeed at the very center of the Snopes trilogy: it leads to Mink's being sentenced to twenty-five years in the state penitentiary. When he comes out, he is bent on revenging himself on Flem, who did not help when he could have.

4. If the short story is particularly well suited to present a conflict reaching a crisis, so that the focus is on the critical points and less on the development leading up to them or following later, this point is obvious.

5. Nature itself seems to resist all of Cotton's attempts to get rid of the corpse and to kill the dog. His own nature also makes him feel subconsciously guilty, even though he would never admit this guilt.

6. When the story was revised and reused in *The Hamlet,* Mink Snopes replaced Cotton as the murderer.

7. In *The Hamlet* Mink is a married man, and this strange—to say the least—relationship with his wife adds important dimensions to his character and to his behavior within the frame of the story.

8. Hereafter references to *Uncollected Stories* are abbreviated *US.*

9. This is elaborated and vastly expanded in *The Hamlet* to motivate Mink's reaction better. Mink lost his case, while Cotton in fact won. He, more than Cotton, has obvious reasons for wishing Houston dead. Cotton's killing of Houston thus becomes even more unreasonable and inexplicable, although he has much more subtle reasons for his action.

10. See Leonidas M. Jones, "Faulkner's 'The Hound.'"

11. Most of the story is indeed a description of the hardships following the murder, and the very fact that Houston's hound is impossible to kill may indicate that it is used as a symbol for Cotton's conscience. L. M. Jones sees it this way.

12. Cotton has made up his mind to do something, and it is virtually impossible for him to yield to any outside forces and give up what he has planned.

## CHAPTER 9: MOUNTAIN VICTORY

1. James B. Meriwether, "Faulkner's Correspondence with *The Saturday Evening Post,*" 468.

2. "Faulkner's Correspondence with *The Saturday Evening Post,*" 470.

3. Perhaps the reduction in "the size of our numbers" described in a letter from the *Post* to Faulkner on January 21, 1931, is part of the reason, although it cannot alone explain the delay, since the editor is optimistic and also says "things are brightening up some now." See "Faulkner's Correspondence with *The Saturday Evening Post,*" 475.

4. From the manuscript for "Mountain Victory," held at the University of Virginia.

5. The text of this deleted passage was printed in the *Mississippi Quarterly,* 32 (1979), 482–83.

6. Even in my own studies of Faulkner's short stories it surprised me some years ago to discover that most comments on this story had disappeared during revision and editing. I tried to make up for some of this unintentional neglect in a lecture in 1990 (see Skei 1992). James Ferguson (1991) makes the point in his introduction that "Mountain Victory" has been largely ignored in his short story study (1), but although the title of the story is mentioned everywhere in Ferguson's book, the study does not really contain a reading of the story as such. The story is almost nonexistent in Carothers's study of Faulkner's short stories (Carothers 1985).

7. Ferguson makes this point, and I quite agree with him. But then again, Faulkner's rhetoric would not really be "Faulknerian" if he did not exaggerate just this practice. See Ferguson 1991, 139.

8. See Bernard Knieger, "Faulkner's 'Mountain Victory, 'Doctor Martino,' and 'There Was a Queen.'"

9. Such adjectives are used to describe the girl in the manuscript version of the story and in part 4 of the typescript version, both held at the University of Virginia. In these early versions she is represented as typically feminine, while she is more individualized in the final, published versions.

## CHAPTER 10: PANTALOON IN BLACK

1. Faulkner wrote to his publisher in 1941 and outlined a volume of collected short stories, "general theme being relationship between white and black races here" (*Selected Letters,* 139).

2. Olga Vickery makes this point, finding that the stories are related through their connection with the plantation. This, then, in Vickery's opinion is one of the unifying elements that makes *Go Down, Moses* a "loosely connected novel." See Vickery 1964, 125.

3. See for instance John Limon, "The Integration of Faulkner's *Go Down, Moses.*"

4. Joanna Creighton (1977) says that the story was only "slightly revised from the account published in *Harper's* in 1940" (115), which means that the story is of little interest for her work, which concerns Faulkner's revisions. It is important that there are links between "Pantaloon in Black" and other stories in the volume and that these links are present also in the magazine text (especially the name of Rider's landlord and the reference to Lucas's fire on the hearth).

5. I am indebted to Sandra Lee Kleppe for this use of Bakhtin to establish the basic function of the protagonist in "Pantaloon in Black." Her lecture at the symposium on Faulkner's short fiction, "Reconstructing Faulkner's 'Pantaloon in Black'" (collected in Skei 1997), is an attempt to approach the topic of race

without the sort of cultural blindness which she finds in most other readings of this text.

6. I am referring here to Richard Gray's lecture, "Across the Great Divide: Race and Revision in *Go Down, Moses*," at the symposium on Faulkner's short fiction in Oslo, 1995, collected in Skei 1997.

7. James Early (1977) finds that the story is "marred by the insistent use of a crude Negro dialect which prevents readers from immersing themselves entirely in the mind of the stricken husband" (12). Rider is not allowed to tell his own story, and only when we are allowed to hear him talk is dialect used, which limits its use so much that Early's remark is unwarranted and unfair.

8. On the surface this refers to the emptiness of the place now that Mannie is gone; the house does not exist without her. But it also carries symbolic overtones of another gate, beyond which he may join Mannie. Faulkner's short story "Beyond," about a postmortal experience, was originally called "Beyond the Gate."

9. No reference should be necessary, since Faulkner used such and related expressions all through his career. His Nobel prize address contains a whole collection of them.

10. I am indebted to Sandra Lee Kleppe for the reference to *The Sound and the Fury*, even though she does not speculate on its importance to the extent that I do here.

11. Richard Gray, "Across the Great Divide: Race and Revision in *Go Down, Moses*," 10.

12. On the basis of a similar interpretation of "Pantaloon in Black," Brooks calls the story "Wordsworthian." See Brooks 1963, 254–55.

## CHAPTER 11: RED LEAVES

1. Because of the differences between the extant carbon typescript and the *Post* text, it is very likely that Faulkner typed a new, clean version which he mailed to the *Post*, and that the existing carbon typescript thus represents the version before this final typescript, which would then probably have been used for the magazine's typesetting.

2. The dates are given at the opening of the second of the four sections in the *Post* version of the story.

3. This indicates that I disagree with Gilbert Muller's observation that the change to six sections better controls "the pastoral pace of the narrative" (Muller 1974, 243n.2; see also Jones 1994, 322).

4. For a relation of Faulkner's Indian tales to historical and sociological facts, see Lewis M. Dabney, *The Indians of Yoknapatawpha*.

5. Here the inconsistent genealogical information is given.

6. Gene M. Moore's paper "'European Finery' and Cultural Survival in Faulkner's 'Red Leaves'" was delivered at the International Faulkner Symposium in Oslo in 1995 and was collected in Skei, ed., *William Faulkner's Short Fiction: An International Symposium*.

7. Gwynn and Blotner, eds., *Faulkner in the University*, 39.

8. Doom, or Ikkemotubbe, is the oldest of the three Chickasaw chiefs we

encounter in Faulkner's Indian stories, followed by Issetibbeha, and then Moketubbe. The genealogy is not clear, however, and while Issetibbeha is the son of Doom in "Red Leaves" he is the uncle of Doom in "A Justice," where Doom is the son of Issetibbeha's sister.

9. See G. W. Sutton, "Primitivism in the Fiction of William Faulkner," 122. The term is of course also used by numerous other critics.

10. Edmond L. Volpe, "Faulkner's 'Red Leaves': The Deciduation of Nature," 130. Other critics make similar points.

11. Irving Howe, *William Faulkner: A Critical Study*, 267.

12. See Duane Gage, "William Faulkner's Indians," particularly the last paragraph.

13. See Noel Polk's 1975 *Mississippi Quarterly* review of two book-length studies of Faulkner's Indians, Lewis M. Dabney's *The Indians of Yoknapatawpha* and Nigliazzo's Ph.D. dissertation "Faulkner's Indians" (University of New Mexico, 1973).

14. G. H. Muller, "The Descent of the Gods: Faulkner's 'Red Leaves' and the Garden of the South," finds that the community in "Red Leaves" must restore "an ecumenical function in life" (249). The entrapment Muller finds in the story he interprets as symbolic of "man's fall from grace. Man has lost sight of the holy Garden and this failure of vision estranges him from possibility of salvation" (248).

15. Muller has apparently forgotten this when he describes the story as a parable on Paradise lost.

16. The slave has lived a quiet and leisurely life; he has not had to toil and sweat like the other black slaves in the Indian camp, and he shows little resistance to nature and its forces when he has to get away to avoid being sacrificed.

## CHAPTER 12: A ROSE FOR EMILY

1. Critics—including myself—may have exaggerated the importance of this fact; Faulkner had, after all, published four novels, including *The Sound and the Fury*, at the time "A Rose for Emily" appeared. And to be absolutely accurate, Faulkner had published in the *Double Dealer*, which had a small but national circulation, in his New Orleans period.

2. See, for example, Ferguson 1991, 13, 33.

3. *Selected Letters*, 34.

4. See also Blotner's annotation in *Selected Letters*, 35.

5. Discussed also in Skei 1981, 51–52, based on the manuscript and carbon typescript in the University of Virginia collection.

6. In some of Faulkner's best stories, such as "Dry September," Faulkner conceived of the story in parts even at the first manuscript stage, and in "Red Leaves" and "Mountain Victory" the division into sections came early and enabled the author to alter the final impressions of these stories by creating new sections ("Red Leaves") or by leaving out a whole section ("Mountain Victory"). The need for sectional division in these three stories is a result of shifting narrative perspectives, whereas "A Rose for Emily" greatly profits from the use of sections because of its long time span.

7. Faulkner's artistic growth within the limits of this single short story is

remarkable, yet it should not be taken as proof of his "growing sophistication as an artist," as Millgate (1966) argues (264), unless the revisions were much later than the extant manuscript and typescript. If an earlier typescript, perhaps one from 1927, were available, the evidence for growth might have been significant even when limited to one story only. We also know that Faulkner's growth did not protect him from writing overworked and overly explicit stories later on. Also, it is tempting to speculate what this remarkable "growth" within the confines of "A Rose for Emily" would be worth if evidence turned up to show that he revised the story because *Forum* asked him to do so and perhaps even suggested which parts to delete or condense. Editors often contribute significantly to what critics seem to think of as subjective, individual growth, maturation, and sophistication, which they then use to show a steady development toward better things.

8. Because of the enormous amount of criticism devoted to this story, it is virtually impossible to rely on or even make use of previous interpretations except in an indirect sense, since I have obviously been influenced by this criticism. See Jones 1994, 87–141, for a detailed survey of criticism and interpretation of "A Rose for Emily."

9. See John B. Cullen (in collaboration with Floyd C. Watkins), *Old Times in the Faulkner Country*, 71.

10. Gwynn and Blotner, eds., *Faulkner in the University*, 185.

11. I fully agree with Diane Jones's assessment of the uneven quality of the criticism of "A Rose for Emily" and would strongly recommend that future critics do their homework before publishing comments on this story, even if this means looking up and reading much that is not really worth one's time and effort. See Jones 1994, 133.

12. For an elaboration of this point, see Helen E. Nebeker, "Emily's Rose of Love: Thematic Implications of Point of View in Faulkner's 'A Rose for Emily.'"

13. Theorists of narrative have speculated that the motivation to narrate a story in the first person is "existential," yet in "A Rose for Emily" the first-person narrator is so marginal as a character in his own story and obscures and hides his own position so cleverly that it may well be that the final impression is of third-person narration with little distance to the events narrated. At any rate the concept of "community point of view" is too general to be of much use in the reading and interpretation of this story.

14. Cleanth Brooks tried to establish a chronology for "A Rose for Emily" and has shown impatience with typical misreadings which have led to impossible chronologies, where, among other things, Emily's death takes place long after the year when the story was published. See Brooks 1978, 284–88, 382–84.

15. This is indeed the explanation given by the narrator and also the understanding shared by the young men of the town.

16. The description of Miss Emily's house among the new garages, cotton gins, and gasoline pumps is symbolic of the isolation in which she comes to live, which in its turn may lessen the society's implied criticism of her living with a dead and unburied past. Critics have found that "the necrophilia of an entire society that lived with a dead but unburied past" is implied in the story. See for example Magalaner and Volpe, "Society in 'A Rose for Emily,'" 17.

17. Miss Emily's resistance to normal behavior includes a resistance to

change. Accordingly she wanted to keep her past alive and to keep her lover even if he had to be dead to remain hers. In R. B. West's words, she has undertaken "to regulate the natural time-universe" (West 1949, 242). In more general terms "A Rose for Emily" states that man must cope with his time, past and present, and that he cannot ignore the present and make time stand still or otherwise yield to his demands.

18. "The distance between reality and illusion has blurred out," according to Brooks and Warren, *Understanding Fiction*, 351.

19. Emily does "as people will," but she is compulsively possessive and clearly a case of abnormal psychology. Within the story Emily very rarely acts out of character; the only time is perhaps when she has to let her father be buried.

20. Gwynn and Blotner, eds., *Faulkner in the University*, 59.

## CHAPTER 13: SPOTTED HORSES

1. James Ferguson (1991) states that "with the exception of the Cotton-Mink Snopes-Houston story, there is no other comparable portion of Faulkner's work on which he labored over so long a period" (25). Ferguson obviously includes Faulkner's work on the manuscript and typescript for *The Hamlet* in this assessment, but if we restrict our comment to the short story material, Faulkner had to experiment with so many narrative techniques and so many levels of language and style through numerous versions, beginning really with *Father Abraham*, that no other story is comparable to "Spotted Horses" in this respect. See Skei 1981, 43–47, for an extended discussions of this material, including Faulkner's first notes about the Snopeses. My discussion in the present volume also takes into account *Father Abraham*, which was not available in 1981.

2. In *William Faulkner: The Short Story Career* I refer to another version of this typescript, paginated 204–220. This is the carbon typescript of the ribbon version discovered in the Rowan Oak papers, all of which I did not have access to then. The complete version of this earliest "As I Lay Dying" is thus eighteen pages. It is reproduced in the first volume of the manuscripts of *The Hamlet*.

3. See Skei 1981, 47, for speculations on an early short story collection. The pagination of this "As I Lay Dying" version clearly indicates a longer manuscript with several stories, although it could hardly be one about "my townspeople," as Faulkner said about the projected collection *A Rose for Emily and Other Stories* at about this time.

4. J. Rea (1970), in an interesting article that may nevertheless be too narrow in its perspective, notes that Faulkner told the story of the spotted horses at least six times: in "Spotted Horses" in *Scribner's* (1931), in "Centaur in Brass" in *American Mercury* (1932), in *The Hamlet* (1940), in *Go Down, Moses* (1942), in *The Town* (1957)—"and in a talk to the English Club at the University of Virginia in 1957." Today we would have to add the version found in *Father Abraham* and also mention all the very different prepublication versions available. Moreover, the appearance of the Texas ponies in Faulkner's writings is worth a study in its own right.

5. Carothers points to the fact that Eula's dowry, the old Frenchman's place, which Flem thus gets his hands on, is not mentioned in "Spotted Horses." An

important element of Flem's later move upwards and away from the village is thus left out (Carothers 1985, 116).

6. The auction took place on a Friday, and we follow its aftermath in Mrs. Littlejohn's boarding house through Saturday night; then we hear about her and Mrs. Armstid on "this morning," which seems not to be the morning after but probably the morning of the next day, since the narrator has been up to Bundren's and back and is now having breakfast, before going to Varner's store and, logically, beginning on his trip to where he is telling his story (probably Jefferson)—most likely on Monday night. His memories should be as vivid and clear as the reader gets them, and the sights and sounds of the ponies have certainly kept them fresh in his mind.

7. For some strange reason Faulkner leaves us uncertain about the baby's sex, referring to the baby as "it" and describing it so that the reader is likely to infer that the child is a boy. In *Father Abraham* and *The Hamlet* there is of course no doubt that the baby is a girl, who would be at the center of the later volumes in the Snopes trilogy.

8. See for instance Matthews 1992, 16–18, and Rea 1970, 160–62.

9. Section divisions in an oral tale seem rather strange, but what we read is of course a written story, perhaps even a writerly text in today's terminology, and if we as readers want to insist on logic and consistency in the oral narrative we might as well allow for a few breaks in the long-winded and apparently uninterrupted narrative.

10. Gwynn and Blotner, eds., *Faulkner in the University,* 66.

11. In *The Hamlet* the fact that the horse has been given away without any bill of sale or note of transfer, in addition to no proof of Flem's partnership in the horse business, makes Tull's case a very difficult one to win.

12. The group of listeners is likely to be located in Jefferson, and in a few years they will get to know Flem Snopes better than most of them will appreciate. Faulkner published "Centaur in Brass" in 1932, the first story about Flem in Jefferson. It is an interesting story in Flem's career, since it is the only text which gives a hint that Flem may not after all be invincible. His eventual downfall in the final volume of the trilogy in 1959 is not indicated by anything Faulkner wrote or said in the 1930s and 1940s.

13. His participation and responsibility are not doubted by any of the buyers or any other people present at the auction; yet the fact that Flem keeps out of sight for some time provides him with an excuse when those who feel cheated come to claim their money back.

14. Quoted from James L. Sanderson, "'Spotted Horses' and the Theme of Social Evil," 704n.

15. Donald Greiner, using the Cowley text of "Spotted Horses," finds the story demonstrates that "a little bit of Snopes resides in everyone," so that even the Snopes in Suratt/Ratliff makes him "stumble into Flem's trap." Greiner's concept of "universal Snopesism" is typical of a strong tendency to read "Spotted Horses" and *The Hamlet* with heavy emphasis on the economic theme. A sociological approach to the Snopes material is obviously warranted, but there is much more to "Spotted Horses" than this, and the concept of "universal Snopesism" is too general to be productive and is based on what I consider a mis-

reading of the texts as well as of the members of the Snopes clan. See Greiner 1968, 1137.

16. Flem fools Suratt (Ratliff in *The Hamlet*) in a deal concerning goats and will fool him again when he sells the old Frenchman's place to Suratt and two of his companions. The last episode is rendered more completely in "Lizards in Jamshyd's Courtyard."

17. See Donald E. Houghton, "Whores and Horses in Faulkner's 'Spotted Horses.'"

18. Malcolm Cowley "created" his own version of "Spotted Horses," excerpted from *The Hamlet,* for *The Viking Portable Faulkner* (1946). Cowley regarded the spotted horses episode in the novel as superior to the magazine short story. He suggested minor cuts in the text from the novel, and Faulkner agreed to the changes; thus a second (or third) "Spotted Horses" was created. It has later been anthologized numerous times in such anomalies as *Three Short Novels.* I cannot find any acceptable reason for dealing with any other version of this material than the original magazine printing, reprinted and thus easily accessible now in *Uncollected Stories,* in a study of Faulkner's short fiction. This does pose one serious problem, though: Critics in their comments and interpretations almost invariably refer to the text in or from *The Hamlet,* and even if the material is basically the same, its narrative handling is so different that much of the commentary is useless for my purpose of studying the original (and only) short story text using this material.

## CHAPTER 14: THAT EVENING SUN

1. The March 1931 issue of *American Mercury* is further described by Norman Holmes Pearson in "Faulkner's Three Evening Suns."

2. See Meriwether 1971, 308–9. Leo Manglaviti has also commented on the various versions of this short story in his "Faulkner's 'That Evening Sun' and Mencken's 'Best Editorial Judgment.'"

3. Norman Holmes Pearson (1954) discusses the significance of some of the restorations; see especially page 65.

4. The paragraph is found in the *Mercury* text on page 267, column 2. Norman Pearson comments on what he considers the appropriateness of removing this paragraph on pages 66–67 of his essay. Pearson thinks that both Hemingway and Faulkner understood that "what is created by presentation need not be repeated by statement" (67), and since the impingement of lives had been established by the story itself, the paragraph in which it is "repeated" and "stated" became unnecessary. Pearson seems to misunderstand what the story itself is, what the narrative perspective permits the text to do, and his distinction between presentation and statement is all too simple. *Mimesis* and *diegesis* have never been meant to be so easily distinguishable or so far apart.

5. The last sentence is omitted in the published versions: "'I'm going to tell on you,' Jason said." Quoted from manuscript at Yale by Pearson (64).

6. Critics have been able to see and prove the story to be primarily Nancy's, or even Caddy's, while others have put emphasis on the double perspective of child character and grown-up narrator to the exclusion of other interests. There

may, indeed, be more extreme readings of this story than of any other story in the Faulkner canon.

7. Information from Manglaviti 1972, 654. The line reads, "Ara hand that touched her, I'd cut it off."

8. E. B. Harrington (1952), in a very early and otherwise interesting reading of "That Evening Sun," thinks that Faulkner "erred in choosing to have Quentin narrate the story fifteen years after the action of it" but is pleased to discover in the story a style "admirably suited to the story" and not "what one would have expected from an adult" (55).

9. R. M. Slabey argues for "an ingeniously organized double plot" in the story. See Slabey 1964, 181.

10. Careful study of syntax, style, and voice in "That Evening Sun" reveals the obvious and at times obtrusive influence of the adult narrator on the language in the parts of the story where the child's perspective seems to be maintained. See May Cameron Brown (1976), especially page 350.

11. Karl F. Zender's "Sight and Marginality in 'That Evening Sun'" refers to the widespread use of the metaphors of sight and visibility in American literature and the need to deconstruct the opposition even in our reading of this short story, so that we not only, as liberalists and humanists, understand Nancy as victim and our responsibility but begin to see from her perspective, see with her, as black and as woman (Zender 1997).

12. The extra effect—and not only an ambiguous one—of naming Nancy's husband Jesus is used for serious as well as humorous reasons throughout the story. Quentin explains to Caddy and to us that Nancy means the other Jesus, when she moans "Jeeeeeeeesus" in her sound-making, and when Caddy earlier innocently suggests that Nancy may be waiting in the kitchen "for Jesus to come and take her home" (CS, 293), the double reference is almost too obvious.

13. The black characters are often given this function; without resorting to any kind of logical or coherent explanation they feel or sense danger.

14. The story is "Mistral." See These 13, 313.

15. There is no need to be concerned with the inconsistency between the short story and The Sound and the Fury. According to a Compson genealogy based on the novel, no twenty-four-year-old Quentin could tell any story.

## CHAPTER 15: VICTORY

1. Blotner quotes from this letter to Mrs. Murry Falkner (October 7, 1925), concluding that "the two manuscript fragments and the two typescripts which remain [of "Victory"] suggest that he may have begun the story not long after his return from Europe" (Blotner 1974, I:692). See also Selected Letters, 28–29.

2. In the fifty-one-page typescript Faulkner gives an exposition in which we are told what to make of Alec Gray's life:

Alexander Gray's background, like his life, falls into three parts, each of which is summed up in an individual who not only typifies each generation with all a generation's surface differences from the preceding or succeeding one, but who being interchangeable one with another, sums up and typifies a manner, a habit of thought and conduct that dates back to the first ship ever built on Clyde. It is necessary to say something of Alexander Gray's background, for without this background there might well have been an Alexander Gray, but this story would not be his. (*William Faulkner Manuscripts 9: These 13*)

This is a prose impossible for a short story, and a kind of apology for Faulkner's habit of using capsule stories to give a character's background. In "Victory" this explicit attempt to explain or even interpret the story which is to follow is later replaced by a complex set of double flashbacks, so that after the opening scene in France it takes the narrative a long time to return to the time of its opening scene.

3. Since "Crevasse" is not a part of "Victory" but still bears a close relationship to the longer story from which it was cut, a brief discussion will be given in this footnote: There is reason to suggest that the nameless soldiers and officers in "Crevasse" are Scottish, and it would be possible to guess that Alec Gray is among them. In this story whatever dream the men may have had about war has become a nightmare. A small infantry patrol marches over a battlefield where the stillness is complete; the grass is "dead-looking" and "gorselike" and forms "bayonets" which "saber" the men's legs (*CS*, 467). The stillness is profound and ominous, and in this ghostly nightmare of a landscape the earth suddenly begins to move and the whole patrol disappears underground. Twelve men die instantly, and the fourteen who are alive move through a valley of death, searching desperately for an exit. When the men try to dig a tunnel to get out of the trap they "burrow furiously, with whimpering cries like dogs" (*CS*, 473), but this hope is contradicted by everything else in the story. Even religious ceremony cannot function as a defense against the horrors of war. War is shown as demoralizing, dehumanizing, and the last note struck in this intense story of horror and desolation is one of meaninglessness and somber despair. The last sentence reads, "Above his voice the wounded man's gibberish rises, meaningless and unemphatic and sustained" (*CS*, 474). This may be compared to the last paragraph in *The Sound and the Fury*. Faulkner apparently liked this kind of ending, and it is indeed very effective. His ending of "Victory" is far less convincing.

4. There are thus many important parallels between "Carcassonne" and "Victory," although I am not certain that they prove much more than Faulkner's propensity for certain rather remarkable images and comparisons. All through *These 13* some of Faulkner's idiosyncrasies can be found, and if taken too seriously we may create a unity in this volume which is not really there.

5. The strongest irony in this part of the text seems to drown in the long and rather uninteresting description of Gray's dining with a Swiss man in his hotel. The Swiss takes for granted that Gray had not participated in the war but insists that he himself, like all others, has suffered.

6. A statement such as "there was something the matter with the eyes of so many people, men and women too, in Europe since four years now" (*CS*, 431), points forward to the gas attack described later in the story in addition to show-

ing how war tends to affect the civilian population, too, and not only the soldiers.

7. One of the typescripts shows Alec Gray as even more bestial in this situation. His glance is described as "wild" and "mad," and the following sentence has been left out in the printed version: "He heard bones, and his teeth glared in the corpse-glow" (*William Faulkner Manuscripts 9: These 13*).

8. What this means, or how it can be said to be consistent with Alec's behavior and self-understanding as exemplified elsewhere in the text, is a real problem. I cannot help but think that the story could easily have done without this kind of philosophy.

9. William Van O'Connor uses this designation. See O'Connor 1968, 67.

10. Raleigh W. Smith is close to a reading of "Victory" in such terms, quoting extensively from very conservative and extratextual thoughts about the endurance theme in Faulkner as voiced by M. E. Bradford. See Smith 1970 and Bradford 1962.

11. See Raleigh W. Smith, Jr., "Faulkner's 'Victory': The Plain People of Clydebank." Toward the end of his article Smith quotes from M. E. Bradford's 1962 article on "The Tall Men" and concludes: "Faulkner's plain people are normative because they almost invariably hold to this standard of endurance in *humility* and pride. This aspect of the endurance theme in Faulkner, the endurance of one's personal heritage, Alec Gray rejects. He is therefore damned" (249).

## CHAPTER 16: WASH

1. In a letter to Malcolm Cowley (probably November 1948), Faulkner lists "Wash" among the "Middle Ground" stories (Cowley 1966, 117). In Faulkner's letter to Robert K. Haas in the fall of 1948, "Wash" is not mentioned. See *Selected Letters*, 274–75.

2. This statement is of course limited to stories reused in novels prior to the publication of *Collected Stories*. "Centaur in Brass" would be used in a novel after it had been included in *Collected Stories*.

3. Cowley, *The Faulkner-Cowley File*, 196–98. Quoted from *Selected Letters*, 197.

4. Jack F. Stewart (1969) accused "mapmakers and chroniclers" of Faulkner's literary landscape to "have been so intent on 'the figure in the carpet,' as Olga W. Vickery calls the central design, that they have failed to give individual pieces that "close textual scrutiny that . . . they deserve" (586). Despite the relatively limited attention in relation to the story's high quality, "Wash" has been mentioned, commented on, referred to in many studies of Faulkner's novels, which is both reasonable and obvious given its significance in relation to *Absalom, Absalom!*

5. Sutpen returns from the the Civil War in 1865; for five years Wash and Sutpen discuss the war. Milly is eight when the war breaks out, fifteen when Sutpen seduces her (1868), and two years later her child is born (1870) in the story's present. Stewart is inaccurate in his dating of the events (Stewart 1969, 588).

6. Sutpen compares nicely with the "dead pilots" after World War I, described in stories such as "Ad Astra" and, notably, "All the Dead Pilots." In Faulkner's fiction characters break and deteriorate if they have experienced or performed something great, which they later are incapable of living up to. Poverty, unemployment, and boredom often lead to drastic and tragic consequences.

7. Notice the implicit reference to the lines from *Macbeth*, which provides the title for *The Sound and the Fury*. The description also indicates the setting of the stage within the story, for the final act of a tragedy.

8. That Wash had borrowed the scythe three months ago to clear away the weeds is mentioned three times in the course of the story, and in due time the scythe is used, in a different meaning, to cut the "rank weeds" that should have been cleared away a long time ago. There is no sign in the text that Wash should have placed the scythe in this strategic position deliberately, and so it is rather strange that the length of time since he borrowed the scythe—and the fact that he borrowed it from Sutpen—should be emphasized through repetitive use.

# Bibliography

Ackerman, R. D. 1974. "The Immolation of Isaac McCaslin." *Texas Studies in Literature and Language,* 16, 557–65.

Adams, Richard P. 1968. *Faulkner: Myth and Motion.* Princeton, N.J.: Princeton University Press.

Allen, Walter. 1981. *The Short Story in English.* New York: Oxford University Press.

Arensberg, Mary, and Sara E. Schyfter. 1986/1987. "Hairoglyphics in Faulkner's 'A Rose for Emily'/Reading the Primal Trace." *Boundary,* 2, 15, 123–34.

Bache, W. B. 1954. "Moral Awareness in 'Dry September.'" *Faulkner Studies,* 3, 53–57.

Backman, Melvin. 1966. *Faulkner: The Major Years: A Critical Study.* Bloomington: Indiana University Press.

Bakhtin, Michail. 1981. *The Dialogic Imagination: Four Essays by M. M. Bakhtin.* Austin: University of Texas Press.

Barber, Marion. 1973. "The Two Emilys: A Ransom Suggestion to Faulkner?" *Notes on Mississippi Writers,* 5, 103–05.

Barnes, Daniel R. 1972. "Faulkner's Emily and Hawthorne's Old Maid." *Studies in Short Fiction,* 9, 373–77.

Barstad, Joel I. 1983. "Faulkner's 'Pantaloon in Black.'" *Explicator,* 41.3, 51–53.

Barth, J. Robert. 1964. "Faulkner and the Calvinist Tradition." *Thought,* 39, 100–20.

———, ed. 1972. *Religious Perspectives in Faulkner's Fiction: Yoknapatawpha and Beyond.* Notre Dame, Ind.: University of Notre Dame Press.

Basic, Sonja. 1997. "Stories vs. Novels: The Narrative Strategies." In Skei, ed., *William Faulkner's Short Fiction: An International Symposium,* 63–73.

Bassett, John. 1972. *William Faulkner: An Annotated Checklist of Criticism.* New York: David Lewis.

———. 1975. *William Faulkner: The Critical Heritage.* Boston & London: Routledge & Kegan Paul.

Baumbach, Jonathan, and Arthur Edelstein. 1968. *Moderns and Contemporaries: Nine Masters of the Short Story.* New York: Random House.

Beck, Warren. 1961. *Man in Motion: Faulkner's Trilogy.* Madison: University of Wisconsin Press.

———. 1976. *Faulkner: Essays.* Madison: University of Wisconsin Press.

Beidler, P.G. 1973. "A Darwinian Source for Faulkner's Indians in 'Red Leaves.'" *Studies in Short Fiction,* 10, 421–23.

Benet, W. R. 1934. "Fourteen Faulkner Stories." *Saturday Review,* 21 April, 645.

Bennet, Ken. 1985. "The Language of the Blues in Faulkner's 'That Evening Sun.'" *Mississippi Quarterly,* 38, 339–42.

Benson, Jackson J. 1982. "Quentin Compson: Self-Portrait of a Young Artist's Emotions." In *Critical Essays on William Faulkner: The Compson Family,* ed. Arthur F. Kinney. Boston: G. K. Hall, 214–30 (orig. pub. 1971).

Benson, W. R. 1966. "Faulkner for the High School: 'Turnabout.'" *English Journal,* 55, 867–69, 874.

Bethea, Sally. 1974. "Further Thoughts on Racial Implications in Faulkner's 'That Evening Sun.'" *Notes on Mississippi Writers,* 6, 87–92.

Billingslea, Oliver. 1991. "Fathers and Sons: The Spiritual Quest in Faulkner's 'Barn Burning.'" *Mississippi Quarterly,* 44.3, 287–308.

Birney, E. 1938. "The Two William Faulkners." *Canadian Forum,* 18, 84–85.

Bleikasten, André. 1973. *Faulkner's As I Lay Dying.* Bloomington: Indiana University Press.

———. 1976. *The Most Splendid Failure: Faulkner's The Sound and the Fury.* Bloomington: Indiana University Press.

———. 1990. *The Ink of Melancholy: Faulkner's Novels from The Sound and the Fury to Light in August.* Bloomington: Indiana University Press.

———. 1997. "'It Still Wasn't Enough': The Novelist as Failed Short Story Writer." In Skei, ed., *William Faulkner's Short Fiction: An International Symposium,* 19–28.

Blotner, Joseph. 1964. *William Faulkner's Library: A Catalogue.* Charlottesville: University Press of Virginia.

———. 1974. *Faulkner: A Biography.* (2 Vols.) New York: Random House; London: Chatto and Windus.

———. 1977. *Selected Letters of William Faulkner.* New York: Random House.

———. 1984. *Faulkner: A Biograpy.* (1 Vol.) New York: Random House.

———1997. "Children in Faulkner's Short Stories." In Skei, ed., *William Faulkner's Short Fiction: An International Symposium,* 82–89.

Blythe, Hal. 1989. "Faulkner's 'A Rose for Emily.'" *Explicator,* 47.2, 49–50.

Bockting, Ineke. 1997. "Whiteness and the Love of Color: The Development of a Theme in Faulkner's *Go Down, Moses.*" In Skei, ed., *William Faulkner's Short Fiction: An International Symposium,* 197–211.

Bomze, Joann. 1983–84. "Faulkner's 'Mountain Victory': The Triumph of the 'Middle Ground.'" *CEA Critic,* 46, 9–11.

Booth, Wayne C. 1961. *The Rhetoric of Fiction.* Chicago: University of Chicago Press.

Bradford, Melvin E. 1962. "Faulkner's 'Tall Men,'" *South Atlantic Quarterly,* 61 (Winter), 29—39.

———. 1964. "Faulkner and the Great White Father." *Louisiana Studies,* 3, 323–29.

———. 1965. "'Spotted Horses' and the Short Cut to Paradise: A Note on the Endurance Theme in Faulkner." *Louisiana Studies,* 4, 324–31.

———. 1966. "Faulkner's 'That Evening Sun.'" *CEA Critic,* 28, 1, 3.

———. 1967–68. "Certain Ladies of Quality: Faulkner's View of Women and the Evidence of 'There Was a Queen.'" *Arlington Quarterly,* 1.2, 106–39.

———. 1968. "Faulkner's 'Elly': An Exposé." *Mississippi Quarterly,* 21, 179–87.

———. 1973. "An Aesthetic Parable: Faulkner's 'Artist at Home.'" *Georgia Review,* 27, 175–81.

———. 1974. "That Other Patriarchy: Observations on Faulkner's 'A Justice.'" *Modern Age,* 18, 266–71.

———. 1981. "The Knight and the Artist: Tasso and Faulkner's 'Carcassonne.'" *South Central Bulletin,* 41.4, 88–90.

———. 1983. "The Anomaly of Faulkner's World War I Stories." *Mississippi Quarterly,* 36.3, 243–62.

———. 1987. "A Late Encounter: Faulkner's 'Mountain Victory.'" *Mississippi Quarterly,* 40, 373–81.

Bride, Sister Mary. 1962. "Faulkner's 'A Rose for Emily.'" *Explicator,* 20, item 78.

Brinkmeyer, Robert. 1997. "A Fighting Faith: Faulkner's Democratic Ideology, and the World War II Home Front." In Skei, ed., *William Faulkner's Short Fiction: An International Symposium,* 306–15.

Brodsky, Louis Daniel. 1984. "The Textual Development of William Faulkner's 'Wash': An Examination of Manuscripts in the Brodsky Collection." *Studies in Bibliography,* 37, 248–81.

———. 1988. *Faulkner: A Comprehensive Guide to the Brodsky Collection.* Vol. 5: Manuscripts and Documents. Jackson: University Press of Mississippi.

Brooks, Cleanth. 1963. *William Faulkner: The Yoknapatawpha Country.* New Haven and London: Yale University Press.

———. 1971. *A Shaping Joy: Studies in the Writer's Craft.* New York: Harcourt Brace.

———. 1972. "Faulkner and History." *Mississippi Quarterly,* 25, Supplement, 3–14.

———. 1973. "A Note on Faulkner's Early Attempts at the Short Story." *Studies in Short Fiction,* 10, 381–88.

———. 1978a. "The Sense of Community in Yoknapatawpha Fiction." *The University of Mississippi Studies in English,* 15, 3–18.

———. 1978b. *William Faulkner: Toward Yoknapatawpha and Beyond.* New Haven and London: Yale University Press.

———. 1983. *William Faulkner: First Encounters.* New Haven: Yale University Press.

———. 1987. *On the Prejudices, Predilections, and Firm Beliefs of William Faulkner.* Baton Rouge: Louisiana State University Press.

———, and Robert Penn Warren. 1971. *Understanding Fiction.* Englewood Cliffs, N.J.: Prentice-Hall.

Broughton, Panthea Reid. 1974. *William Faulkner: The Abstract and the Actual.* Baton Rouge: Louisiana State University Press.

Brown, Calvin S. 1966. "Faulkner's Manhunts: Fact into Fiction." *Georgia Review,* 20, 388–95.

Brown, May Cameron. 1976. "Voice in 'That Evening Sun': A Study of Quentin Compson." *Mississippi Quarterly*, 29, 347–60.

Brown, Suzanne Hunter. 1989. "Appendix A: Reframing Stories." In *Short Story Theory at a Crossroads*, ed. Susan Lohafer and Jo Ellyn Clarey. Baton Rouge: Louisiana State University Press.

Brylowski, Walter. 1968. *Faulkner's Olympian Laugh: Myth in the Novels*. Detroit: Wayne State University Press.

Bungert, Hans. 1971. *William Faulkner und die humoristische Tradition des Amerikanischen Südens*. Heidelberg: Carl Winter Universitätsverlag.

Burduck, Michael L. 1990. "Another View of Faulkner's Narrator in 'A Rose for Emily.'" *University of Mississippi Studies in English*, n.s., 8, 209–11.

Callen, Shirley. 1963. "Planter and Poor White in *Absalom, Absalom!*, 'Wash,' and *The Mind of the South*." *South Central Bulletin*, 23.4, 24–36.

Campbell, Harry Modean, and Ruel E. Forster. 1971. *William Faulkner: A Critical Appraisal*. New York: Cooper Square. (orig. 1951).

Cantwell, Robert. 1985. "Introduction [to *Sartoris*]." *Critical Essays on William Faulkner: The Sartoris Family*, ed. Arthur F. Kinney. Boston: G. K. Hall, 146–60 (orig. pub. 1953).

Carey, Glenn O. 1964. "Social Criticism in Faulkner's 'Dry September.'" *English Record*, 15.2, 27–30.

Carothers, James B. 1981. "The Myriad Heart: The Evolution of the Faulkner Hero." *"A Cosmos of My Own": Faulkner and Yoknapatawpha 1980*, ed. Doreen Fowler and Ann J. Abadie. Jackson: University Press of Mississippi, 252–83.

———. 1985. *William Faulkner's Short Stories*. Ann Arbor: UMI Research Press.

———. 1992. "Faulkner's Short Story Writing and the Oldest Profession." In *Faulkner and the Short Story: Faulkner and Yoknapatawpha, 1990*, ed. Evans Harrington and Ann J. Abadie. Jackson: University Press of Mississippi, 38–61.

———. 1997. "Short Story Backgrounds for *Absalom, Absalom!*" In Skei, ed., *William Faulkner's Short Fiction: An International Symposium*, 129–38.

Cleman, John L. 1977. "'Pantaloon in Black': Its Place in *Go Down, Moses*." *Tennessee Studies in Literature*, 22, 170–81.

Clements, Arthur L. 1962. "Faulkner's 'A Rose for Emily.'" *Explicator*, 20, item 78.

Coburn, Mark D. 1974. "Nancy's Blues: Faulkner's 'That Evening Sun.'" *Perspective*, 17.3, 87–92.

Coindreau, Maurice E. 1971. *The Time of William Faulkner*, ed. George McMillan Reeves. Columbia: University of South Carolina Press. Includes foreword by Michel Gresset.

Collins, Carvel. 1954. "A Note on the Conclusion of 'The Bear.'" *Faulkner Studies*, 2, 58–60.

Connoly, Thomas E. 1988. *Faulkner's World: A Directory of His People and Synopses of Actions in His Published Works*. Lanham, Md.: University Press of America.

Cook, Sylvia Jenkins. 1976. *From Tobacco Road to Route 66: The Southern Poor White in Fiction*. Chapel Hill: University of North Carolina Press.

Coughlan, Robert. 1972. *The Private World of William Faulkner*. New York: Cooper Square (orig. pub. 1954).

Cowley, Malcolm. 1946. "Introduction." In *The Viking Portable Faulkner*. New York: Viking Press.

———. 1966. *The Faulkner-Cowley File: Letters and Memories 1944–1962*. New York: Viking Press.

Cox, Leland H. 1982. *William Faulkner: Biographical and Reference Guide*. Detroit: Gale Research.

Crane, John K. 1985. "But the Days Grow Short: A Reinterpretation of Faulkner's 'Dry September.'" *Twentieth Century Literature*, 31, 410–20.

Creighton, Joanne V. 1977. *William Faulkner's Craft of Revision: The Snopes Trilogy, "The Unvanquished" and "Go Down, Moses."* Detroit: Wayne State University Press.

Cullen, John B., and Floyd C. Watkins. 1975. *Old Times in the Faulkner Country*. Baton Rouge: Louisiana State University Press (orig. pub. 1961).

Curry, Renée R. 1994. "Gender and Authorial Limitation in Faulkner's 'A Rose for Emily.'" *Mississippi Quarterly*, 47.3, 391–402.

Dabney, Lewis M. 1974. *The Indians of Yoknapatawpha: A Study in Literature and History*. Baton Rouge: Louisiana State University Press.

Davis, Scottie. 1972. "Faulkner's Nancy: Racial Implications in 'That Evening Sun.'" *Notes on Mississippi Writers*, 5, 30–32.

Davis, Thadious M. 1987. "From Jazz Syncopation to Blues Elegy: Faulkner's Development of Black Characterization." In *Faulkner and Race: Faulkner and Yoknapatawpha, 1986*, ed. Doreen Fowler and Ann J. Abadie. Jackson: University Press of Mississippi, 70–92.

Davis, W. V. 1974. "Another Flower for Faulkner's Bouquet: Theme and Structure in 'A Rose for Emily.'" *Notes on Mississippi Writers*, 7, 34–38.

Day, Douglas. 1961. "The War Stories of William Faulkner." *Georgia Review*, 15, 385–94.

Dessner, Lawrence Jay. 1984. "William Faulkner's 'Dry September': Decadence Domesticated." *College Literature*, 11, 151–62.

Dillon, R. T. 1973. "Some Sources for Faulkner's Version of the First Air War." *American Literature*, 44, 629–37.

Donaldson, Susan. 1992. "Contending Narratives: *Go Down, Moses* and the Short Story Cycle." In Evans Harrington and Ann J. Abadie, ed. *Faulkner and the Short Story*. Jackson: University Press of Mississippi.

Donaldson, Susan. 1997. "Dangerous Women and Gothic Debates: Faulkner, Welty, and Tales of the Grotesque." In Skei, ed., *William Faulkner's Short Fiction: An International Symposium*, 106–16.

Douglas, Ellen. 1981. "Faulkner's Women." In *"A Cosmos of My Own": Faulkner and Yoknapatawpha 1980*, ed. Doreen Fowler and Ann J. Abadie. Jackson: University Press of Mississippi, 149–67.

Duvall, John N. 1990. *Faulkner's Marginal Couple: Invisible, Outlaw, Unspeakable Communities*. Austin: University of Texas Press.

Early, James. 1972. *The Making of Go Down, Moses*. Dallas: Southern Methodist University Press.

Eddins, Dwight. 1982. "Metahumour in Faulkner's 'Spotted Horses.'" *Ariel*, 13.1, 23–31.

Edwards, C. H., Jr. 1974. "Three Literary Parallels to Faulkner's 'A Rose for Emily.'" *Notes on Mississippi Writers*, 7, 21–25.

Emerson, O. B. 1984. *Faulkner's Early Literary Reputation in America*. Ann Arbor: UMI Research Press.

Everett, Walter K. 1969. *Faulkner's Art And Character*. Woodbury, N.Y.: Barron's Educational Series.

Faulkner, Howard J. 1973. "The Stricken World of 'Dry September.'" *Studies in Short Fiction*, 10, 47–50.

Faulkner, William. 1931. *These 13*. New York: Jonathan Cape and Harrison Smith.

———. 1934. *Doctor Martino and Other Stories*. New York: Harrison Smith and Robert Haas.

———. 1940. *The Hamlet*. New York: Random House.

———. 1942. *Go Down, Moses*. New York: Random House.

———. 1950. *Collected Stories*. New York: Random House.

———. 1966. *Essays, Speeches & Public Letters*, ed. James B. Meriwether. New York: Random House.

———. 1979. *Uncollected Stories*, ed. Joseph Blotner. New York: Random House.

———. 1987a. *William Faulkner Manuscripts 9: These 13*, ed. Noel Polk. New York: Garland.

———. 1987b. *William Faulkner Manuscripts 11: Doctor Martino and Other Stories*, ed. Thomas L. McHaney. New York: Garland.

———. 1987c. *William Faulkner Manuscripts 15 (Vols. I & II): The Hamlet*, ed. Thomas L. McHaney. New York: Garland.

Ferguson, James. 1991. *Faulkner's Short Fiction*. Knoxville: University of Tennessee Press.

Fisher, Marvin. 1960. "The World of Faulkner's Children." *University of Kansas City Review*, 27, 13–18.

Ford, Arthur L. 1962. "Dust and Dreams: A Study of Faulkner's 'Dry September.'" *College English*, 24, 219–20.

Forkner, Ben. 1983. "The Titular Voice in Faulkner's 'Pantaloon in Black.'" *Les Cahiers de la Nouvelle*, 1, 39–48.

Franklin, Phyllis. 1968. "Sarty Snopes and 'Barn Burning.'" *Mississippi Quarterly*, 21 (Summer), 189–93.

Frazer, Winifred L. 1986. "Faulkner and Womankind 'No Bloody Moon.'" In *Faulkner and Women: Faulkner and Yoknapatawpha, 1985*, ed. Doreen Fowler and Ann J. Abadie. Jackson: University Press of Mississippi, 162–79.

Frey, Leonard H. 1953. "Irony and Point of View in 'That Evening Sun.'" *Faulkner's Studies*, 2, 33–40.

Friedman, Norman. 1958. "What Makes a Short Story Short?" *Modern Fiction Studies*, 4, 103–17.

Funk, Robert W. 1972. "Satire and Existentialism in Faulkner's 'Red Leaves.'" *Mississippi Quarterly*, 25, 339–48.

Gage, Duane. 1974. "William Faulkner's Indians." *American Indian Quarterly,* 1, 27–33.

Garrison, Joseph M., Jr. 1979. "'Bought Flowers' in 'A Rose for Emily.'" *Studies in Short Fiction,* 16, 341–44.

———. 1976. "The Past and the Present in 'That Evening Sun.'" *Studies in Short Fiction,* 13, 371–73.

Gerard, Albert. 1954. "Justice in Yoknapatawpha County: Some Symbolic Motifs in Faulkner's Later Writing." *Faulkner Studies,* 2, 49–57.

Gerlach, John. 1985. *Toward the End: Closure and Structure in the American Short Story.* University: University of Alabama Press.

Gerstenberger, Donna, and Frederick Garber. 1969. "William Faulkner, 'Dry September.'" In *Microcosm: An Anthology of the Short Story,* ed. Donna Gerstenberger and Frederick Garber. San Francisco: Chandler, 406–7.

Gidley, Mick. 1973. "Elements of the Detective Story in William Faulkner's Fiction." *Journal of Popular Culture,* 7, 97–123.

———. 1990. "Sam Fathers's Fathers: Indians and the Idea of Inheritance." In *Critical Essays on William Faulkner: The McCaslin Family,* ed. Arthur F. Kinney. Boston: G. K. Hall, 121–31.

Gladstein, Mimi Reisel. 1986. *The Indestructible Woman in Faulkner, Hemingway, and Steinbeck.* Ann Arbor: UMI Research Press.

Going, William T. 1958a. "Faulkner's 'A Rose for Emily.'" *Explicator,* 16, item 27.

———. 1958b. "Chronology in Teaching 'A Rose for Emily.'" *Exercise Exchange,* 5, 8–11.

Gold, Joseph. 1966. *William Faulkner: A Study in Humanism from Metaphor to Discourse.* Norman: University of Oklahoma Press.

Gray, Richard. 1997. "Across the Great Divide: Race and Revision in *Go Down, Moses.*" In Skei, ed., *William Faulkner's Short Fiction: An International Symposium,* 185–93.

Greiner, Donald J. 1968. "Universal Snopesism: The Significance of 'Spotted Horses.'" *English Journal,* 57, 1133–37.

Gresset, Michel. 1985. *A Faulkner Chronology,* trans. Arthur B. Scharff. Jackson: University Press of Mississippi.

———, and K. Ohashi, 1987. *Faulkner: After the Nobel Prize.* Kyoto: Yamaguchi.

Griffin, William J. 1956. "How to Misread Faulkner: A Powerful Plea for Ignorance." *Tennessee Studies in Literature,* 1, 27–34.

Guerard, Albert J. 1976. *The Triumph of the Novel: Dickens, Dostoevsky, Faulkner.* New York: Oxford University Press.

Guillain, Aurélie. 1997. "Waiting for the End. Eliminating Digressions and Representing Repression in Four Short Stories by William Faulkner: 'Elly,' 'The Brooch,' 'Red Leaves,' 'Hair.'" In Skei, ed., *William Faulkner's Short Fiction: An International Symposium,* 29–37.

Günter, Bernd. 1973. "William Faulkner's 'Dry September.'" *Die Neueren Sprachen,* 22, 607–16.

Gwin, Minrose C. 1990. *The Feminine and Faulkner: Reading (Beyond) Sexual Difference.* Knoxville: University of Tennessee Press.

Gwynn, Frederick L., and Joseph Blotner, eds. 1959. *Faulkner in the University.*

244     Bibliography

*Class Conferences at the University of Virginia 1957–1958.* Charlottesville: University Press of Virginia.

Hagopian, John V. 1962. "'A Rose for Emily.'" In *Insight I: Analyses of American Literature,* ed. Hagopian and Martin Dolch. Frankfurt am Main: Hirschgraben-Verlag, 42–50.

——. 1962. "'That Evening Sun.'" *Insight I: Analyses of American Literature,* ed. Hagopian and Martin Dolch. Frankfurt am Main: Hirschgraben-Verlag, 50–55.

——, and Martin Dolch. 1964. "Faulkner's 'A Rose for Emily.'" *Explicator,* 6, item 68.

Hamblin, Robert W. 1979. "Before the Fall: The Theme of Innocence in Faulkner's 'That Evening Sun.'" *Notes on Mississippi Writers,* 11, 86–94.

——. 1989. "Carcassonne in Mississippi: Faulkner's Geography of the Imagination." In *Faulkner and the Craft of Fiction. Faulkner and Yoknapatawpha 1987,* ed. Doreen Fowler and Ann J. Abadie. Jackson: University of Mississippi Press.

——, and Louis Daniel Brodsky. 1979. *Selections from the William Faulkner Collection of Louis Daniel Brodsky: A Descriptive Catalogue.* Charlottesville: University Press of Virginia.

Happel, Nikolaus. 1962. "William Faulkners 'A Rose for Emily.'" *Die Neueren Sprachen,* 9, 396–404.

Harrington, Evans B. 1952. "Technical Aspects of William Faulkner's 'That Evening Sun.'" *Faulkner Studies,* 1, 54–59.

Harter, Carol Clancey. 1970. "The Winter of Isaac McCaslin: Revisions and Irony in Faulkner's 'Delta Autumn.'" *Journal of Modern Literature,* 1, 209–25.

Hayes, Ann L. 1961. "The World of *The Hamlet.*" In *Studies in Faulkner.* Ed. Ann L. Hayes et al. Carnegie Series in English 6. Pittsburgh: Department of English, Carnegie Institute of Technology, 3–16.

Hays, Peter L. 1988. "Who Is Faulkner's Emily?" *Studies in American Fiction,* 1, 105–10.

Heck, Francis S. 1981. "Faulkner's 'Spotted Horses': A Variation of a Rabelaisian Theme." *Arizona Quarterly,* 37.2, 166–72.

Heilman, Robert B. 1950. *Modern Short Stories: A Critical Anthology.* New York: Harcourt, Brace.

Heller, Terry. 1972. "The Telltale Hair: A Critical Study of William Faulkner's 'A Rose for Emily.'" *Arizona Quarterly,* 28, 301–18.

Hendricks, William O. 1977. "'A Rose for Emily': A Syntagmatic Analysis." *PTLA Journal for Descriptive Poetics and Theory of Literature,* 2, 257–95.

Hermann, John. 1970. "Faulkner's Heart's Darling in 'That Evening Sun.'" *Studies in Short Fiction,* 7, 320–23.

Hernadi, Paul. 1972. *Beyond Genre: New Directions in Literary Classification.* Ithaca and London: Cornell University Press.

Hiles, Jane. 1985. "Kinship and Heredity in Faulkner's 'Barn Burning.'" *Mississippi Quarterly,* 38.3, 329–37.

Hill, A. A. 1964. "Three Examples of Unexpectedly Accurate Indian Lore." *Texas Studies in Literature and Language,* 6, 80–83.

Hinkle, James. 1984. "Some Yoknapatawpha Names." In *New Directions in*

*Faulkner Studies: Faulkner and Yoknapatawpha, 1983,* ed. Doreen Fowler and Ann J. Abadie. Jackson: University Press of Mississippi, 172–201.

Hoffman, Frederick J. 1966. *William Faulkner.* Revised edition. New York: Twayne.

Hoffmann, Gerhard. 1997. "The Comic and the Humoristic, the Satiric and the Grotesque Modes of Representation: Faulkner's Fusion of Perspectives in *The Hamlet.*" In Skei, ed., *William Faulkner's Short Fiction: An International Symposium,* 139–63.

Holland, Norman N. 1972. "Fantasy and Defense in Faulkner's 'A Rose for Emily.'" *Hartford Studies in Literature,* 4, 1–35.

———. 1975. *5 Readers Reading.* New Haven: Yale University Press.

Holmes, Edward M. 1966. *Faulkner's Twice-Told Tales: His Re-use of His Material.* The Hague: Mouton.

Houghton, Donald E. 1970. "Whores and Horses in Faulkner's 'Spotted Horses.'" *Midwest Quarterly,* 11, 361–69.

Howe, Irwing. 1975. *William Faulkner: A Critical Study.* Revised and enlarged edition. Chicago: University of Chicago Press (orig. pub. 1952).

Howell, Elmo. 1959. "Colonel Sartoris Snopes and Faulkner's Aristocrats." *Carolina Quarterly,* 11 (Summer), 13–19.

———. 1961. "Faulkner's 'A Rose for Emily.'" *Explicator,* 19, item 26.

———. 1962. "William Faulkner and Tennessee." *Tennessee Historical Quarterly,* 21, 251–62.

———. 1966. "A Note on Faulkner's Emily as a Tragic Heroine." *Serif,* 3, 13–15.

———. 1967a. "William Faulkner and the Mississippi Indians." *Georgia Review,* 21, 386–96.

———. 1967b. "Faulkner's Wash Jones and the Southern Poor White." *Ball State University Forum,* 8, 8–12.

———. 1967c. "President Jackson and William Faulkner's Choctaws." *Chronicles of Oklahoma,* 45, 252–58.

———. 1970. "William Faulkner's Chickasaw Legacy: A Note on 'Red Leaves.'" *Arizona Quarterly,* 26, 293–303.

Hunt, John W. 1982. "The Disappearance of Quentin Compson." In *Critical Essays on William Faulkner: The Compson Family,* ed. Arthur F. Kinney. Boston: G. K. Hall, 366–80.

———. 1973. *William Faulkner: Art in Theological Tension.* New York: Haskell House (orig. pub. 1965).

Hunter, Edwin R. 1973. *William Faulkner: Narrative Practice and Prose Style.* Washington, D.C.: Windhover.

Hunter, William B., Jr. 1980. "A Chronology for Emily." *Notes on Modern American Literature,* 4, item 18.

Hönnighausen, Lothar. 1997. "'Pegasusrider and Literary Hack': Portraits of the Artist in Faulkner's Short Fiction ('Carcassonne' and 'Artist at Home')," in Skei, ed., *William Faulkner's Short Fiction: An International Symposium,* 275–80.

———, ed. 1989. *Faulkner's Discourse. An International Symposium.* Tübingen: Niemeyer, Hönnighausen.

Inge, Thomas M. 1970. "Introduction." In *William Faulkner: "A Rose for Emily,"* ed. Inge. Columbus, Ohio: Merrill's Casebooks, 1–7.

Ingram, Forrest L. 1971. *Representative Short Story Cycles of the Twentieth Century: Studies in a Literary Genre.* The Hague and Paris: Mouton.

Inscoe, John C. 1987. "Faulkner, Race, and Appalachia." *South Atlantic Quarterly,* 86, 244–53.

Irwin, John T. 1975. *Doubling & Incest, Repetition & Revenge: A Speculative Reading of Faulkner.* Baltimore and London: Johns Hopkins University Press.

Isaacs, Neil D. 1963. "Götterdämmerung in Yoknapatawpha." *Tennessee Studies in Literature,* 8, 47–55.

Jacobs, John T. 1982. "Ironic Allusions in 'A Rose for Emily.'" *Notes on Mississippi Writers,* 14, 77–79.

Jäger, Dietrich. 1968. "Der 'verheimlichte Raum' in Faulkners 'A Rose for Emily' und Brittings 'Der Schneckenweg.'" *Literatur in Wissenschaft und Unterricht,* 1, 108–16.

Jehlen, Myra. 1976. *Class and Character in Faulkner's South.* New York: Columbia University Press.

Johnson, C. W. M. 1948. "Faulkner's 'A Rose for Emily.'" *Explicator,* 5, item 45.

Johnson, Ira. 1972. "Faulkner's 'Dry September' and Caldwell's 'Saturday Afternoon': An Exercise in Practical Criticism." In *Tradition and Innovation. Littérature et paralittérature.* Nancy: Actes du Congrès de Nancy, 269–78.

Johnston, Kenneth G. 1974. "The Year of Jubilee: Faulkner's 'That Evening Sun.'" *American Literature,* 46, 93–100.

Jones, Anne Goodwyn. 1997. "Penetrating Faulkner: Masculinity and Discourse in Selected Short Fictions." In Skei, ed., *William Faulkner's Short Fiction: An International Symposium,* 38–48.

Jones, Diane Brown. 1994. *A Reader's Guide to the Short Stories of William Faulkner.* New York: G. K. Hall.

Jones, Leonidas M. 1957. "Faulkner's 'The Hound.'" *Explicator,* 15, item 37.

Karl, Frederick R. 1989. *William Faulkner: American Writer.* New York: Weidenfeld and Nicolson.

Kartiganer, Donald M. 1979. *The Fragile Thread: The Meaning of Form in Faulkner's Novels.* Amherst: University of Massachusetts Press.

———. 1997. "Learning to Remember: Faulkner's 'Rose of Lebanon.'" In Skei, ed., *William Faulkner's Short Fiction: An International Symposium,* 49–59.

Kazin, Alfred. 1962. *Contemporaries.* Boston: Little Brown.

Kent, George E. 1974. "The Black Woman in Faulkner's Works, With the Exclusion of Dilsey." *Phylon,* 35, 430–41.

Kerr, Elizabeth M. 1962. "William Faulkner and the Southern Concept of Woman." *Mississippi Quarterly,* 15, 1–16.

———. 1976. *Yoknapatawpha: Faulkner's "Little Postage Stamp of Native Soil."* Revised edition. New York: Fordham University Press (orig. pub. 1969).

———. 1979. *William Faulkner's Gothic Domain.* Port Washington, N.Y.: Kennikat Press.

———. 1983. *William Faulkner's Yoknapatawpha: "A Kind of Keystone in the Universe."* New York: Fordham University Press.

Kinney, Arthur F. 1978. *Faulkner's Narrative Poetics: Style as Vision.* Amherst: University of Massachusetts Press.

———. 1980. "Faulkner's Narrative Poetics and *Collected Stories.*" *Faulkner Studies*, 1, 58–79.

———. 1984. "'Topmost in the Pattern': Family Structure in Faulkner." In *New Directions In Faulkner Studies: Faulkner and Yoknapatawpha, 1983*, ed. Doreen Fowler and Ann J. Abadie. Jackson: University Press of Mississippi, 143–71.

———. 1989. "The Family-Centered Nature of Faulkner's World." *College Literature*, 16.1, 83–101.

Kirk, Robert W., and Marvin Klotz. 1963. *Faulkner's People: A Complete Guide and Index to Characters in the Fiction of William Faulkner*. Berkeley and Los Angeles: University of California Press.

Kleppe, Sandra Lee. 1997. "Reconstructing Faulkner's 'Pantaloon in Black.'" In Skei, ed., *William Faulkner's Short Fiction: An International Symposium*, 212–21.

Knieger, Bernard. 1972. "Faulkner's 'Mountain Victory,' 'Doctor Martino,' and 'There Was a Queen.'" *Explicator*, 30, item 45.

Kobler, J. F. 1974. "Faulkner's 'A Rose for Emily.'" *Explicator*, 32, item 65.

Krefft, James H. 1978. "A Possible Source for Faulkner's Indians: Oliver La Farge's Laughing Boy." *Tulane Studies in English*, 23, 187–92.

Kurtz, Elizabeth Carney. 1986. "Faulkner's 'A Rose for Emily.'" *Explicator*, 44.2, item 40.

Kuyk, Dirk., Jr., Betty M. Kuyk, and James A. Miller. 1986. "Black Culture in William Faulkner's 'That Evening Sun.'" *Journal of American Studies*, 20, 33–50.

Landeira, Ricardo López. 1975. "'Aura,' 'The Aspern Papers,' 'A Rose for Emily': A Literary Relationship." *Journal of Spanish Studies: Twentieth Century*, 3, 125–43.

Lang, Béatrice. 1976. "'Dr. Martino': The Conflict of Life and Death." *Delta*, 3, 23–33.

Langford, Beverly Young. 1973. "History and Legend in William Faulkner's 'Red Leaves.'" *Notes on Mississippi Writers*, 6, 19–24.

Leary, Lewis. 1973. *William Faulkner of Yoknapatawpha County*. New York: Thomas Y. Crowell.

Lee, Jim. 1961. "The Problem of Nancy in Faulkner's 'That Evening Sun.'" *South Central Bulletin*, 21, 49–50.

Levins, Lynn Gattell. 1976. *Faulkner's Heroic Design: The Yoknapatawpha Novels*. Athens: University of Georgia Press.

Levitt, Paul. 1973. "An Analogue for Faulkner's 'A Rose for Emily.'" *Papers on Languages and Literature*, 9, 91–94.

Limon, John. 1986. "The Integration of Faulkner's *Go Down, Moses.*" *Critical Inquiry*, 12. 2, 422–38.

Lind, Ilse Dusoir. 1978. "Faulkner's Women." In *The Maker and the Myth: Faulkner and Yoknapatawpha, 1977*, ed. Evans Harrington and Ann J. Abadie. Jackson: University Press of Mississippi, 89–104.

Littler, Frank A. 1982. "The Tangled Thread of Time: Faulkner's 'A Rose for Emily.'" *Notes on Mississippi Writers*, 14, 80–86.

Lohafer, Susan, and Jo E. Clarey, eds. 1989. *Short Story Theory at a Crossroads*. Baton Rouge: Louisiana State University Press.

Long, Elizabeth. 1985. *The American Dream and the Popular Novel*. Boston: Routledge & Kegan Paul.

Longley, John L., Jr. 1963. *The Tragic Mask: A Study of Faulkner's Heroes*. Chapel Hill: University of North Carolina Press.

Lothe, Jakob. 1997. "Narrative, Character and Plot: Theoretical Observations Related to Two Short Stories by Faulkner." In Skei, ed., *William Faulkner's Short Fiction: An International Symposium*, 74–81.

Lupack, Barbara Tepa. 1981. "The Two Tableaux in Faulkner's 'A Rose for Emily.'" *Notes on Contemporary Literature*, 11.3, 6–7.

McDermott, John V. 1976. "Faulkner's Cry for Healing Measure: 'Dry September.'" *Arizona Quarterly*, 32, 31–34.

McGlynn, Paul D. 1969. "The Chronology of 'A Rose for Emily.'" *Studies in Short Fiction*, 6, 461–62.

McHaney, Pearl. 1997. "Eudora Welty on Faulkner Short Fiction: 'Not Meteors, but Comets.'" In Skei, ed., *William Faulkner's Short Fiction: An International Symposium*, 93–105.

McHaney, Thomas L. 1975. *William Faulkner's The Wild Palms: A Study*. Jackson: University Press of Mississippi.

———. 1976. *William Faulkner: A Reference Guide*. Boston, Mass.: G. K. Hall.

———. 1997. "'Beyond' and BEYOND and *beyond*." In Skei, ed., *William Faulkner's Short Fiction: An International Symposium*, 289–305.

Magalaner, Marvin, and Edmond L. Volpe. 1961. "Society in 'A Rose for Emily.'" In *Teachers Manual to Accompany Twelve Short Stories*. New York: McMillan.

Malin, Irving. 1957. *William Faulkner: An Interpretation*. Stanford: Stanford University Press.

———. 1975. *Man Collecting: Manuscripts and Printed Works of William Faulkner in the University of Virginia Library*. Charlottesville: University of Virginia Library.

Manglaviti, Leo M. J. 1972. "Faulkner's 'That Evening Sun' and Mencken's 'Best Editorial Judgement.'" *American Literature*, 43, 649–54.

Martin, W. R. 1989. "Faulkner's Pantaloon and Conrad's Gaspar Ruiz." *Conradiana*, 21.1, 47–51.

Massey, Linton R., comp. 1968. *Man Working, 1919–1962: William Faulkner: A Catalogue of the William Faulkner Collections at the University of Virginia*. Charlottesville: Bibliographical Society of the University of Virginia.

Matthews, Brander. 1976. "The Philosophy of the Short Story." In May, ed., *Short Story Theories* (orig. pub. 1901).

Matthews, John T. 1989. "Faulkner's Narrative Frames." In *Faulkner and the Craft of Fiction: Faulkner and Yoknapatawpha, 1987*, ed. Doreen Fowler and Ann J. Abadie. Jackson: University Press of Mississippi, 71–79.

———. 1992. "Shortened Stories: Faulkner and the Market." In *Faulkner and the Short Story: Faulkner and Yoknapatawpha, 1990*, ed. Evans Harrington and Ann J. Abadie. Jackson: University Press of Mississippi, 3–37.

———. 1997. "Faulkner's Short Stories and New Deal Interference." In Skei, ed., *William Faulkner's Short Fiction: An International Symposium*, 222–29.

May, Charles E. 1984. "The Nature of Knowledge in Short Fiction." *Studies in Short Fiction*, 21.1, 327–38.

———, ed. 1976. *Short Story Theories*. Athens: Ohio University Press.

Meindl, Dieter. 1974. *Bewusstsein als Schicksal: Zu Struktur und Entwicklung von William Faulkners Generationenromanen*. Stuttgart: Metzler.

Mellard, James M. 1986. "Faulkner's Miss Emily and Blake's 'Sick Rose': 'Invisible Worm,' Nachträglichkeit, and Retrospective Gothic." *Faulkner Journal*, 2, 37–45.

Meriwether, James B. 1971a. *The Literary Career of William Faulkner: A Bibliographical Study*. Columbia: University of South Carolina Press (orig. pub. 1961).

———. 1971b. "The Short Fiction of William Faulkner: A Bibliography." *Proof*, 1.

———. 1973. "Faulkner's Correspondence with *Scribner's Magazine*." *Proof*, 3, 253–82.

———. 1977a. "Faulkner's Correspondence with *The Saturday Evening Post*." *Mississippi Quarterly*, 30, 461–75.

———. 1977b. "The Books of William Faulkner." *Mississippi Quarterly*, 30, 417–28.

———. 1979. "An Unpublished Episode from 'A Mountain Victory.'" *Mississippi Quarterly*, 30, 461–75.

———, and Michael Millgate, eds. 1968. *Lion in the Garden. Interviews with William Faulkner 1926–1962*. New York: Random House.

Millgate, Michael. 1966. *William Faulkner*. New York: Barnes & Noble (orig. pub. 1961).

———. 1971. *The Achievement of William Faulkner*. New York: Vintage Books (orig. pub. 1966).

———. 1980. "Faulkner's First Trilogy: *Sartoris, Sanctuary*, and *Requiem for a Nun*." In *Fifty Years of Yoknapatawpha: Faulkner and Yoknapatawpha 1979*, ed. Doreen Fowler and Ann J. Abadie. Jackson: University Press of Mississippi, 90–109.

———. 1987. "'A Novel: Not an Anecdote': Faulkner's *Light in August*." In *New Essays on Light in August*, ed. Millgate. Cambridge: Cambridge University Press, 31–53.

———. 1997. "Was Malcolm Cowley Right? The Short Stories in Faulkner's Non-episodic Novels." In Skei, ed., *William Faulkner's Short Fiction: An International Symposium*, 164–72.

Milum, Richard A. 1974a. "Ikkemotubbe and the Spanish Conspiracy." *American Literature*, 46, 389–91.

———. 1974b. "The Title of Faulkner's 'Red Leaves.'" *American Notes and Queries*, 13, 58–59.

———. 1978. "Faulkner's 'Carcassonne': The Dream and the Reality." *Studies in Short Fiction*, 15, 133–38.

Miner, Ward L. 1963. *The World of William Faulkner*. New York: Cooper Square (orig. pub. 1952).

Minter, David. 1980. *William Faulkner: His Life and Work*. Baltimore: Johns Hopkins University Press.

———. 1992. "'Carcassonne,' 'Wash,' and the Voices of Faulkner's Fiction." In *Faulkner and the Short Story: Faulkner and Yoknapatawpha, 1990*, ed. Evans Harrington and Ann J. Abadie. Jackson: University Press of Mississippi, 78–107.

———. 1997. "Faulkner's Imagination and the Logic of Reiteration: The Case of 'The Old People.'" In Skei, ed., *William Faulkner's Short Fiction: An International Symposium*, 230–43.

Mitchell, C. 1965. "The Wounded Will of Faulkner's Barn Burner." *Modern Fiction Studies*, 11, 185–89.

Momberger, Philip. 1975. "Faulkner's 'Country' as Ideal Community." In *Individual And Community: Variations on a Theme in American Fiction*, ed. Kenneth H. Baldwin and David K. Kirby. Durham: Duke University Press, 112–36.

———. 1978. "Faulkner's 'The Village' and 'That Evening Sun': The Tale in Context." *Southern Literary Journal*, 11.1, 20–31.

Moore, Gene M. 1997. "'European Finery' and Cultural Survival in Faulkner's 'Red Leaves.'" In Skei, ed., *William Faulkner's Short Fiction: An International Symposium*, 263–68.

Moore, Janice Townley. 1983. "Faulkner's 'Dry September.'" *Explicator*, 411, 47–48.

Moreland, Richard C. 1990. *Faulkner and Modernism: Rereading and Rewriting*. Madison: University of Wisconsin Press.

Morris, Wesley, and Barbara Alverson Morris. 1989. *Reading Faulkner*. Madison: University of Wisconsin Press.

Morrison, Gail Moore. 1983. "Never Done No Weepin When You Wanted to Laugh." *Mississippi Quarterly*, 36, 461–74.

Muller, Gilbert H. 1974. "The Descent of the Gods: Faulkner's 'Red Leaves'" and the Garden of the South." *Studies in Short Fiction*, 11, 243–49.

———. 1975. "Faulkner's 'A Rose for Emily.'" *Explicator*, 33, item 79.

Nebeker, Helen. 1970a. "Emily's Rose of Love: Thematic Implications of Point of View in Faulkner's 'A Rose for Emily.'" *Bulletin of the Rocky Mountain Modern Language Association*, 24, 3–13.

———. 1970b. "Emily's Rose of Love: A Postscript." *Bulletin of the Rocky Mountain Modern Language Association*, 24, 190–91.

———. 1971. "Chronology Revised." *Studies in Short Fiction*, 8, 471–73.

Nicolaisen, Peter. 1997. "The Quality of the Real in Hemingway's 'My Old Man' and Faulkner's 'Barn Burning.'" In Skei, ed., *William Faulkner's Short Fiction: An International Symposium*, 117–25.

Nicolet, W. P. 1975. "Faulkner's 'Barn Burning.'" *Explicator*, 34, item 25.

Nigliazzo, Marc A. 1973. *Faulkner's Indians*. Ph.D. dissertation. Ann Arbor: University Microfilms.

Nilon, Charles H. 1965. *Faulkner and the Negro*. New York: Citadel Press.

———. 1981. "Blacks in Motion." In *"A Cosmos of My Own": Faulkner and Yoknapatawpha 1980*, ed. Doreen Fowler and Ann J. Abadie. Jackson: University Press of Mississippi, 227–51.

————. 1965. *Faulkner and the Negro*. New York: Citadel Press.

Noble, Donald R. 1973. "Faulkner's 'Pantaloon in Black': An Aristotelean Reading." *Ball State University Forum*, 14, 16–19.

O'Connor, Frank. 1962. *The Lonely Voice. A Sketch of the Short Story*. Cleveland: World.

O'Connor, William Van. 1970. "The State of Faulkner Criticism." In Inge, ed., *William Faulkner: "A Rose for Emily,"* 44–45 (orig. pub. 1952).

————. 1968. *The Tangled Fire of William Faulkner*. New York: Gordian Press (orig. pub. 1954).

————. 1969. *William Faulkner*. Revised edition. Minneapolis: University of Minnesota Press (orig. pub. 1959).

O'Donnell, George Marion. 1939. "Faulkner's Mythology." *Kenyon Review*, 1, 285–99.

O'Nan, Martha. 1970. "William Faulkner's 'Du Homme.'" *Laurel Review*, 10.2, 26–28.

Page, Sally R. 1972. *Faulkner's Women: Characterization and Meaning*. Deland, Fla.: Everett/Edwards.

Pearson, Norman Holmes. 1954. "Faulkner's Three Evening Suns." *Yale University Library Gazette*, 29, 61–70.

————. 1962. "The American Writer and the Feeling for Community." *American Studies Inaugural Lecture, Alabama*.

Peavy, Charles D. 1971. *Go Slow Now: Faulkner and the Race Question*. Eugene: University of Oregon Books.

Perkins, Hoke. 1987. "'Ah Just Cant Quit Thinking': Faulkner's Black Razor Murderers." In *Faulkner and Race: Faulkner and Yoknapatawpha, 1986*, ed. Doreen Fowler and Ann J. Abadie. Jackson: University Press of Mississippi, 222–35.

Perrine, Laurence. 1985. "'That Evening Sun': A Skein of Uncertainties." *Studies in Short Fiction*, 22, 295–307.

Perry, Menakhem. 1979. "Literary Dynamics: How the Order of a Text Creates Its Meanings [With an Analysis of Faulkner's 'A Rose for Emily']." *Poetics Today*, 1, 35–64, 311–61.

Peters, Erskine. 1983. *William Faulkner: The Yoknapatawpha World and Black Being*. Darby, Penn.: Norwood Editions.

Petersen, Carl. 1975. *Each in Its Ordered Place: A Faulkner Collector's Notebook*. Ann Arbor: Ardis.

Petry, Alice Hall. 1986. "Faulkner's 'A Rose for Emily.'" *Explicator*, 44.3, 52–54.

Pilkington, John. 1981. *The Heart of Yoknapatawpha*. Jackson: University Press of Mississippi.

Pitcher, E. W. 1981. "Motive and Metaphor in Faulkner's 'That Evening Sun.'" *Studies in Short Fiction*, 18, 131–35.

Plyaut, Edwige. 1997. "'That One Man Should Die,' or The Figure of the Scapegoat in 'Uncle Willy' and 'A Bear Hunt.'" In Skei, ed., *William Faulkner's Short Fiction: An International Symposium*, 269–74.

Polk, Noel. 1975. "Book Review." *Mississippi Quarterly*, 28.3, 387–92.

————. 1981. *Faulkner's Requiem for a Nun: A Critical Study*. Bloomington: Indiana University Press.

———. 1984a. "William Faulkner's 'Carcassonne.'" *Studies in American Fiction,* 12, 1, 29–43.

———. 1984b. "'The Dungeon Was Mother Herself': William Faulkner: 1927–1931." *New Directions in Faulkner Studies: Faulkner and Yoknapatawpha, 1983,* ed. Doreen Fowler and Ann J. Abadie. Jackson: University Press of Mississippi, 61–93.

Pothier, Jacques. 1986. "History and Family Stories in Faulkner from *Absalom, Absalom!* to *The Mansion.*" In *Faulkner and History,* ed. Javier Coy and Michel Gresset. Salamanca: Edicions Universidad de Salamanca, 181–95.

———. 1997. "Black Laughter: Poor White Short Stories Behind *Absalom, Absalom!* and *The Hamlet.*" In Skei, ed., *William Faulkner's Short Fiction: An International Symposium,* 173–84.

Powers, Lyall H. 1980. *Faulkner's Yoknapatawpha Comedy.* Ann Arbor: University of Michigan Press.

Pratt, Mary Louise. 1981. "The Short Story: The Long and Short of it." *Poetics,* 10, 175–94.

Pryse, Marjorie. 1979. *The Mark and the Knowledge: Social Stigma in Classic American Fiction.* Columbus: Ohio State University Press.

Putzel, Max. 1975. "Race: Faulkner's 'Red Leaves.'" *Studies in Short Fiction,* 12, 133–38.

———. 1977. "Faulkner's Short Story Sending Schedule." *Papers of the Bibliographical Society of America,* 71, 98–105.

———. 1985. *Genius of Place: William Faulkner's Triumphant Beginnings.* Baton Rouge: Louisiana State University Press.

Rabbets, John. 1989. *From Hardy to Faulkner: Wessex to Yoknapatawpha.* New York: St. Martin's.

Ragan, David Paul. 1987. *William Faulkner's Absalom, Absalom!: A Critical Study.* Ann Arbor: UMI Research Press.

Ramsey, Allen. 1990. "'Spotted Horses' and Spotted Pups." *Faulkner Journal,* 5.2, 35–38.

Rea, J. 1970. "Faulkner's 'Spotted Horses.'" *Hartford Studies in Literature,* 2, 157–64.

Reed, Joseph W., Jr. 1973. *Faulkner's Narrative.* New Haven: Yale University Press.

Reid, Ian. 1977. *The Short Story.* London: Methuen.

Richardson, H. Edward. 1969. *William Faulkner: The Journey to Self-Discovery.* Columbia: University of Missouri Press.

Rodman, Isaac. 1993. "Irony and Isolation: Narrative Distance in Faulkner's 'A Rose for Emily.'" *Faulkner Journal,* 8.2, 3–12.

Rogalus, Paul. 1990. "Faulkner's 'Dry September.'" *Explicator,* 48, 211–12.

Rosenman, John B. 1978. "The Heaven and Hell Archetype in Faulkner's 'That Evening Sun' and Bradbury's *Dandelion Wine.*" *South Atlantic Bulletin,* 43, 12–16.

Ross, Danforth. 1970. "From The American Short Story." In Inge, ed., *William Faulkner: "A Rose for Emily,"* 61–62 (orig. pub. 1961).

Ross, Stephen M. 1989a. *Fiction's Inexhaustible Voice: Speech and Writing in Faulkner.* Athens: University of Georgia Press.

———. 1989b. "'Lying beneath Speech': Preliminary Notes on the Representation of Thought in 'Carcassonne.'" In Hönnighausen, ed., *Faulkner's Discourse,* 159–69.

Roth, Russel. 1949. "The Brennan Papers: Faulkner in Manuscript." *Perspective*, 2, 219–24.

Ruppersburg, Hugh M. 1983. *Voice and Eye in Faulkner's Fiction*. Athens: University of Georgia Press.

Sanders, Barry. 1967. "Faulkner's Fire Imagery in 'That Evening Sun.'" *Studies in Short Fiction*, 5, 69–71.

Sanderson, James L. 1968. "'Spotted Horses' and the Theme of Social Evil." *English Journal*, 62, 700–4.

Sayre, Robert. 1997. "The Romantic Critique of the Modern World in the Faulknerian Short Story." In Skei, ed., *William Faulkner's Short Fiction: An International Symposium*, 244–52.

Schaller, Hans-Wolfgang. 1973. *Kompositionsformen im Erzählwerk William Faulkners: Entwicklungszüge von der Kurzprosa zum Roman*. Göttingen: doctoral dissertation.

Scherer, Olga. 1990. "A Dialogic Hereafter: *The Sound and the Fury* and *Absalom, Absalom!*" In *Southern Literature and Literary Theory*, ed. Jefferson Humphries. Athens: University of Georgia Press, 300–17.

Scherting, Jack. 1980. "Emily Grierson's Oedipus Complex: Motif, Motive, and Meaning in Faulkner's 'A Rose for Emily.'" *Studies in Short Fiction*, 17, 397–405.

Schoenberg, Estella. 1977. *Old Tales and Talking: Quentin Compson in Absalom, Absalom! and Related Works*. Jackson: University Press of Mississippi.

Scholes, Robert. 1974. *Structuralism in Literature. An Introduction*. New Haven and London: Yale University Press.

Seyppel, Joachim. 1971. *William Faulkner*. New York: Ungar.

Shaw, Valerie. 1983. *The Short Story. A Critical Introduction*. London and New York: Longman.

Shiroma, Mikio. 1986. "A Rose for Tobe: A New View of Faulkner's First Short Story." *Kyushu American Literature*, 27, 21–27.

Skei, Hans H. 1979a. "A Forgotten Faulkner Story: 'Thrift.'" *Mississippi Quarterly*, 32, 453–60.

———. 1979b. "William Faulkner's Short Story Sending Schedule and His First Short Story Collection; *These 13*: Some Ideas." *Notes on Mississippi Writers*, 11, 64–72.

———. 1981. *William Faulkner: The Short Story Career*. Oslo: Universitetsforlaget.

———. 1985. *William Faulkner: The Novelist as Short Story Writer*. Oslo: Universitetsforlaget.

———. 1992. "Beyond Genre? Existential Experience in Faulkner's Short Fiction." *Faulkner and the Short Story: Faulkner and Yoknapatawpha, 1990*, ed. Evans Harrington and Ann J. Abadie. Jackson: University Press of Mississippi, 62–77.

———, ed. 1997. *William Faulkner's Short Fiction: An International Symposium*. Oslo: Solum.

Skinner, John L. 1985. "'A Rose for Emily': Against Interpretation." *Journal of Narrative Technique*, 15, 42–51.

Slabey, Robert M. 1964. "Quentin Compson's 'Lost Childhood.'" *Studies in Short Fiction*, 1, 173–83.

Slatoff, Walter Jacob. 1976. *Quest for Failure: A Study of William Faulkner.* Westport, Conn.: Greenwood Press (orig. pub. 1960).

Smart, George K. 1976. *Religious Elements in Faulkner's Early Novels.* Coral Gables, Fla.: University of Miami Press.

Smith, Marshall J. 1931. "Faulkner of Mississippi." *Bookman,* 74, 411–17.

Smith, Raleigh W. 1970. "Faulkner's 'Victory': The Plain People of Clydebank." *Mississippi Quaterly,* 23, 241–49.

Snead, James. 1986. *Figures of Division: William Faulkner's Major Novels.* New York: Methuen.

Stafford, T. J. 1968. "Tobe's Significance in 'A Rose for Emily.'" *Modern Fiction Studies,* 14, 451–453.

Stephens, Rosemary. 1971. "Mythical Elements of 'Pantaloon in Black.'" *University of Mississippi Studies in English,* 11, 45–51.

Stevens, Aretta J. 1968. "Faulkner and 'Helen': A Further Note." *Poe Newsletter,* 1, 31.

Stewart, Jack F. 1969. "Apotheosis and Apocalypse in Faulkner's 'Wash.'" *Studies in Short Fiction,* 6, 586–600.

———. 1979. "The Infernal Climate of Faulkner's 'Dry September.'" *Research Studies,* 47, 238–43.

Stewart, James T. 1958. "Miss Havisham and Miss Grierson." *Furman Studies,* 6, 21–23.

Stone, Edward. 1969. *A Certain Morbidness: A View of American Literature.* Carbondale: Southern Illinois University Press.

———. 1960. "Usher, Poquelin, and Miss Emily: The Progress of Southern Gothic." *Georgia Review,* 14, 433–43.

Stonum, Gary Lee. 1979. *Faulkner's Career: An Internal Literary History.* Ithaca and London: Cornell University Press.

Strandberg, Victor. 1981. *A Faulkner Overview: Six Perspectives.* Port Washington, N.Y.: Kennikat Press.

Stronks, James. 1968. "A Poe Source for Faulkner? 'To Helen' and 'A Rose for Emily.'" *Poe Newsletter,* 1.1, 11.

Sullivan, Ruth. 1971. "The Narrator in 'A Rose for Emily.'" *Journal of Narrative Technique,* 1, 159–78.

Summers, Hollis, ed. 1963. *Discussions of the Short Story.* Boston: Heath.

Sunderman, Paula. 1981. "Speech Act Theory and Faulkner's 'That Evening Sun.'" *Language and Style,* 14, 304–14.

Sundquist, Eric J. 1983. *Faulkner: The House Divided.* Baltimore: Johns Hopkins University Press.

Sutton, G. W. 1967. "Primitivism in the Fiction of William Faulkner." Ph.D. dissertation, University of Mississippi.

Széky, Annamária R. 1978. "The Lynching Story." *Studies in English and American* [Budapest], 4, 181–99.

Taylor, Walter. 1972. "Faulkner's Pantaloon: The Negro Anomaly at the Heart of *Go Down, Moses.*" *American Literature,* 44, 430–44.

———. 1983. *Faulkner's Search for a South.* Urbana: University of Illinois Press.

———. 1987. "Yoknapatawpha's Indians: A Novel Faulkner Never Wrote." In

*The Modernists: Studies in Literary Phenomenon,* ed. L. B. Gamache and I. S. MacNiven. Rutherford, N.J.: Fairleigh Dickinson University Press, 202–09.

Tefs, Wayne A. 1974. "Norman N. Holland and 'A Rose for Emily.'" *Journal of Narrative Technique,* 1, 159–78.

Thompson, Lawrence. 1967. *William Faulkner: An Introduction and an Interpretation.* Revised edition. New York: Holt, Reinhart and Winston.

Toolan, Michael. 1984. "'Pantaloon in Black' in *Go Down, Moses:* The Function of the 'Breathing' Motif." *Les Cahiers de la Nouvelle,* 2, 155–66.

Toole, W. B., III. 1963. "Faulkner's 'That Evening Sun.'" *Explicator,* 21, item 52.

Trilling, Lionel. 1931. "Mr. Faulkner's World." *Nation,* 133, 491–92.

Tuck, Dorothy. 1964. *Crowell's Handbook of Faulkner.* New York: Thomas Y. Crowell.

Turner, Darwin T. 1977. "Faulkner and Slavery." In *The South and Faulkner's Yoknapatawpha: The Actual and the Apocryphal,* ed. Evans Harrington and Ann J. Abadie. Jackson: University Press of Mississippi, 62–85.

Tuso, Joseph F. 1968. "Faulkner's 'Wash.'" *Explicator,* 27, item 17.

Utley, Francis Lee, Lynn Z. Bloom, and Arthur F. Kinney. 1971. *Bear, Man, and God: Eight Approaches to "The Bear."* Second edition. New York: Random House.

Vaschenko, Alexandre. 1986. "Woman and the Making of the New World: Faulkner's Short Stories." *Faulkner and Women: Faulkner and Yoknapatawpha, 1985,* ed. Doreen Fowler and Ann J. Abadie. Jackson: University Press of Mississippi, 205–19.

Vickery, John B. 1962. "Ritual and Theme in Faulkner's 'Dry September.'" *Arizona Quarterly,* 18, 5–14.

Vickery, Olga W. 1964. *The Novels of William Faulkner: A Critical Interpretation.* Revised edition. Baton Rouge: Louisiana State University Press (orig. pub. 1959).

Volpe, Edmond L. 1964. *A Reader's Guide to William Faulkner.* New York: Farrar, Straus and Giroux.

———. 1975. "Faulkner's 'Red Leaves': The Deciduation of Nature." *Studies in American Fiction,* 3, 121–31.

———. 1989. "'Dry September': Metaphor for Despair." *College Literature,* 16, 60–65.

Waggoner, Hyatt H. 1966. *William Faulkner: From Jefferson to the World.* Lexington: University of Kentucky Press (orig. pub. 1959).

Wagner, Linda Welshimer. 1975. *Hemingway and Faulkner: Inventors/masters.* Metuchen, N.J.: Scarecrow Press.

Warren, Robert Penn. 1968. "Faulkner: The South, the Negro, and Time." In R. P. Warren, ed., *Faulkner: A Collection of Critical Essays.* Englewood Cliffs: Prentice-Hall.

Watkins, Floyd C. 1954. "The Structure of 'A Rose for Emily.'" *Modern Language Notes,* 69, 508–10.

———, and Thomas Daniel Young. 1959. "Revisions of Style in Faulkner's 'The Hamlet.'" *Modern Fiction Studies,* 5, 327–36.

Watson, James G. 1980a. "Faulkner: The House of Fiction." In *Fifty Years of Yoknapatawpha: Faulkner and Yoknapatawpha 1979*, ed. Doreen Fowler and Ann J. Abadie. Jackson: University Press of Mississippi, 134–58.

———. 1980b. "Faulkner's Short Stories and the Making of Yoknapatawpha County." *Fifty Years of Yoknapatawpha: Faulkner and Yoknapatawpha 1979*, ed. Doreen Fowler and Ann J. Abadie. Jackson: University Press of Mississippi, 202–25.

———. 1987. *William Faulkner: Letters and Fictions*. Austin: University of Texas Press.

Weaks, Mary Louise. 1981. "The Meaning of Miss Emily's Rose." *Notes on Contemporary Literature*, 11.5, 11–12.

Webb, James W., and A. Wigfall Green. 1965. *William Faulkner of Oxford*. Baton Rouge: Louisiana State University Press.

Weiss, Daniel. 1963. "William Faulkner and the Runaway Slave." *Northwest Review*, 6, 71–79.

Werner, Craig. 1987. "Minstrel Nightmares: Black Dreams of Faulkner's Dreams of Blacks." In *Faulkner and Race: Faulkner and Yoknapatawpha, 1986*, ed. Doreen Fowler and Ann J. Abadie. Jackson: University Press of Mississippi, 35–57.

West, Ray B., Jr. 1949. "Atmosphere and Theme in Faulkner's 'A Rose for Emily.'" *Perspective*, 2, 239–45.

———. 1948. "Faulkner's 'A Rose for Emily.'" *Explicator*, 7, item 8.

———. 1952. *The Short Story in America 1900–1950*. Chicago: Regnery.

Whicher, Stephen E. 1954. "The Compsons's Nancies: A Note on *The Sound and the Fury* and 'That Evening Sun.'" *American Literature*, 26, 253–55.

Wigfall Green, A. 1932. "William Faulkner at Home." *Sewanee Review*, 40, 294–306.

Wilde, Meta Carpenter, and Orion Borsten. 1976. *A Loving Gentleman: The Love Story of William Faulkner and Meta Carpenter*. New York: Simon and Schuster.

Williams, David. 1977. *Faulkner's Women: The Myth and the Muse*. Montreal and London: McGill-Queen's University Press.

Wilson, G. E. 1971. "Being Pulled Two Ways: The Nature of Sarty's Choice in 'Barn Burning.'" *Mississippi Quarterly*, 24, 279–88.

Wilson, G. R., Jr. 1972. "The Chronology of Faulkner's 'A Rose for Emily' Again." *Notes on Mississippi Writers*, 5, 56, 58–62.

Winchell, Mark Royden. 1983. "For All the Heart's Endeavor: Romantic Pathology in Brow[n]ing and Faulkner." *Notes on Mississippi Writers*, 15, 57–63.

Winslow, Joan D. 1977. "Language and Destruction in Faulkner's 'Dry September.'" *College Language Association Journal*, 20, 380–86.

Wittenberg, Judith Bryant. 1979. *Faulkner: The Transfiguration of Biography*. Lincoln and London: University of Nebraska Press.

———. 1997. "Synecdoche and Strategic Redundance: The 'Integrated Form' of *These 13*." In Skei, ed., *William Faulkner's Short Fiction: An International Symposium*, 281–88.

Wolfe, Ralph Haven, and Edgar F. Daniels. 1964. "Beneath the Dust of 'Dry September.'" *Studies in Short Fiction*, 1, 158–59.

Woodward, Robert H. 1966. "The Chronology of 'A Rose for Emily.'" *Exercise Exchange*, 13, 17–19.

Wright, Austin McGiffert. 1961. *The American Short Story in the Twenties*. Chicago: University of Chicago Press.

———. 1989. "Recalcitrance in the Short Story." In Lohafer and Clarey, eds., *Short Story Theory at a Crossroads*, 115–29.

Yorks, Samuel A. 1961. "Faulkner's Women: The Peril of Mankind." *Arizona Quarterly*, 17, 119–29.

Yunis, Susan S. 1991. "The Narrator of Faulkner's 'Barn Burning.'" *Faulkner Journal*, 6, 2, 23–31.

Zender, Karl F. 1997. "'That Evening Sun': Marginality and Sight." In Skei, ed., *William Faulkner's Short Fiction: An International Symposium*, 253–59.

Ziegler, Heide. 1977. *Existentielles Erleben und kurzes Erzählen: Das Komische, Tragische, Groteske und Mytische in William Faulkners "Short Stories."* Stuttgart: Metzler.

# Index

110, 136, 137, 152, 226n. 3, 228nn. 8, 11
Jones, Leonidas M., 106, 224nn. 10, 11
"Justice, A," 12, 13, 40, 45, 58, 122, 137, 180, 192, 193

Kilchenmann, Ruth, 34
Kleppe, Sandra Lee, 225n. 5, 226n. 10
Knieger, Bernhard, 225n. 8
"Knight's Gambit," 21
*Knight's Gambit*, 16, 17, 18, 20, 21
*Kriegserlebnis*, 48, 203

"Landing in Luck," 7
"Leg, The," 10, 15, 16, 70
"Liar, The," 9
*Light in August*, 10, 91, 95
Limon, John, 225n. 3
"Lion," 18, 19
Liveright, Horace, 151
"Lizards in Jamshyd's Courtyard," 16, 177, 231n. 16
"Lo!," 17, 23, 116, 206
"Love," 8

*Macbeth* (Shakespeare), 235n. 7
Magalaner, Marvin, 228n. 16
Manglaviti, Leo, 178, 231n. 2, 232n. 7
*Mansion, The*, 24
Matthews, Brander, 34, 219n. 7
Matthews, John T., 176, 230n. 8
May, Charles, 35, 37, 38, 219nn. 10, 12
*Mayday*, 9
McHaney, Tom, 220n. 1
Mencken, H. L., 178, 179
Meriwether, James B., 27, 69, 178, 194, 219n. 1, 221n. 1, 222n. 1, 224n. 1, 231n. 2
Millgate, Michael, 27, 33, 81, 84, 152, 153, 219nn. 1, 3, 223n. 3, 228n. 7
Minter, David, 80, 212, 216, 221n. 4, 222n. 8
*Miss Zilphia Gant*, 11, 15
"Mississippi," 9, 27
"Mistral," 10, 12, 14, 24, 223n. 5

"Monk," 18, 21
"Moonlight," 8
Moore, Gene M., 226n. 6
*Mosquitoes*, 69
"Mountain Victory," 15, 24, 45, 84, 97, 108–23, 137, 205, 212, 225nn. 4, 6, 227n. 6
"Mr. Acarius," 25
"Mule in the Yard," 17, 47
Muller, Gilbert, 226n. 3, 227n. 14
"Music—Sweeter Than the Angels Sing," 9
"My Grandmother Millard and General Bedford Forrest and the Battle of Harrykin Creek," 22
myth, 18, 26, 38, 44, 45, 86, 92, 122, 136, 139, 142, 145, 168, 193

"Name for the City, A," 24
narrated monologue, 40
narrative technique, 7, 14, 42, 65, 207
  control, 5, 47, 60
  handling, 23, 45, 48, 71, 166, 183
  perspective, 93, 100, 142, 155, 177, 182
  strategy, 38, 39, 89, 90, 154, 167
  voice, 36, 44, 61, 126, 155, 180, 181, 197
Nebeker, Helen, 228n. 12
"Never Done No Weeping When You Wanted to Laugh," 178
*New Stories from the South 1996*, 11
*New Orleans Sketches*, 7, 8
"New Orleans," 8
Nigliazzo, Marc A., 227n. 13
*Notes on a Horsethief*, 24
"Nympholepsy," 8

Ober, Harold, 55, 57, 124, 220n. 2
O'Connor, Frank, 35, 39
O'Connor, William Van, 27, 234n. 9
O'Donnell, George Marion, 220n. 6
"Odor of Verbena, An," 18
Ohashi, Kenzaburo, 220n. 13
"Old People, The," 19, 20, 136
omnicient narration, 59, 61, 89, 97, 160, 208